The Princeton Review®

$y = 2x^2 - 5x + 3$ $x = 0$ $y = 3$

B. 12 f rentd $3 shoes

8 games   24 games
32 game

PSAT™ 8/9

PREP

with 2 Practice Tests

$32\overline{)176}$

$y = -3x + 13$ $y = -3(2y + 9) + 13$

$x - 2y = 9$ $y = -6y - 18 + 13$

The Staff of The Princeton Review

PrincetonReview.com

$x = 2y + 9$ $y = -6y - 5$

$7y = -5$

$y = -2$ $y = -5/7$

5.5
$32\overline{)176}$
$8\overline{)160}$
$256\overline{)160}$

Penguin
Random
House

The Princeton Review
110 East 42nd Street, 7th Floor
New York, NY 10017

E-mail: editorialsupport@review.com

Published in the United States by Penguin Random House LLC,
New York, and in Canada by Random House of Canada,
a division of Penguin Random House Ltd., Toronto.

ISBN: 978-0-525-57016-5
eBook ISBN: 978-0-525-57026-4
ISSN: 2693-0722

Editorial

Rob Franek, Editor-in-Chief
David Soto, Director of Content Development
Stephen Koch, Student Survey Manager
Deborah Weber, Director of Production
Gabriel Berlin, Production Design Manager
Selena Coppock, Managing Editor
Aaron Riccio, Senior Editor
Meave Shelton, Senior Editor
Chris Chimera, Editor
Eleanor Green, Editor
Orion McBean, Editor
Patricia Murphy, Editorial Assistant

Random House Publishing Team

Tom Russell, VP, Publisher
Alison Stoltzfus, Publishing Director
Amanda Yee, Associate Managing Editor
Ellen Reed, Production Manager
Suzanne Lee, Designer

Editor: Chris Chimera
Production Editors: Emma Parker and Liz Dacey
Production Artist: Gabriel Berlin

Printed in the United States of America.

10 9 8 7 6 5 4 3 2 1

Acknowledgments

Special thanks to Amy Minster, Sara Kuperstein, and Cynthia Ward for their contributions to this edition, as well as Aaron Lindh for his expert guidance.

Thanks also to Anne Bader, Kevin Baldwin, Gabby Budzon, Nicole Cosme, Lori DesRochers, Anne Goldberg-Baldwin, Cat Healey, Brad Kelly, Jomil London, Dave McKenzie, Danielle Perrini, Benjamin Tallon, Jess Thomas, and Jimmy Williams.

The Princeton Review would also like to thank Gabriel Berlin, Emma Parker, and Liz Dacey for their time and attention to each page.

Special thanks to Adam Robinson, who conceived of and perfected the Joe Bloggs approach to standardized tests, and many other techniques in this book.

1) 1 pizza   6 pizza
4 people   ✓

2) $50 \leq x < 60$

$$\frac{50 \leq 4x < 60}{4}$$

$\begin{array}{r} 3 \\ 59 \\ 4 \\ \hline 236 \end{array}$ (B)   ✓

24 people
$\frac{3}{\boxed{72}}$ D

$200 < x < 240$

3) $312 + 220 + 216$ 4.) $\frac{15}{100}$ 78.20   ✓
(b.)   5.) A (48.8)   15.

6. B   7.

$\frac{7}{50} = \frac{x}{14878}$ 14.2, 13.8, 12.6, 13, 4, 11.5, X

11.5, 12.6, $\overset{13.1}{13.4}$, 13.8, 14.2

$12.6 + 13.4$

median = 13   Mean = 13.1

12.6   A. $\frac{17}{70} = \frac{x}{325}$ 80

B

Contents

Handwritten annotations (top): $37g + 3c = 600$

$37 : 3 = 600$ (with S, C above)

$\frac{1.25}{1.25} = 2.50$ (addition)

$x = min$

$\frac{3}{37} = \frac{x}{600-x}$

Get More (Free) Content vii

Part I: Orientation 1

1   What Is the PSAT 8/9? 3

2   General Strategies 13

Part II: Practice Test 1 21

3   Practice Test 1 23

4   Practice Test 1: Answers and Explanations 71

Part III: PSAT 8/9 Prep 105

5   Reading Comprehension 107

6   Introduction to the Writing and Language Strategy 143

7   Punctuation 151

8   Words 169

9   Questions 183

10 Math Basics 199

11 Math Techniques 237

12 Advanced Math 267

Part IV: Drill Answers and Explanations 285

Practice Test 2 .... Online

Practice Test 2: Answers and Explanations .... Online

Handwritten annotations (left and bottom):

$10. \; \curlyvee$

$y = \frac{m}{9} \times 9$

$gy = m$

$37x + 3x = 600$

5261.87

5231.87

$8.) \; A$

$9.)$

$B), D) A)$

$X + 0.085x = 5231.87$

$1.085x = 5231.87$

Handwritten (center/right): 18 $6\,in$ 42 A

$6ft$ 14

$3\overline{)42}$, $\frac{3}{12}$, $\frac{1}{2}$ foot

$\frac{6}{36}$ $\frac{1}{6}$

$\frac{3x}{37x}$

Get More (Free) Content
at PrincetonReview.com/prep

As easy as 1·2·3

1 Go to PrincetonReview.com/prep and enter the following ISBN for your book:

9780525570165

2 Answer a few simple questions to set up an exclusive Princeton Review account. *(If you already have one, you can just log in.)*

3 Enjoy access to your **FREE** content!

Once you've registered, you can...

- Get our take on any recent or pending updates to the PSAT 8/9

- Take a full-length practice PSAT, SAT, and/or ACT

- Get valuable advice about the college application process, including tips for writing a great essay and where to apply for financial aid

- If you're still choosing between colleges, use our searchable rankings of *The Best 386 Colleges* to find out more information about your dream school.

- Access comprehensive study guides and a variety of printable resources, including: an additional practice test, explanations, and a bubble sheet.

- Check to see if there have been any corrections or updates to this edition

Need to report a potential **content** issue?

Contact **EditorialSupport@review.com** and include:

- full title of the book
- ISBN
- page number

Need to report a **technical** issue?

Contact **TPRStudentTech@review.com** and provide:

- your full name
- email address used to register the book
- full book title and ISBN
- Operating system (Mac/PC) and browser (Firefox, Safari, etc.)

Look For These Icons Throughout The Book

 PROVEN TECHNIQUES

 APPLIED STRATEGIES

 WATCH OUT

 ANOTHER APPROACH

17.) 839
+157.5
$\boxed{1000.5}$

$200x + 350y = 24000$
$200x + 400y = 4800000$

Part I
Orientation

$-50 = -477600$

955200

$x + 2y = 130$

1 What Is the PSAT 8/9?
2 General Strategies

1p   2p
$x + y = 130$

$200x + 350y = 24000$
$20x + 35y = 2400$
$20x + 2y = 2600$

$15y = -20$

$10x - 6y = 2.7$
$-10x + 7y = 1.6$
$-13y = 1.1$

$35x - 12y = 18.9$
$+60x - 14y = 9.6$
$95x = 28.5$
$x = 0.3$

Chapter 1
What Is the PSAT 8/9?

The PSAT 8/9 is a standardized test given to eighth and ninth graders to give them a "preliminary" idea of how well they could do on SAT question types. This chapter will give you a general overview of the test and how it is used, along with the basics to start your preparation. Finally, we'll take a glimpse at the other tests in College Board's Suite of Assessments: the PSAT 10, PSAT/NMSQT, and the SAT.

PSAT 8/9

Just like the SAT and the other PSAT tests, the PSAT 8/9, which is designed for eighth and ninth graders, contains a Reading Test, a Writing and Language Test, and a Math Test. In terms of the main areas of focus, the content of each section is comparable among the different versions of the PSAT and the SAT.

Although Reading and Writing and Language are two separate sections and two different sets of skills, College Board uses both sections to produce a single Evidence-Based Reading and Writing score. According to College Board, the Evidence-Based Reading and Writing section asks you to "interpret, synthesize, and use evidence found in a wide range of sources." The bottom line: be prepared to justify your selected answer with evidence from the passage and/or graph provided. This test is still not about making up anything, but finding the correct answer based on the text.

College Board also claims that the Math Test "focuses in-depth on two essential areas of math: Problem Solving and Data Analysis, and Heart of Algebra." The bottom line: expect to see Algebra I (and maybe some Algebra II) and questions with charts, graphs, data tables, scatter-plots, or other forms of data representation provided.

The Math Test is split into two sections: one in which a calculator may be used and one in which it may not be used. Even though a calculator is allowed in one section, it is up to the test-taker to determine whether the calculator will be helpful in solving a question. According to College Board, "students who make use of structure or their ability to reason will probably finish before students who use a calculator." The bottom line: show your work and use the calculator for tedious calculations, but a calculator will not be necessary to solve a majority of the questions.

All questions in the Evidence-Based Reading and Writing section are multiple choice. Most of the Math Test questions are multiple choice, with 18 percent of all Math Test questions in the Grid-In, or student-produced, format. For each question answered correctly, one raw point is earned, and there is no penalty for an incorrect response or a question left blank. The bottom line: don't leave anything blank!

What's with All These Scores?

The PSAT 8/9 (and the PSAT 10, PSAT/NMSQT, and SAT) are designed (according to College Board) to reflect how prepared you are for college and for the working world. While we at The Princeton Review may take issue with that claim, this idea does inform both how College Board recommends you prepare and why there are so many different scores on your score report.

College Board maintains that the best way to prepare for the test is to:

- take challenging courses
- do your homework
- prepare for tests and quizzes
- ask and answer lots of questions

College admissions advisors want a "well-rounded" picture of the applicant, so College Board has done its best to meet the demand with its suite of tests. The PSAT 8/9 is more for schools to determine how well-prepared eighth- and ninth-graders are for the other PSATs and the SAT. The PSAT 8/9 provides a measurement of four Evidence-Based Reading and Writing subscores (Command of Evidence, Words in Context, Standard English Conventions, and Expression of Ideas), and two Math subscores (Heart of Algebra as well as Problem Solving and Data Analysis).

In addition to the six subscores reported, College Board now provides two cross-test scores to offer more insight: one score for Analysis in History/Social Studies and another for Analysis in Science. Remain calm; these scores are gathered only from select questions that deal with relevant subject matter and are not actual entire test sections. We will go into PSAT 8/9 scoring in more detail later.

When Is the PSAT 8/9 Given?

The PSAT 8/9 is offered by schools. Schools choose the date to offer the test; this date can be anytime between late September and the end of April, excluding the first two weeks of April.

How Do I Sign Up for the PSAT 8/9?

You don't have to do anything to sign up for the PSAT 8/9; your school will do all the work for you. Test registration fees can vary from school to school, so be sure to check with your school counselor if you have questions about how much the PSAT 8/9 will cost you.

What About Students with Special Needs?

If you have a diagnosed learning, physical, or cognitive disability, you will probably qualify for accommodations on the PSAT 8/9. However, it's important that you get the process started early. The first step is to speak to your school counselor who handles accessibility and accommodations. Only he or she can file the appropriate paperwork. You'll also need to gather some information (documentation of your condition) from a licensed practitioner and some other information from your school. Then your school counselor will file the application for you.

You will need to apply for accommodations only once; with that single application you'll qualify for accommodations on the PSAT 8/9, PSAT 10, PSAT/NMSQT, SAT, SAT Subject Tests, and AP Exams. The one exception to this rule is that if you change school districts, you'll need to have a counselor at the new school refile your paperwork.

Does the PSAT 8/9 Play a Role in College Admissions?

No! The PSAT 8/9 plays no role in college admissions. It's really just a practice test for the SAT.

What Happens to the Score Report from the PSAT 8/9?

Only you and your school will receive copies of your score report. It won't be sent to colleges.

What Does the PSAT 8/9 Test?

As you begin your prep, it's useful to remember that the PSAT 8/9 is not a test of aptitude, how good of a person you are, or how successful you will be in life. The PSAT 8/9 simply tests how well you take the PSAT 8/9 (and, by extension, how well you would have performed on the PSAT 10, PSAT/NMSQT, or SAT, if you had taken one of those tests instead). That's it. And performing well on the PSAT 8/9 is a skill that can be learned like any other. The Princeton Review was founded more than 40 years ago on this very simple idea, and—as our students' test scores show—our approach is the one that works.

These tests can be extremely daunting. However, remember that any standardized test is a coachable test. A beatable test. Just remember:

The PSAT 8/9 doesn't measure the stuff that matters. It measures neither intelligence nor the depth and breadth of what you're learning in school. The PSAT 8/9 is an opportunity to start preparing for the tests that *do* matter: the PSAT/NMSQT and the SAT.

Who Writes the PSAT 8/9?

The PSAT is created by College Board. You might think that the people at College Board are educators, professors of education, or teachers. They're not. They are people who just happen to make a living writing tests. In fact, they write hundreds of tests, for all kinds of organizations.

The folks at College Board aren't really paid to educate; they're paid to make and administer tests. And even though you may pay them to take the PSAT 8/9, you're not their customer. The actual customers College Board caters to are the colleges, which get the information they want at no cost, and the middle and high schools, which are often judged based on how well their students do on these tests. Because you, the student, are not College Board's customer, you should take everything that College Board says with a grain of salt and realize that its testing "advice" isn't always the best advice. (Getting testing advice from College Board is a bit like getting baseball advice from the opposing team.)

Every test reflects the interests of the people who write it. If you know who writes the test, you will know a lot more about what kinds of answers will be considered "correct" answers on that test.

WHAT IS THE PRINCETON REVIEW?

The Princeton Review is the nation's leading test-preparation company. In just a few years, we became the nation's leader in SAT preparation, primarily because our techniques work. We offer courses and private tutoring for all of the major standardized tests, and we publish a series of books to help in your search for the right school. If you'd like more information about our programs or books, give us a call at 800-2-Review, or check out our website at PrincetonReview.com.

HOW TO USE THIS BOOK

This book is divided into five parts. The first three parts of the book contain Practice Test 1, general testing strategies, and question-specific problem-solving instruction. Use the first practice test as a diagnostic to see which sections of the test you need to work on when you read through the content chapters. The last part of the book contains drill answers and explanations. After working through the content chapters and checking your answers and the explanations to the chapter drills, take Practice Test 2 (downloadable in your online Student Tools) and apply everything you've learned to improve your score. The Session-by-Session Study Guide starting on page 8 will give you a plan of attack for these tests and the rest of the book. There is no single plan that will fit everyone, so be prepared to adapt the plan and use it according to your own needs.

Practice Test 1 will give you an idea of your strengths and weaknesses, both of which can be sources of improvement. If you're already good at something, additional practice can make you great at it; if you're not so good at something, what you should do about it depends on how important it is. If the concept is one that frequently appears on the test, you should spend a lot of time on it; if it comes up only once in a while, you should spend very little time working on it and remember that it's something you should either put off until you've completed easier things or skip entirely.

How do you know what's important? We'll tell you throughout this book when we discuss techniques like Plugging In and so forth, but you can also get an idea of what to focus on simply by observing how this book is laid out. The most important concepts appear first in each section of the book. For example, if you're shaky on reading comprehension, you know you'll need to devote some time to Reading questions because there are 42 such questions on the test. But if you're not so confident when it comes to Growth and Decay, don't panic: Growth and Decay questions appear only in the Advanced Math chapter, which tells you that this topic isn't as much of a priority as Plugging In or Math Basics.

Time Management

To manage your PSAT 8/9 preparation, make use of the study guide on the following pages. This guide will break down the seemingly daunting task of PSAT 8/9 prep into bite-sized pieces we call "sessions." We have mapped out tasks for each session to be sure you get the most out of this book. The tests will be the first and last sessions, so you should be sure to plan to have about two and a half hours for these sessions. Most other sessions will last between an hour and two hours, so plan to take a short break in the middle, and if it looks like the session is going to exceed two hours, feel free to stop and pick up where you left off on the next day.

When You Take a Practice Test

You'll see when to take practice tests in the session outlines. Here are some guidelines for taking these tests:

- Time yourself strictly. Use a timer, watch, or stopwatch that will ring, and do not allow yourself to go over time for any section. If you try to do so on the real test, your scores will probably be canceled.

- Take a practice test in one sitting, allowing yourself breaks of no more than two minutes between sections. You need to build up your endurance for the real test, and you also need an accurate picture of how you will do. However, do take 5-minute breaks after the Reading and Math (No Calculator) sections. On the real test you will have these breaks, so it's important not to skip them on the practice tests.

- Always take a practice test using an answer sheet with bubbles to fill in, just as you will for the real test. For the practice test in this book and the one online, use the answer sheets provided in your online Student Tools, which you can feel free to print. You need to be comfortable transferring answers to the separate sheet because that's another skill that will be required on test day.

- Each bubble you choose should be filled in thoroughly, and no other marks should be made in the answer area.

- As you fill in the bubble for a question, check to be sure you are on the correct number on the answer sheet. If you fill in the wrong bubble on the answer sheet, it won't matter if you've worked out the problem correctly in the test booklet. All that matters to the machine scoring the test is the No. 2 pencil mark.

Session-by-Session Study Guide

Session Zero You're doing this session right now. Finish reading the first chapter, so you'll know what the test is about, why it is important for you to take, and what to expect from the rest of this book. This step probably won't take you long, so if you have two-and-a-half hours free after you complete Chapter 1, you can go on to Session One and take the first practice test.

Session One Take Practice Test 1 and score it. You'll use this result to get an idea of how many questions on each section you should attempt before guessing strategically, and the parts of each section you should concentrate on. Note that our explanations refer to concepts discussed elsewhere in this book, so you may want to wait until after Session Four before reviewing this test.

Session Two Work through Chapter 2 of the Orientation and Chapter 5, Reading Comprehension.

Session Three Read Chapter 6, Introduction to the Writing and Language Strategy, along with Chapter 7, Punctuation.

Session Four Work through the Math Basics in Chapter 10 and the corresponding drills.

Session Five Work through the Math Techniques section in Chapter 11 and associated drills. Take a look at Chapter 8, Words.

Session Six Review Advanced Math, Chapter 12. As you work through this chapter, be sure to apply techniques like Plugging In that you learned in Chapter 11. Since these techniques are central to doing well on the math sections, you can never practice them too much.

Session Seven Work through Chapter 9, Questions. This will give you a good idea of how the PSAT will put together all the things you've gone over for the Writing and Language section of the test.

Session Eight Take Practice Test 2. Use the techniques you've been practicing throughout the book. Score your test and go through the explanations, focusing on where you may have missed the opportunity to use a technique and your decisions about whether you should have attempted a question or not, given your pacing goals and Personal Order of Difficulty.

Some of the terminology in the study guide may be unfamiliar to you now, but don't worry, you'll get to know it soon. Also, you'll want to refer back to this study guide at each session to keep yourself on track.

One important note: In the Math chapters of this book, some sample questions do not appear in numerical order within a chapter. For example, you might see a question 4 followed by a question 14. This is because on the Math sections of the PSAT 8/9, a higher question number generally indicates a higher level of difficulty (this is not the case with Reading or Writing and Language). Chapter 2 has great advice on how to crack some of the most difficult questions.

How Is the PSAT 8/9 Structured and Scored?

Category	PSAT 8/9

Components	• Evidence-Based Reading and Writing:
	  ◦ Reading
	  ◦ Writing and Language
	• Math
	  ◦ Calculator
	  ◦ No Calculator

Number of Questions, Time by Section	• Reading
	  ◦ 42 questions over 5 passages
	  ◦ 55 minutes
	• Writing and Language
	  ◦ 40 questions over 4 passages
	  ◦ 30 minutes
	• Math (No Calculator)
	  ◦ 13 questions (10 Multiple-Choice, 3 Grid-In)
	  ◦ 20 minutes
	• Math (Calculator)
	  ◦ 25 questions (21 Multiple-Choice, 4 Grid-In)
	  ◦ 40 minutes

Scoring	• Rights-only scoring (a point for a correct answer but no deduction for an incorrect answer; blank responses have no impact on score)
Score Reporting	• Scored on a scale of 240–1440 that will be the sum of the two section scores (Evidence-Based Reading and Writing as well as Math) that range from 120–720
Subscore Reporting	• Subscores for every test, providing added insight for students, parents, educators, and counselors
Answer Choices	• 4 answer choices for multiple-choice questions

The PSAT 8/9 was created in the wake of major changes to both the SAT and PSAT in the 2015–2016 school year. As we will discuss below, the PSAT 8/9, PSAT, and SAT are more similar than different. According to College Board, the PSAT redesign of 2015 raised the complexity of questions across the board. For the Reading and Writing and Language Tests, this refers in part to the way in which all questions are now connected to full passages, which are written at the same level as writing expected in introductory college and vocational training programs. This means that there will be a good amount of history- and science-based reading material. Further, the PSAT claims to test your ability to demonstrate a full understanding of a source's ideas. On the PSAT 8/9, the texts are *slightly* less complex and the questions *slightly* more straightforward, but the test overall gives an accurate preview of what you'll see on the PSAT and the SAT.

Scoring Your Practice Tests

As you can see, scoring is a little tricky. That's why we provide scoring tables to help you determine your approximate score. When we say that the score is "approximate," we mean that the score is accurate for that particular test. However, the number of questions you need to get right or wrong to earn a certain score can vary depending on the PSAT 8/9's scale from test to test. For example, if you miss 10 Math questions and get a 620 on a practice test, that does not necessarily mean that 10 missed Math questions on an actual exam will result in a 620 as well; you may get that score from missing 8 questions or 12 questions.

Moreover, the scope of math content tests a specific set of problem-solving and analytical topics, focusing on algebra and data analysis in the PSAT 8/9. You will also encounter Grid-In questions, and you will face topics that are specifically geared to test your ability to use a calculator as well as those for which calculators are not permitted.

The Math Test is divided into two sections, one without a calculator, with 13 questions over the course of 20 minutes, followed by one with a calculator, with 25 questions administered in 40 minutes. Because of the tight time limits, you should work as efficiently as possible. To help you do this, even if you answer a question correctly, we recommend that you review the explanations for the problems in the drills and the practice tests. You may discover techniques that help to shave seconds from your solutions. A large part of what's being tested is your ability to use the appropriate tools in a strategic fashion, and while there may be multiple ways to solve a given problem, you'll want to focus on the most efficient approach.

Scoring on the PSAT 8/9

The PSAT 8/9 is scored on a scale of 240–1440, which is the sum of the two area scores that range from 120–720. The two areas are the Evidence-Based Reading and Writing portion and the Mathematics portion. Wrong answers to multiple-choice questions are not penalized, so you're advised never to leave a question blank—even if that means blindly picking a letter and bubbling it in for any uncompleted questions before time runs out.

In addition to the overall total score and the section scores, you'll find several subscores on your PSAT 8/9 score report.

Analysis in History/Social Studies and **Analysis in Science** cross-test scores are generated based on questions from all three of the subject tests (Math included!). These cross-test scores assess the cross-curricular application of the tested skills to other contexts. Relax! This doesn't mean that you have to start cramming dates and anatomy—every question can be answered from the context of a given reading passage or the data included in a table or figure. The only changes have to do with the content of the passages and questions themselves. For example, Reading questions on a passage about a historical event or a Math question that describes a science experiment (but is ultimately still testing math skills) would fall into these cross-test scores.

Additionally, the Math Test is broken into two categories. The **Heart of Algebra** subscore looks specifically at how well students understand how to handle algebraic expressions, work with a variety of algebraic equations, and relate real-world scenarios to algebraic principles. **Problem Solving and Data Analysis** focuses more on interpretation of mathematical expressions, graphical analysis, and data interpretation. Your ability to understand what a question is asking will come in handy here. Finally, there are few questions that showcase the higher-level math that's been added to the test, from quadratics and their graphs to the creation of functions. Although these questions might not correlate directly to a subscore, 6 of these miscellaneous types will show up on the test.

In the Verbal portions of the test, the **Command of Evidence** subscore measures how well you can translate and cite specific lines that back up your interpretation, while the **Words in Context** subscore ensures that you can select the best definition for how a word is used in a passage. The Writing and Language Test additionally measures **Expression of Ideas**, which deals with revising language in order to make more logical and cohesive arguments, and **Standard English Conventions**, which assesses your ability to conform to the basic rules of English grammar, punctuation, and usage.

HOW DOES THE PSAT 8/9 DIFFER FROM THE PSAT AND SAT?

College Board has created what they call a "Suite of Assessments" that starts with the PSAT 8/9. One of the ideas behind these tests is that each test prepares you for the next. To that end, the tests are more similar than different.

The tests do get longer as you move from test to test, but the differences are relatively slight. Reading on the PSAT 8/9 has 42 questions in 55 minutes; the PSAT has 47 questions in 60 minutes; and the SAT has 52 questions in 65 minutes. In other words, as you move from test to test, you'll see 5 more questions (one more question per passage) and have 5 more minutes to answer those questions.

Writing and Language has 40 questions in 30 minutes on the PSAT 8/9, whereas both the PSAT and SAT have 44 questions and 35 minutes. Finally, Math has a total of 38 questions in 60 minutes on the PSAT 8/9, 48 questions in 70 minutes on the PSAT, and 58 questions in 80 minutes on the SAT. Each test has 10 more questions and 10 more minutes than the previous level.

Here's a breakdown of how the tests differ:

	PSAT 8/9	PSAT 10; PSAT/ NMSQT	SAT
Structure	4 sections	4 sections	4 sections (+ optional Essay)
Length	2 hours 25 minutes	2 hours 45 minutes	3 hours (+ 50 minutes for Essay)
Purpose	Prepare for the PSAT and SAT	National Merit Scholarship Qualifying	College admissions
Scoring	240–1440	320–1520	400–1600

What Does the PSAT 8/9 Score Mean for My PSAT and SAT Scores?

The PSAT 8/9 is scored on a 1440 scale, whereas the PSAT is scored on a 1520 scale and the SAT on a 1600 scale. However, because the PSAT 8/9, PSAT, and SAT are aligned by College Board to be scored on the same scale, your PSAT 8/9 score indicates the approximate PSAT or SAT score you would earn were you to have taken the PSAT or SAT on that same day.

Study

If you were getting ready to take a biology test, you'd study biology. If you were preparing for a basketball game, you'd practice basketball. So, if you're preparing for the PSAT 8/9 (and eventually the PSAT and SAT), study the PSAT 8/9. The PSAT 8/9 can't test everything, so concentrate on learning what it does test.

How Much Should I Prepare for the PSAT 8/9?

The PSAT 8/9 gives you insight into the PSAT and SAT. Your goal should be to prepare enough so that you feel more in control of the test and have a better testing experience. (Nothing feels quite as awful as being dragged through a testing experience unsure of what you're being tested on or what to expect—except perhaps dental surgery.) The other reason to prepare for the PSAT 8/9 is that it will give you some testing skills that will help you begin to prepare for the tests that actually count, namely the SAT and SAT Subject Tests.

The bottom line is this: the best reason to prepare for the PSAT 8/9 is that it will help you get an early start on your preparation for the SAT.

PSAT 10 AND PSAT/NMSQT

Though these tests go by different names, they are identical in terms of both number of questions and time limits per section. The major differences are who takes the test and when: the PSAT 10 is taken by 10th-graders and schools choose a date in the spring, whereas the PSAT/NMSQT is taken by 11th-graders on one of two or three specified dates in October. Additionally, the PSAT 10 does not qualify you for National Merit Scholarship consideration, but the PSAT/NMSQT does.

Just as with the PSAT 8/9 and the SAT, the PSAT 10 and PSAT/NMSQT include Evidence-Based Reading and Writing sections and Math Tests. As you progress through College Board's "Suite of Assessments," the passages become more complex, and the Math content expands to include more nonlinear equations, some geometry, and even complex numbers. However, the core skills you learn in preparing for the PSAT 8/9 will apply directly to these tests.

Chapter 2
General Strategies

The first step to cracking the PSAT 8/9 is to know how best to approach the test. The PSAT 8/9 is not like the tests you've taken in school, so you need to learn to look at it in a different way. This chapter will show test-taking strategies that immediately improve your score. Make sure you fully understand these concepts before moving on to the following chapters. Good luck!

BASIC PRINCIPLES OF CRACKING THE TEST

What the College Board Is Good At

The folks at the College Board have been writing standardized tests for more than 80 years, and they write tests for all sorts of programs. They have administered the test so many times that they know exactly how you will approach it. They know how you'll attack certain questions, what sort of mistakes you'll probably make, and even what answer you'll be most likely to pick. Freaky, isn't it?

However, the College Board's strength is also a weakness. Because the test is standardized, the PSAT 8/9 has to ask the same type of questions over and over again. Sure, the numbers or the words might change, but the basics don't. With enough practice, you can learn to think like the test-writers. But try to use your powers for good, okay?

The PSAT 8/9 Isn't School

Our job isn't to teach you math or English—leave that to your supersmart school teachers. Instead, we're going to teach you what the PSAT 8/9 is and how to crack the PSAT 8/9. You'll soon see that the PSAT 8/9 involves a very different skill set.

> **No Penalty for Incorrect Answers!**
> You will NOT be penalized on the PSAT 8/9 for any wrong answers. This means you should always guess, even if this means choosing an answer at random.

Be warned that some of the approaches we're going to show you may seem counterintuitive or unnatural. Some of these strategies may be very different from the way you learned to approach similar questions in school, but trust us! Try tackling the problems using our techniques, and keep practicing until they become easier. You'll see a real improvement in your score.

Let's take a look at the questions.

Cracking Multiple-Choice Questions

What's the capital of Azerbaijan?

Give up?

Unless you spend your spare time studying an atlas, you may not even know that Azerbaijan is a real country, much less what its capital is. If this question came up on a test, you'd have to skip it, wouldn't you? Well, maybe not. Let's turn this question into a multiple-choice question—just like all the questions on the PSAT 8/9 Reading Test and Writing and Language Test, and the majority of questions you'll find on the PSAT 8/9 Math Test—and see if you can figure out the answer anyway.

1

The capital of Azerbaijan is

A) Washington, D.C.

B) Paris.

C) London.

D) Baku.

The question doesn't seem that hard anymore, does it? Of course, we made our example extremely easy. (By the way, there won't actually be any questions about geography on the PSAT 8/9 that aren't answered by the accompanying passage.) But you'd be surprised by how many people give up on PSAT 8/9 questions that aren't much more difficult than this one just because they don't know the correct answer right off the top of their heads. "Capital of Azerbaijan? Oh, no! I've never heard of Azerbaijan!"

These students don't stop to think that they might be able to find the correct answer simply by eliminating all of the answer choices they know are wrong.

You Already Know Almost All of the Answers

All but a handful of the questions on the PSAT 8/9 are multiple-choice questions, and every multiple-choice question has four answer choices. One of those choices, and only one, will be the correct answer to the question. You don't have to come up with the answer from scratch. You just have to identify it.

How will you do that?

Look for the Wrong Answers Instead of the Right Ones

Why? Because wrong answers are usually easier to find than the right ones. After all, there are more of them! Remember the question about Azerbaijan? Even though you didn't know the answer off the top of your head, you easily figured it out by eliminating the three obviously incorrect choices. You looked for wrong answers first.

In other words, you used the Process of Elimination, which we'll call POE for short. This is an extremely important concept, one we'll come back to again and again. It's one of the keys to improving your PSAT 8/9 score. When you finish reading this book, you will be able to use POE to answer many questions that you may not fully understand.

The great artist Michelangelo once said that when he looked at a block of marble, he could see a statue inside. All he had to do to make a sculpture was to chip away everything that

It's Not About Circling the Right Answer

Physically marking in your test booklet what you think of certain answers can help you narrow down choices, take the best possible guess, and save time! Try using the following notations:

- ✔ Put a check mark next to an answer you like.
- ~ Put a squiggle next to an answer you kinda like.
- ? Put a question mark next to an answer you don't understand.
- A̶ Cross out the letter of any answer choice you KNOW is wrong.

You can always come up with your own system. Just make sure you are consistent.

wasn't part of it. You should approach difficult PSAT 8/9 multiple-choice questions in the same way, by chipping away everything that's not correct. By first eliminating the most obviously incorrect choices on difficult questions, you will be able to focus your attention on the few choices that remain.

PROCESS OF ELIMINATION (POE)

There won't be many questions on the PSAT 8/9 in which incorrect choices will be as easy to eliminate as they were on the Azerbaijan question. But if you read this book carefully, you'll learn how to eliminate at least one choice on almost any PSAT 8/9 multiple-choice question, if not two or even three choices.

What good is it to eliminate just one or two choices on a four-choice PSAT 8/9 question?

Plenty. In fact, for most students, it's an important key to earning higher scores. Here's another example:

2

The capital of Qatar is

A) Paris.

B) Dukhan.

C) Tokyo.

D) Doha.

On this question, you'll almost certainly be able to eliminate two of the four choices by using POE. That means you're still not sure of the answer. You know that the capital of Qatar has to be either Doha or Dukhan, but you don't know which.

Should you skip the question and go on? Or should you guess?

Close Your Eyes and Point

There is no guessing penalty on the PSAT 8/9, so you should bubble something for every question. If you get down to two answers, just pick one of them. There's no harm in doing so.

You're going to hear a lot of mixed opinions about what you should bubble or whether you should bubble at all. Let's clear up a few misconceptions about guessing.

FALSE: Don't answer a question unless you're absolutely sure of the answer.

You will almost certainly have teachers and school counselors who tell you this. Don't listen to them! While the SAT used to penalize students for wrong answers prior to 2016, no tests in the current "Suite of Assessments" do this now. Put something down for every question: you might get a freebie.

FALSE: If you have to guess, guess (C).

This is a weird misconception, and obviously it's not true. As a general rule, if someone says something really weird-sounding about the PSAT 8/9, it's safest not to trust that information. (And we at The Princeton Review have gone through every PSAT and SAT and found that there isn't a "better" letter to guess, so just pick your favorite!)

FALSE: Always pick the [fill in the blank].

Be careful with directives that tell you that this or that answer or type of answer is always right. It's much safer to learn the rules and to have a solid guessing strategy in place.

As far as guessing is concerned, we do have a small piece of advice. First and foremost, make sure of one thing:

> Answer every question on the PSAT 8/9. There's no penalty for wrong answers.

LETTER OF THE DAY (LOTD)

Sometimes you won't be able to eliminate any answers, and other times there will be questions that you won't have time to look at. For those, we have a simple solution. Pick a "letter of the day," or LOTD (from A to D), and use that letter for all the questions for which you weren't able to eliminate any choices.

This is a quick and easy way to make sure that you've bubbled in an answer for every test question. It also has some potential statistical advantages. If all the answers show up about one-fourth of the time and you guess the same answer every time you have to guess, you're likely to get a couple of freebies.

LOTD should absolutely be an afterthought; it's far more important and helpful to your score to eliminate answer choices. But for those questions you don't know at all, LOTD is better than full-on random guessing or no strategy at all.

PACING

LOTD should remind us about something very important: there's a very good chance that you won't answer every question on the test. Instead, work at a pace that lets you avoid careless mistakes, and don't stress about the questions you don't get to.

Think about it this way. There are 5 passages and 42 questions on the Reading Test. You have 55 minutes to complete those questions. Now, everyone knows that the Reading Test is super long and boring, and 42 questions in 55 minutes probably sounds like a ton. The great news is that you don't have to work all 42 of these questions. After all, do you think you read most effectively when you're in a huge rush? You might do better if you worked only four of the passages and LOTD'd the rest. There's nothing in the test booklet that says that you can't work at your own pace.

Let's say you do all 42 Reading questions and get half of them right. What raw score do you get from that? That's right: 21.

Now, let's say you do only three of the 8-question Reading passages and get all of them right. It's conceivable that you could because you've now got all this extra time. What kind of score would you get from this method? You bet: 24—and maybe even a little higher because you'll get a few freebies from your Letter of the Day.

In this case, and on the PSAT 8/9 as a whole, slowing down can get you more points. Unless you're currently scoring in the 650+ range on the two sections, you shouldn't be working all the questions. We'll go into this in more detail in the later chapters, but for now remember this:

> Slow down, score more. You're not scored on *how many questions you answer*. You're scored on *how many questions you answer correctly*. Doing fewer questions can mean more correct answers overall!

EMBRACE YOUR POOD

Embrace your what now? POOD! It stands for "Personal Order of Difficulty." One of the things that the College Board has dispensed with altogether is a strict Order of Difficulty—in other words, an arrangement of problems that puts easy ones earlier in the test than hard ones. It is true that the Math sections are loosely arranged this way, but to College Board, "difficult" just means that more students are likely to get it wrong. In the absence of this Order of Difficulty (OOD), you need to be particularly vigilant about applying your *Personal* Order of Difficulty (POOD).

Think about it this way. There's someone writing the words that you're reading right now. So what happens if you are asked, *Who is the author of PSAT 8/9 Prep?* Do you know the answer to that question? Maybe not. Do we know the answer to that question? Absolutely.

So you can't exactly say that that question is "difficult," but you can say that certain people would have an easier time answering it.

As we've begun to suggest with our Pacing, POE, and Letter of the Day strategies, The Princeton Review's strategies are all about making the test your own, to whatever extent that is possible. We call this idea POOD because we believe it is essential that you identify the questions that you find easy or hard and that you work the test in a way most suitable to your goals and strengths.

As you familiarize yourself with the rest of our strategies, keep all of this in mind. You may be surprised to find out how you perform on particular question types and sections. This test may be standardized, but the biggest improvements are usually reserved for those who can treat the test in a personalized, nonstandardized way.

Summary

○ When you don't know the right answer to a multiple-choice question, look for wrong answers instead. They're usually easier to find.

○ When you find a wrong answer choice, eliminate it. In other words, use Process of Elimination, or POE.

○ There's no penalty for wrong answers, so there's no reason NOT to guess.

○ There will likely be at least a few questions you simply don't get to or where you're finding it difficult to eliminate even one answer choice. When this happens, use the LOTD (Letter of the Day) strategy.

○ Pace yourself. Remember, you're not scored on the number of questions you answer, but on the number of questions you answer correctly. Take it slow and steady.

○ Make the test your own. When you can work the test to suit your strengths (and use our strategies to overcome any weaknesses), you'll be on your way to a higher score.

Part II
Practice Test 1

3   Practice Test 1
4   Practice Test 1: Answers and Explanations

Chapter 3
Practice Test 1

Reading Test

55 MINUTES, 42 QUESTIONS

Turn to Section 1 of your answer sheet to answer the questions in this section.

Each passage or pair of passages below is followed by a number of questions. After reading each passage or pair, choose the best answer to each question based on what is stated or implied in the passage or passages and in any accompanying graphics (such as a table or graph).

Questions 1-8 are based on the following passage.

Excerpts from *The Kite Runner* by Khaled Hosseini, ©2003 by TKR Publications, LLC. Used by permission of Riverhead, an imprint of Penguin Publishing Group, a division of Penguin Random House, LLC. All rights reserved.

The kite-fighting tournament was an old winter tradition in Afghanistan. It started early in the morning on the day of the contest and didn't end until
Line only the winning kite flew in the sky – I remember
5 one year the tournament outlasted daylight. People gathered on sidewalks and roofs to cheer for their kids. The streets filled with kite fighters, jerking and tugging on their lines, squinting up to the sky, trying to gain position to cut the opponent's line. Every kite fighter
10 had an assistant – in my case, Hassan – who held the spool and fed the line…

Over the years, I had seen a lot of guys run kites. But Hassan was by far the greatest kite runner I'd ever seen. It was downright eerie the way he always got to
15 the spot the kite would land *before* the kite did, as if he had some sort of inner compass.

I remember one overcast winter day, Hassan and I were running a kite. I was chasing him through neighborhoods, hopping gutters, weaving through
20 narrow streets. I was a year older than him, but Hassan ran faster than I did, and I was falling behind. "Hassan! Wait!" I yelled, my breathing hot and ragged.

He whirled around, motioned with his hand. "This way!" he called before dashing around another corner.
25 I looked up, saw that the direction we were running was opposite to the one the kite was drifting.

"We're losing it! We're going the wrong way!" I cried out.

"Trust me!" I heard him call up ahead. I reached
30 the corner and saw Hassan bolting along, his head down, not even looking at the sky, sweat soaking through the back of his shirt. I tripped over a rock and fell – I wasn't just slower than Hassan but clumsier too; I'd always envied his natural athleticism. When
35 I staggered to my feet, I caught a glimpse of Hassan disappearing around another street corner. I hobbled after him, spikes of pain battering my scraped knees.

I saw we had ended up on a rutted dirt road near Isteqlal Middle School. There was a field on one side
40 where lettuce grew in the summer, and a row of sour cherry trees on the other. I found Hassan sitting cross-legged at the foot of one of the trees, eating from a fistful of dried mulberries.

"What are we doing here?" I panted, my stomach
45 roiling with nausea.

He smiled. "Sit with me, Amir agha."

I dropped next to him, lay on a thin patch of snow, wheezing. "You're wasting our time. It was going the other way, didn't you see?"
50 Hassan popped a mulberry in his mouth. "It's coming," he said. I could hardly breathe and he didn't even sound tired. "How do you know?" I said.

"I know."…

"Here it comes," Hassan said, pointing to the sky.
55 He rose to his feet and walked a few paces to his left. I looked up, saw the kite plummeting toward us. I heard footfalls, shouts, an approaching melee of kite runners.

CONTINUE

But they were wasting their time. Because Hassan
stood with his arms wide open, smiling, waiting for the
60 kite. And may God – if He exists, that is – strike me
blind if the kite didn't just drop into his outstretched
arms.

1

Which choice best describes a main theme of the
passage?

A) Trusting a friend may be wise, even when it goes
against reason.

B) Victory comes from hard work.

C) Competition brings out the best in each
competitor.

D) It is best to be cautious when the outcome is
uncertain.

2

The author includes the second paragraph (lines
12–16) most likely to

A) provide background on the characters by
recounting how Hassan became a skilled kite
runner.

B) create a sense of anticipation by emphasizing the
history of competitiveness between Hassan and
the narrator.

C) introduce the relationship between the characters
described in the passage by emphasizing the
narrator's impression of Hassan's skill.

D) provide context for the story by describing the
time period during which the events take place.

3

Which choice best supports the narrator's description
of Hassan as "the greatest kite runner I'd ever seen"
(lines 13–14)?

A) Line 12 ("Over the…kites")

B) Lines 14–16 ("It was…compass")

C) Line 21 ("I was…behind")

D) Lines 56–57 ("I heard…runners")

4

As used in line 16, "inner compass" most strongly
suggests that Hassan

A) has a natural gift for kite running.

B) is able to navigate in a strange city.

C) is guided by his strong morals.

D) is cheating at the kite-fighting competition.

5

As used in line 22, "ragged" most nearly means

A) fast.

B) loud.

C) rough.

D) fevered.

6

After Hassan and the narrator reach the middle
school, Hassan's actions suggest that he

A) is upset that the narrator found him.

B) is confident that he will catch the kite.

C) sits down to let the narrator catch up with him.

D) ran the wrong way to let the narrator catch the kite.

7

Which choice provides the best evidence for the
answer to the previous question?

A) Lines 9–11 ("Every kite…line")

B) Lines 47–48 ("I dropped…wheezing")

C) Lines 48–49 ("You're wasting…see")

D) Lines 50–51 ("Hassan popped…said")

8

According to the passage, while the kite is falling,
there is a sound of

A) wind whipping the kite's fabric.

B) Hassan calling out to the narrator.

C) the group of competitors coming closer.

D) parents cheering for their children.

CONTINUE

Questions 9-16 are based on the following passage and supplementary material.

This passage is adapted from Elaina Zachos, "Can Pokémon Go Get Players Into National Parks?" ©2016 by *National Geographic*. In the game "Pokémon Go," players use mobile devices to find and catch characters with names such as "Charmander" and "Pikachu." The game uses GPS and augmented reality to make the characters appear as if they are in the player's real-world location.

They walk among us. Shuffling along sidewalks, mesmerized by the smartphones cradled in their hands. Some have earbuds in, seemingly oblivious to *Line* the physical world around them. They are Pokémon
5 Go players, and they are on one mission: They've gotta catch 'em all. From teenage girls to police officers, it seems like everyone is hopping on the augmented reality bandwagon to hunt down their first Charmanders, Squirtles, and Bulbasaurs. Recently
10 ranked as the most popular game in U.S. history, the phenomenon has made its way through civilization and is now venturing into uncharted territory: national parks.

With lush trees and mountain ranges, national
15 parks are not the easiest places to find cell reception or Wi-Fi. Because of this, Barb Maynes, public information officer at Olympic National Park, says she hasn't heard reports of people playing Pokémon Go. Acadia National Park also hasn't reported any
20 activity. But some visitors centers, which have Wi-Fi, double as pokégyms, or places where players can battle each other and level up. On Tuesday, Tim Rains, a public affairs specialist at Glacier National Park, caught his first Pokémon—a Bulbasaur—near Glacier's Apgar
25 Visitor Center. Lynda Doucette, a lead interpretive ranger at Great Smoky Mountains National Park, says the park's landscape obstructs cell service. But she and her colleagues have found at least five Pokéstops, landmarks where players can collect useful items, and
30 a Pokégym. They've identified at least 12 Pokémon, including Zubats and Squirtles.

"One of our goals as part of the National Park Service Centennial is to connect with and create the next generation of park visitors, supporters, and
35 advocates," Rains writes in an email. "Games that use geolocation are a new and emerging opportunity to bring new audiences to the park."

Pokémon Go also has an educational component to it. Great Smoky Mountains's Mountain Farm

40 Museum has three Pokéstops. When found, historical text will pop up on screen, and players can tap an icon to learn more before returning to the game. There's also a Twitter account called Pokémon Archaeology devoted to recording Pokémon in
45 historical settings. "It gets people out there," Doucette says. "I think it's an opportunity to bring a new audience to a site."

But as play increases, injuries abound. Already, players have been hurt after falling or walking into
50 obstacles while cruising for critters. So far, though, national parks aren't implementing any policies against the game. Instead, Emily Davis, a public affairs officer at Grand Canyon National Park, says rangers will continue to remind visitors to be aware of their
55 surroundings on their quests to track down new Pokémon. "I don't anticipate that we're going to have any new rules implemented," Doucette says. "It's the same safety concerns we've had before this game."

Overall, Pokémon Go may become a new way to
60 explore historic parks, which tend to be dead spots for technology. In Washington, D.C., rangers will even soon be getting in on the game by leading a "Catch the Mall Pokémon Hunt," according to the National Mall and Memorial Parks Facebook page.
65 "On top of reminding visitors to be safe during their visit, we are also asking them to be respectful of the solemn monuments and to avoid wandering into off-limits areas," Tom Crosson, chief of public affairs for the National Park Service, writes in an email.

70 Who knows? Maybe Pikachu could end up on Mount Rushmore one day.

CONTINUE

Top 10 National Parks, Recreation Visits
2017 to 2018

Great Smoky   11,338,893 ————————————————— 11,421,200 Great Smoky
Mountains NP   Mountains NP

                                                6,380,495 Grand Canyon NP

Grand Canyon NP   6,254,238

Zion NP   4,504,812 ———————————————— 4,590,493 Rocky Mountain NP
Rocky Mountain NP 4,437,215   4,320,033 Zion NP
Yosemite NP   4,336,890   4,115,000 Yellowstone NP
Yellowstone NP   4,116,524   4,009,436 Yosemite NP
Acadia NP   3,509,271 ———————————————— 3,537,575 Acadia NP
Olympic NP   3,401,996   3,491,151 Grand Teton NP
Grand Teton NP   3,317,000   3,104,455 Olympic NP
Glacier NP   3,305,512 ———————————————— 2,965,309 Glacier NP

                      2017   2018

9

The main idea of the passage is that

A) national park rangers are concerned about possible injuries due to Pokémon Go.

B) visitors to national parks are discouraged by the lack of Wi-Fi and other technology.

C) people who play Pokémon Go are more likely to visit national parks.

D) Pokémon Go may encourage players to explore and learn about national parks.

10

As used in line 33, "create" most nearly means

A) design.

B) birth.

C) foster.

D) help.

11

As used in line 36, "emerging" most nearly means

A) developing.

B) appearing.

C) becoming.

D) unexpected.

12

The author uses the example in lines 39–42 ("Great Smoky . . . game") mainly to support the assertion that Pokémon Go

A) requires parks to increase safety measures to protect visitors from injury.

B) can inform Pokémon Go players about the national parks.

C) was created for the National Park Service Centennial.

D) was demanded by an increasing number of visitors to the park.

CONTINUE

13

Which choice provides the best evidence for the answer to the previous question?

A) Lines 32–35 ("One of . . . email")

B) Lines 35–37 ("Games that...park")

C) Lines 38–39 ("Pokémon Go . . . it")

D) Lines 50–56 ("So far . . . Pokémon")

14

In the passage, Lynda Doucette indicates that

A) Pokémon Go players in national parks do not raise unique safety concerns.

B) Pokémon Go players ignore animals and natural features.

C) new visitors to national parks will mainly be Pokémon Go players.

D) Pokémon Go players may injure themselves and other national park visitors.

15

Which choice provides the best evidence for the answer to the previous question?

A) Lines 25–30 ("Lynda Doucette . . . Pokégym")

B) Lines 45–47 ("It gets . . . site")

C) Lines 48–50 ("But as . . . critters")

D) Lines 56–58 ("I don't . . . game")

16

According to the graph, in 2018, there were more visits to Olympic National Park than to

A) Zion National Park.

B) Yellowstone National Park.

C) Glacier National Park.

D) Grand Canyon National Park.

CONTINUE

Questions 17-25 are based on the following passage and supplementary material.

This passage is adapted from Adel Heenan, Andrew S. Hoey, Gareth J. Williams, and Ivor D. Williams, "Understanding the conditions that foster coral reefs' caretaker fish," originally published in 2016 by *The Conversation*: https://theconversation.com/.

Coral reefs are among the most valuable natural assets on Earth. They provide an estimated US$375 billion worth of goods and services every year, such as
Line supporting fisheries and protecting coasts. But reefs
5 face many stresses and shocks, from local threats like overfishing, habitat damage and pollution to the global impacts of climate change. Many scientists are working to identify management strategies that can effectively buffer reefs against the array of threats that challenge
10 them.

Herbivorous fish (species that eat plants) are critical for healthy coral reefs because they help to regulate the constant competition for space between corals and seaweeds. Hard corals and other reef-
15 building organisms form hard skeletons out of calcium carbonate, while fleshy organisms such as seaweeds and algal turfs (thick mats of short algae) grow on the surfaces of these hard structures. By feeding on seaweeds and algal turfs, herbivorous fish prevent these
20 organisms from smothering reefs.

Recent studies have stressed the importance for coral reef conservation of protecting herbivorous fish, which are heavily fished in many parts of the world. But in a new study, we found that populations of
25 herbivorous fish vary widely from site to site, and are strongly influenced by factors including temperature and island type. This means that strategies to protect these important species may not work unless they take local conditions into account, and no single strategy is
30 likely to work everywhere.

Fishing has caused widespread reductions in herbivorous fish populations on coral reefs around the world. Because fishing has had such pervasive global effects, it is hard to separate human impacts from the
35 natural biophysical and environmental drivers of these fish populations.

But we need to make this distinction if we want to understand why herbivores might be naturally more prevalent in some places than others, and to measure
40 true human-related depletion effects accurately. More

specifically, in this study we wanted to know whether it was reasonable to expect the same amount of these fishes in areas where environmental conditions are very different.

45 All herbivorous fish are not equal. Depending on what they eat, they perform different roles that contribute to the functioning of coral reefs, much in the same way that lawn mowers and hedge trimmers perform different tasks in your garden. To understand
50 how these fishes differ in their response to the environment, we classified fishes in our study based on their functional roles, defined by what they eat and how they eat it.

For example, browsers eat fleshy seaweeds;
55 detritivores comb algal turfs, feeding on a variety of fine plant and animal matter; and scrapers and excavators scrape hard surfaces on the reef, clearing space for corals to colonize. Large excavators, such as big parrotfish, are considered to be particularly
60 important.

Since the groups of herbivores we studied play different functional roles on reefs, healthy reefs are likely to need diverse populations of grazing fishes. Browsers and large parrotfish are most sensitive to
65 human impacts, so our results suggest that we may need new strategies to protect these species.

Our findings also show that a coral reef's environmental setting strongly influences the number and diversity of herbivorous caretaker species that it
70 can support. For instance, browsers that feed directly on macroalgae are naturally increased in cooler locations, while detritivores that selectively remove detritus from algal turfs (thus keeping the turfs clean) have increased population sizes in warmer areas.

75 Agencies that manage coral reefs are increasingly turning to local-scale interventions to help make these sensitive ecosystems more sustainable. Some may adopt policies that focus on herbivores, such as the marine reserve on the Hawaiian island of
80 Maui where herbivores, but not other species, are protected from fishing. Our results show that it is important to treat herbivores as a diverse group with different roles and vulnerabilities, and to think about the environmental context as we design strategies to
85 protect them.

CONTINUE

Figure 1

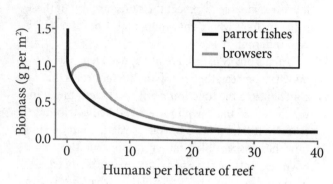

Humans per hectare of reef

Figure 2

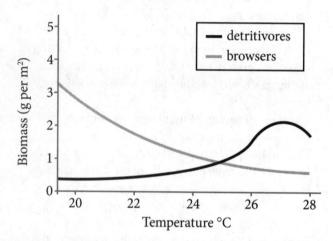

Temperature °C

17

Which statement best describes the overall structure of the passage?

A) The authors outline various types of herbivorous fish, and then explain how they interact together.

B) The authors trace the history of research on herbivorous fish, and then explain the impact of that research.

C) The authors describe an event that occurs on coral reefs, and then explain what caused the event.

D) The authors explain the relationship between coral reefs and herbivorous fish, and then detail a study's findings about that relationship.

18

Based on the passage, the authors' perspective on studying coral reefs is that it is

A) confusing to find varying amounts of seaweed and algal turf in reefs.

B) difficult to understand why the fish populations varied in different reefs.

C) important to protect a valuable resource.

D) controversial to study human effects on the reefs.

19

As used in line 5, "shocks" most nearly means

A) surprises.

B) jolts.

C) disturbances.

D) reactions.

20

According to the passage, conservation efforts should take local conditions into account because populations of herbivorous fish

A) are affected by competing species.

B) are influenced by their habitats.

C) are not influenced by water temperature.

D) do not protect other important species.

21

Which choice provides the best evidence for the answer to the previous question?

A) Lines 21–23 ("Recent studies...world")

B) Lines 24–27 ("But in a new...type")

C) Lines 27–30 ("This means...everywhere")

D) Lines 33–36 ("Because fishing...populations")

CONTINUE

22

What does the authors' use of the word "drivers" (line 35) suggest about the fish population?

A) Human and natural factors affect the fish population.

B) The feeding habits of fish are influenced by multiple factors.

C) Fishing has forced fish populations to move to new locations around the globe.

D) Fish populations have not changed significantly in response to human activity.

23

Which choice best supports the conclusion that different types of herbivorous fish perform different roles in the reef environment?

A) Lines 40–44 ("More specifically…different")

B) Line 45 ("All herbivorous…equal")

C) Lines 54–58 ("For example…colonize")

D) Lines 58–60 ("Large excavators…important")

24

Based on the graphs, which of the following groups includes the greatest biomass of herbivorous fish?

A) Detritivores when the water temperature is 28 degrees Celsius

B) Parrotfishes when there are 0 humans per hectare of reef

C) Browsers and parrotfishes when there are 40 humans per hectare of reef

D) Browsers when the water temperature is 20 degrees Celsius

25

Which idea from the passage is supported by the information in the graphs?

A) Herbivorous fish eat different types of seaweed.

B) Certain types of herbivorous fish are affected by the presence of humans.

C) Herbivorous fish perform different functional roles in coral reefs.

D) Conservation of herbivorous fish has increased their populations.

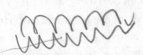

Questions 26-34 are based on the following passage.

This passage is adapted from the speech "The Noble Mansion of Free India" from *The Penguin Book of Twentieth-Century Speeches* edited by Brian MacArthur, Copyright ©1992 by Brian MacArthur. Used by permission of Viking Books, an imprint of Penguin Publishing Group, a division of Penguin Random House LLC. All rights reserved. The speech was given by Jawaharlal Nehru, the first Prime Minister of India, to the members of India's first Parliament on August 14, 1947, when India was about to become independent from the United Kingdom.

At the dawn of history India started on her unending quest, and trackless centuries are filled with her striving and the grandeur of her success
Line and her failures. Through good and ill fortune alike
5 she has never lost sight of that quest or forgotten the ideals which gave her strength. We end today a period of ill fortune and India discovers herself again. The achievement we celebrate today is but a step, an opening of opportunity, to the greater triumphs and
10 achievements that await us. Are we brave enough and wise enough to grasp this opportunity and accept the challenge of the future?

Freedom and power bring responsibility. The responsibility rests upon this Assembly, a sovereign
15 body representing the sovereign people of India. Before the birth of freedom we have endured all the pains of labour and our hearts are heavy with the memory of this sorrow. Some of those pains continue even now. Nevertheless, the past is over and it is the
20 future that beckons to us now.

That future is not one of ease or resting but of incessant striving so that we may fulfill the pledges we have so often taken and the one we shall take today. The service of India means the service of the millions
25 who suffer. It means the ending of poverty and ignorance and disease and inequality of opportunity. The ambition of the greatest man of our generation has been to wipe every tear from every eye. That may be beyond us, but as long as there are tears and suffering,
30 so long our work will not be over.

And so we have to labour and to work, and work hard, to give reality to our dreams. Those dreams are for India, but they are also for the world, for all the nations and peoples are too closely knit together today
35 for any one of them to imagine that it can live apart. Peace has been said to be indivisible; so is freedom, so is prosperity now, and so also is disaster in this

One World that can no longer be split into isolated fragments.
40 It is a fateful moment for us in India, for all Asia and for the world. A new star rises, the star of freedom in the East, a new hope comes into being, a vision long cherished materializes. May the star never set and that hope never be betrayed! We rejoice in that freedom,
45 even though clouds surround us, and many of our people are sorrow stricken and difficult problems encompass us. But freedom brings responsibilities and burdens and we have to face them in the spirit of a free and disciplined people.
50 The future beckons to us. Whither do we go and what shall be our endeavour? To bring freedom and opportunity to the common man, to the peasants and workers of India; to fight and end poverty and ignorance and disease; to build up a prosperous,
55 democratic and progressive nation, and to create social, economic and political institutions which will ensure justice and fullness of life to every man and woman.

We have hard work ahead. There is no resting for
60 any one of us till we redeem our pledge in full, till we make all the people of India what destiny intended them to be. We are citizens of a great country on the verge of bold advance, and we have to live up to that high standard. All of us, to whatever religion we may
65 belong, are equally the children of India with equal rights, privileges and obligations. We cannot encourage communalism or narrow-mindedness, for no nation can be great whose people are narrow in thought or in action.
70 To the nations and peoples of the world we send greetings and pledge ourselves to cooperate with them in furthering peace, freedom and democracy. And to India, our much-loved motherland, the ancient, the eternal and the ever-new, we pay our reverent homage
75 and we bind ourselves afresh to her service.

CONTINUE ▶

26

The main purpose of the passage is to

A) inspire the Assembly to work diligently to help India prosper.

B) persuade Indian citizens to take advantage of new opportunities.

C) comfort those who lost a great deal in the fight for independence.

D) seek advice from the Assembly about India's next steps.

27

Which choice best summarizes the passage?

A) The common people of India suffered many hardships to gain freedom, and they must organize to achieve true equality.

B) The nations of the world have prospered and failed together throughout history.

C) The citizens of India will be sorrowful and burdened until they realize their dreams.

D) Gaining independence is a great accomplishment, but India's leaders must dedicate themselves to help the country achieve its full potential.

28

Nehru includes the statement in lines 4–6 ("Through good…strength") most likely to convey the idea that

A) India's people have been true to their values even during times of hardship.

B) India's quest will succeed even though the past has been difficult.

C) India has been led by people with strong ideals throughout history.

D) the people of India must honor their nation's values no matter the circumstances.

29

Nehru's purpose for using the words "birth" and "pains" in lines 16–17 is most likely to

A) admit that sorrowful memories will continue even in happier times.

B) support the argument that the new era of freedom will be joyful.

C) compare the heavy labor of the past with the easy road ahead.

D) imply that something positive came from a difficult experience.

30

Nehru implies that for India to succeed, the members of Parliament must

A) accept what fate may have in store for the country.

B) celebrate both India's past and future steps toward success.

C) work continually to fulfill their obligations to India's people.

D) encourage the common people to keep their promises to each other.

31

Which choice provides the best evidence for the answer to the previous question?

A) Lines 8–10 ("The achievement…us")

B) Lines 21–23 ("That future…today")

C) Lines 40–41 ("It is…world")

D) Lines 70–72 ("To the…democracy")

CONTINUE

32

Based on the passage, which choice most closely describes Nehru's perspective on opportunity?

A) Once freedom is achieved, there is no need to work for greater economic opportunity.

B) Opportunities for personal prosperity must be balanced with opportunities for national prosperity.

C) A responsible government works to bring about equal opportunity for all its people.

D) Equal economic opportunity is not as essential as religious equality.

33

As used in line 68, "narrow" most nearly means

A) thin.

B) fine.

C) limited.

D) tight.

34

Which of the following does Nehru suggest is most important to ensure that India reaches its potential?

A) Evaluating good and ill fortune

B) Honoring and serving India

C) Remembering forgotten ideals

D) Seeking advice from other nations

CONTINUE

Questions 35-42 are based on the following passages.

Passage 1 is adapted from Clara Moskowitz, "Mysterious Neutrinos Get New Mass Estimate." Adapted with permission. Copyright ©2019 *Scientific American*, a division of Nature America, Inc. All rights reserved. Passage 2 is adapted from Davide Castelvecchi, "Physicists close in on elusive neutrino's mass." ©2019 by Springer Nature.

Passage 1

Neutrinos, some of nature's weirdest fundamental particles, are nearly massless—emphasis on nearly. They were predicted to be completely massless,
Line but experiments roughly 20 years ago found they
5 surprisingly do have some mass. Just how much has remained a mystery. Now a new calculation based on cosmological observations places an upper limit on how heavy the lightest kind of neutrino can be.

The new mass limit comes from a supercomputer
10 calculation that combined data on the distribution of galaxies throughout the universe, the remnants of the first light released after the big bang and supernova measurements that reflect the expansion rate of the cosmos. The analysis also used laboratory data on
15 neutrinos to arrive at an estimate of the maximum weight of the smallest one: 0.086 electron volt, or 0.000 00000000000000000000000000000015 kilogram— making it at least six million times lighter than an electron.
20 "What they have done is really nice work," says Olga Mena of the Institute of Corpuscular Physics in Spain, who has worked on similar calculations. André de Gouvêa, a theoretical physicist at Northwestern University, says, "It's a slightly more detailed analysis
25 of cosmological data than people had done before. It's quite a nice paper."

The estimate complements other efforts to weigh neutrinos that focus on laboratory experiments. For instance, a project called the Karlsruhe Tritium
30 Neutrino (KATRIN) experiment in Germany aims to measure neutrino mass by observing beta decays in which a neutron transforms into a proton by releasing a neutrino and an electron. By carefully measuring the energy of the electron, scientists can infer the
35 mass of the neutrino. In contrast to cosmology-based estimates, which include uncertainties from assumptions about unknowns such as dark matter and dark energy, this kind of experiment is more direct.

Ultimately, scientists must compare the results
40 from all these different methods. "Only by combing all the possible ways of measuring the neutrino mass will we have a finite and robust answer," Mena says. But if the estimates differ, some scientists say, all the better. "One thing that's exciting is: What if we
45 make a measurement from cosmology, and we get an answer that doesn't agree with particle physics measurements?" de Gouvêa says. "That would be indicative of the fact that there's something in this picture that's just wrong. Maybe there's something
50 wrong with our understanding of the early universe. Or maybe there's something unusual about the mechanism for neutrino masses, like the mass depends on where you are or when you make the measurement. It sounds crazy, but it's possible."

Passage 2

55 An experiment in Germany has made the most precise measurement yet of the maximum mass of neutrinos — light subatomic particles that are so devilishly difficult to measure that physicists have only been able to estimate the upper limit of their mass.
60 The first results from the Karlsruhe Tritium Neutrino (KATRIN) experiment in southwestern Germany reveal that neutrinos weigh at most 1.1 electronvolts (eV). This measurement is a two-fold improvement over previous upper-
65 bound measurements of 2 eV. Guido Drexlin, co-spokesperson for the KATRIN collaboration, presented the results on 13 September at a conference in Toyama, Japan.

KATRIN collected data over a few weeks of its
70 initial run in April and May. The detector monitored the nuclear decay of a heavy isotope of hydrogen called tritium. During this process, a neutron turns into a proton and emits an electron and a neutrino. KATRIN cannot detect the neutrinos directly. Instead,
75 it measures the range of energies of the electrons that shoot around inside a 23-metre-long, blimp-shaped chamber, which is the largest ultra-high-vacuum system in the world. This measurement reveals the range of energies of the unseen neutrinos, which in
80 turn reveals their mass.

During the next five years, Drexlin's collaboration plans to make continuous improvements to KATRIN's sensitivity that could enable it to make an actual

CONTINUE

measurement of a neutrino's mass — or to narrow the
85 range of the estimate as far as the machine's sensitivity
will allow. Cosmological observations suggest that the
mass of neutrinos could be 0.1 eV or lighter.

35

Based on Passage 1, what can be reasonably inferred
about neutrinos?

A) A person holding one would not be able to feel its
weight.

B) They have surprised scientists more than any
other particle has.

C) They provide a direct measurement of the mass of
the early universe.

D) Calculating their size helps determine the charge
of other particles.

36

Which choice from Passage 1 provides the best
evidence for the answer to the previous question?

A) Lines 3–5 ("They were…mass")

B) Lines 14–19 ("The analysis…electron")

C) Lines 33–35 ("By carefully…neutrino")

D) Lines 40–44 ("Only by…better")

37

The author uses the word "weirdest" in line 1 most
likely to

A) point out problems with previous observations.

B) indicate that neutrinos can be puzzling.

C) suggest the unusual nature of recent experiments.

D) describe previous observations as awkward.

38

As used in line 42, "robust" most nearly means

A) exact.

B) healthy.

C) reliable.

D) vigorous.

39

The last paragraph of Passage 2 serves mainly to

A) support the claim that scientists have studied
particles for many years.

B) explain the methods scientists will use to measure
neutrinos.

C) celebrate the researchers' achievements.

D) describe future research possibilities.

40

What main purpose do Passages 1 and 2 share?

A) To share discoveries about one type of particle

B) To describe how researchers develop new
measurement tools

C) To summarize what physicists have learned about
subatomic particles

D) To persuade scientists to make more accurate
measurements

CONTINUE

41

The authors of Passage 1 and Passage 2 would most likely agree that

A) researchers have not given neutrinos as much attention as they deserve.

B) indirect measurements will replace direct observation in scientific study.

C) any valuable discovery raises more questions than it answers.

D) subatomic particles do not always keep the same form.

42

Which choice from Passage 2 provides the best evidence for the answer to the previous question?

A) Lines 55–59 ("An experiment…mass")

B) Lines 63–65 ("This measurement…eV")

C) Lines 72–73 ("During this…neutrino")

D) Line 74 ("KATRIN cannot…directly")

STOP

If you finish before time is called, you may check your work on this section only.
Do not turn to any other section.

Writing and Language Test

30 MINUTES, 40 QUESTIONS

Turn to Section 2 of your answer sheet to answer the questions in this section.

Questions 1-10 are based on the following passage.

Expanding Europe's Understanding

In 1295, Italian explorer and trader Marco Polo returned to his home of Venice after 24 years of travel along the Silk Road to China. He brought with him precious gems—such as **1** diamonds, rubies, and, sapphires—as well as a Chinese navigation device: the compass. Polo also **2** carried, alongside the diamonds, rubies, sapphires, and compass, knowledge

1

A) NO CHANGE
B) diamonds, rubies, and
C) diamonds; rubies and
D) diamonds, rubies; and

2

A) NO CHANGE
B) carried in addition to the diamonds, rubies, sapphires, and compass
C) carried
D) carried, aside from the diamonds, rubies, sapphires, and compass,

CONTINUE

he had **3** gained; from his journey east. He introduced the ideas of paper currency and burning coal for heat, and he showed Europeans that their societies were not the only advanced civilizations. **4**

Polo, along with his father and uncle, had set out to deliver items to China, a journey that took them over three years to complete. Upon arriving in China, Polo became appointed as a diplomat to assist the ruler Kublai Khan. In this **5** role as a diplomat, Polo traveled extensively in the Chinese empire and throughout Asia. He encountered

3

A) NO CHANGE
B) gained. From
C) gained from
D) gained, it was from

4

At this point, the writer is considering adding the following sentence.

> Europeans considered themselves advanced because of the technologies they used, though some had been invented elsewhere.

Should the writer make this addition here?

A) Yes, because it helps show how influential Marco Polo was.
B) Yes, because it provides information that supports what was previously stated about advanced civilizations.
C) No, because it interrupts the discussion of Marco Polo's journey with a largely unrelated detail.
D) No, because it contains information that was previously stated.

5

A) NO CHANGE
B) life,
C) life as a diplomat,
D) role,

CONTINUE

many things that were unknown in **6** Europe.

[1] After returning to Venice with his fortune in gemstones, Polo dictated a detailed tale of his travels to a writer. [2] His book, *The Travels of Marco Polo*, spread across Europe over the next century. [3] Polo's explanation of paper money, which was very different from the European monetary system, relying on heavy gold and silver, **7** was new and intriguing. [4] The geographic information he provided eventually led to the creation of the Fra Mauro map, one of the most significant historical maps and the most accurate at the time. [5] Polo's book also detailed the paper currency used in the East, which he considered to be a superior system. **8**

6

The writer is considering revising the underlined portion to the following.

> Europe, including animals, monetary systems, and technologies.

Should the writer make this revision?

A) Yes, because it gives details that further explain Marco Polo's everyday life in Asia.

B) Yes, because it provides additional relevant information about what Marco Polo learned in his travels.

C) No, because it doesn't fully explain how he communicated with people in Asia.

D) No, because it provides information that is not related to the paragraph's focus on Kublai Khan.

7

A) NO CHANGE

B) were

C) is

D) are

8

To make this paragraph most logical, sentence 3 should be placed

A) where it is now.

B) after sentence 1.

C) after sentence 4.

D) after sentence 5.

CONTINUE

In addition to these specific effects, Polo's travels also inspired other people to explore the world. The curiosity spurred by his tales contributed to the Age of Discovery, a period of European history that involved significant overseas exploration.

9 The original manuscripts of Polo's book are now lost, but approximately 150 copies in different languages still exist. Because these manuscripts were written before the invention of the printing press, the versions all have significant differences. While it may never be known exactly what Polo's original manuscript said, his influence lives on in many areas, **10** including cartography, currency, and exploration.

9

Which sentence, if added here, would most effectively introduce the topic of the paragraph?

A) Christopher Columbus was famously influenced by Polo's travels.

B) The Age of Discovery led to greater geographic understanding but also increased conflict.

C) Some historians have questioned the accuracy of certain details in Polo's book.

D) Sadly, a complete and accurate account of Polo's tales no longer exists.

10

A) NO CHANGE

B) including—

C) including:

D) including;

CONTINUE

Questions 11-20 are based on the following passage.

Crabs Can Navigate

Research has shown that both terrestrial and aquatic animals practice spatial **11** learning, and the ability to navigate a physical environment. Biologists study spatial learning to understand how animals find their way around familiar territory. **12** A team of scientists at Swansea University is hoping to learn more about the spatial learning abilities of both terrestrial and aquatic animals.

Dr. Edward Pope, a marine biologist at Swansea University, said that the new study "is important because we know that insects, especially ants and bees, have some impressive mental abilities but we haven't really looked for them in their aquatic counterparts." The results of the study shed light on how members of an aquatic species navigate **13** they're underwater environment to find things like food. **14**

11

A) NO CHANGE
B) learning. The
C) learning the
D) learning—the

12

Which sentence provides the best transition to the next paragraph?

A) NO CHANGE

B) A team of scientists at Swansea University wants to research the spatial learning abilities of many different aquatic species to better understand spatial learning in shore crabs.

C) A team of scientists at Swansea University recently published a study that assessed the spatial learning abilities of the shore crab, an aquatic creature.

D) A team of scientists at Swansea University is researching why shore crabs need spatial learning abilities to find their way around a physical environment.

13

A) NO CHANGE
B) they are
C) their
D) there

14

The writer is considering revising the paragraph to remove the quotation from Pope. Assuming that the revision would result in a complete sentence, should the quotation be kept or deleted?

A) Kept, because it gives a reason that Pope and his team wanted to study shore crabs.

B) Kept, because it provides necessary details about the scientific approach to Pope's study.

C) Deleted, because it does not contribute to the paragraph's focus on the importance of studying spatial learning abilities in aquatic animals.

D) Deleted, because it gives an unnecessary fact that obscures the paragraph's focus.

CONTINUE

According to Pope, shore crabs frequently navigate complex environments. This fact led him to suspect that the [15] crabs may have complex spatial learning abilities. In order to prove this theory, Pope and his colleagues put a group of shore crabs to the test.

[1] At the end of this period, scientists had observed a decrease in both the time it took each of the 12 crabs to complete the maze and the number of wrong turns each crab took. [2] The team taught 12 shore crabs to navigate an underwater maze, which contained several false paths to the end and one true path. [3] Over a four-week period, scientists placed food only at the end of the true path to reward those crabs that successfully completed the maze. [4] When the crabs were returned to the maze [16] too weak later, [17] you completed the maze in less than eight minutes. [5] To determine the significance of this finding, scientists introduced a second, untrained group of crabs to the maze. [6] Many of the crabs in the second group did not complete the maze, and those that did took much longer to do so than the crabs from the first group did. [18]

15
A) NO CHANGE
B) crabs, perchance,
C) crabs, perhaps,
D) crabs, possibly,

16
A) NO CHANGE
B) two weeks
C) too weeks
D) two weak

17
A) NO CHANGE
B) they
C) he or she
D) it

18
To make this paragraph most logical, sentence 1 should be placed
A) where it is now.
B) after sentence 2.
C) after sentence 3.
D) after sentence 5.

CONTINUE

The difference in performance between the two groups of crabs led the team to conclude that the first group of crabs remembered the topography of the maze. Pope **19** desperately wishes to conduct further research into the way shore crabs navigate in ocean conditions created by climate change. **20** Despite this, the research done by Pope and his team demonstrates that shore crabs have complex spatial learning abilities.

19

A) NO CHANGE

B) dreams with hope that there will be

C) has his heart set on conducting

D) would like to conduct

20

A) NO CHANGE

B) As the research done by Pope and his team demonstrates,

C) As an indication of the research done by Pope and his team,

D) Due to the research done by Pope and his team,

CONTINUE ▶

Questions 21-30 are based on the following passage and supplementary material.

Modern Medicine

Robotic surgery, also known as robot-assisted surgery, is a medical technology in which an advanced robot with arms and small instruments is controlled by a surgeon. This allows the doctor to perform **21** puzzling procedures without having to make significant incisions on **22** patients' bodies. The first surgical robot was created in 1985, but the uses for surgical robots were initially limited. In 2000, the Food and Drug Administration approved the da Vinci system for general laparoscopic surgery. Now, surgical robots have changed the medical **23** industry. They allow doctors to make precise cuts, even from afar.

In the past, a surgeon would have had to make a long cut for most operations. This can result in more blood loss and longer recovery times for patients. With a surgical robot, after he or she makes a tiny cut, a physician **24** have been able to use a camera to see inside the patient. Then, the doctor can use the controls to conduct the surgery with the robot's miniature tools. Since this technology is fairly new, a study was completed in 2018 to determine how doctors are trained to use surgical robots before operating on patients. Of the 71 programs that were surveyed, 99 percent used a robotic simulator, and **25** medical programs used robots in 86 percent of their classes.

Responses of 71 Medical Programs on How They Train Doctors in Robotic Surgery

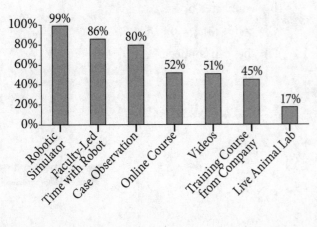

21

A) NO CHANGE
B) twisted
C) mysterious
D) complex

22

A) NO CHANGE
B) patients body's
C) patients bodies'
D) patient's bodies

23

Which choice most effectively combines the sentences at the underlined portion?
A) industry, though they allow
B) industry, which allows
C) industry by allowing
D) industry that allows

24

A) NO CHANGE
B) was
C) is
D) were

25

Which choice most accurately represents the data in the chart?
A) NO CHANGE
B) 86 percent used faculty-led time with a robot.
C) students spent 86 percent of their time using the robots.
D) another 86 percent trained students through observational experience.

CONTINUE ▶

Furthermore, [26] 51 percent of programs used videos as part of their training.

Aside from helping surgeons to make more precise movements, robotic surgery can also allow physicians to conduct surgeries remotely. For example, although an isolated or impoverished region might not have [27] access to an effective local surgeon, if a surgical robot were available it could actually be controlled by a doctor working in another city or even another country. A 2017 study by Dr. Ryan Madder, published in *EuroIntervention*, showed a 95 percent overall success rate for such surgeries. [28] Surprisingly, the study showed that no patients died or had to have procedures repeated before being discharged from the hospital.

Surgical robots can help doctors to make precise movements in complex procedures. [29] For this reason, they also allow doctors to operate on patients from a distance, which saves on travel time and costs. Since patients sometimes need a surgery right away, surgical robotics is a field [30] while connecting people with life-saving technology.

[26]

Which choice most accurately and precisely provides specific data from the chart?
A) NO CHANGE
B) 51 programs
C) some of the participants
D) additional programs surveyed

[27]

A) NO CHANGE
B) access, to an effective local surgeon,
C) access to an effective local surgeon
D) access, to an effective local surgeon

[28]

A) NO CHANGE
B) The study, though,
C) As previously stated, the study
D) The study additionally

[29]

A) NO CHANGE
B) Conversely,
C) As another benefit,
D) Thus,

[30]

A) NO CHANGE
B) connected by
C) connecting with
D) that can connect

CONTINUE

Questions 31-40 are based on the following passage.

Queen Bess

The crowd was **31** gathering, on, September 3, 1922, as Bessie Coleman looked up to see a clear sky, ideal conditions for her air show. She was relieved that the sky was cloudless, and the temperature was mild; the show had already been postponed because of to bad weather. The crowd continued to grow at Curtiss Field in Long Island, NY for Bessie's first American airshow. She took a deep breath as she prepared to fly. The journey to this moment had been long.

Years prior, Bessie had fallen in love with flying while watching newsreels about World War I. **32** At this point of war, technological advancements, especially in aviation, increased, and many images of the war featured pilots and fighter planes. Inspired by these aviators, Bessie applied to many American flight schools but was rejected by each one because of her race and gender. For aspiring aviators, if they were white, they studied in the United States, but if they were black and female, like Bessie, **33** you had to look abroad to find training.

Bessie planned to attend a flight school in France, a more progressive nation than the United States in the early twentieth century. She worked hard, saved money, and learned French. In November 1920, she moved to France and enrolled in the Caudron Brothers' School of Aviation, where she met Gaston and Rene Caudron. These were the **34** instructors, who would train Bessie, in the skills and techniques of aviation. Bessie knew that aviation training was dangerous. **35** She persisted, and on June 15, 1921, she earned her pilot's license.

31

A) NO CHANGE
B) gathering: on
C) gathering on
D) gathering, on

32

A) NO CHANGE
B) At this time
C) During this time
D) For this period

33

A) NO CHANGE
B) she
C) he or she
D) they

34

A) NO CHANGE
B) instructors who would train Bessie
C) instructors who would train Bessie,
D) instructors, who would train Bessie

35

Which choice, if added here, would most effectively explain why Bessie might be cautious?

A) She knew that her training would take more than six months.
B) Even now, flying can be risky for pilots.
C) She had often imagined being in the pilot's seat.
D) She had seen a fellow classmate die in a crash.

[1] When Bessie returned to the United States, she was disappointed by the lack of career opportunities. [2] Once again she was unable to find an instructor in any American school, so she headed back to Europe. [3] Rather than continue her career search, she decided to pursue advanced aviation training. [4] She studied in France, the Netherlands, and Germany to master a range of aerial tricks and stunts. [5] In August 1922, she came back to New York, ready to perform. **36**

At Curtiss Field, Bessie took to the sky and performed daring stunts: barrel rolls, loops, figure eights, and low dives. **37** The crowd cheered loudly **38** because they loved her performance. When she landed, the show may

36

To make this paragraph most logical, sentence 2 should be placed

A) where it is now.

B) after sentence 3.

C) after sentence 4.

D) after sentence 5.

37

At this point, the writer is considering adding the following sentence.

> After World War II, safety concerns about stunt flying curtailed its popularity, so today it is difficult to find a performance that features these particular tricks.

Should the writer make this addition here?

A) Yes, because it adds a detail about the current time to make the passage more relevant to the reader.

B) Yes, because it supports the paragraph's point about the difficulty of the stunts.

C) No, because it is irrelevant to the passage's focus on how Coleman became an aviator.

D) No, because it blurs the paragraph's focus on explaining airshows.

38

A) NO CHANGE

B) because they wanted to see her perform again.

C) to show they enjoyed watching her.

D) DELETE the underlined portion and end the sentence with a period.

CONTINUE

have been over, but her career was only beginning. After that successful debut, Bessie went on to tour the country, showcasing a range of aerial maneuvers and **39** electrifying audiences. **40**

A) NO CHANGE

B) pleasing

C) occupying

D) growing

The writer wants to conclude with a thought that emphasizes the idea of Bessie Coleman as a significant aviator. Which sentence, if added here, would best accomplish this goal?

A) "Queen Bess" continues to be an inspiration for those who want to fly.

B) Bessie Coleman would always remember that first airshow at Curtiss Field.

C) Bessie Coleman always knew that stunt flying would start her career.

D) Though it wasn't her initial goal, Bessie Coleman's decision to return to Europe was the correct one.

STOP

If you finish before time is called, you may check your work on this section only. Do not turn to any other section.

Math Test – No Calculator

20 MINUTES, 13 QUESTIONS

Turn to Section 3 of your answer sheet to answer the questions in this section.

DIRECTIONS

For questions 1–10, solve each problem, choose the best answer from the choices provided, and fill in the corresponding circle on your answer sheet. **For questions 11–13,** solve the problem and enter your answer in the grid on the answer sheet. Please refer to the directions before question 11 on how to enter your answers in the grid. You may use any available space in your test booklet for scratch work.

NOTES

1. The use of a calculator **is not permitted**.
2. All variables and expressions used represent real numbers unless otherwise indicated.
3. Figures provided in this test are drawn to scale unless otherwise indicated.
4. All figures lie in a plane unless otherwise indicated.
5. Unless otherwise indicated, the domain of a given function f is the set of all real numbers x for which $f(x)$ is a real number.

REFERENCE

$A = \pi r^2$
$C = 2\pi r$

$A = \ell w$

$A = \frac{1}{2} bh$

$c^2 = a^2 + b^2$

Special Right Triangles

$V = \ell wh$

$V = \pi r^2 h$

$V = \frac{4}{3}\pi r^3$

$V = \frac{1}{3}\pi r^2 h$

$V = \frac{1}{3}\ell wh$

The number of degrees of arc in a circle is 360.
The number of radians of arc in a circle is 2π.
The sum of the measures in degrees of the angles of a triangle is 180.

CONTINUE

1

A secondhand sports store sells two types of softball equipment: gloves for $20 each and bats for $50 each. On a particular day, the store sold 52 pieces of softball equipment for a total of $1,700. Which system of equations represents the relationship between the number of gloves, g, and the number of bats, b, sold on this day?

A) $\begin{cases} g + b = 1{,}700 \\ 20g + 50b = 52(1{,}700) \end{cases}$

B) $\begin{cases} g + b = 52 \\ 20g + 50b = (1{,}700) \end{cases}$

C) $\begin{cases} g + b = 52 \\ 20g + 50b = 52(1{,}700) \end{cases}$

D) $\begin{cases} 20g = 50b \\ 52g + 52b = (1{,}700) \end{cases}$

2

What is the value of a in the equation $\dfrac{8}{a} = \dfrac{2}{12}$?

A) 16

B) 24

C) 48

D) 106

3

x	0	1	2	3	4
$f(x)$	2	−2	−6	−10	−14

Some values of x and their corresponding $f(x)$ values are shown in the table above. Which of the following functions could represent the relationship between x and $f(x)$?

A) $f(x) = 4x - 2$

B) $f(x) = -2x + 2$

C) $f(x) = -3x + 1$

D) $f(x) = -4x + 2$

CONTINUE

4

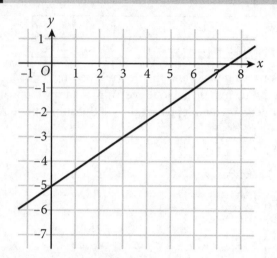

Which of the following equations is graphed on the *xy*-plane above?

A) $y = \frac{2}{3}x - 5$

B) $y = -\frac{2}{3}x + 5$

C) $y = \frac{3}{2}x - 5$

D) $y = -\frac{3}{2}x + 5$

5

$$-9(3t - 3v) + (9t - 13v)$$

Which of the following expressions is equivalent to the expression above?

A) $-18t - 40v$

B) $-18t + 14v$

C) $36t + 14v$

D) $36t - 40v$

6

Which of the following is equivalent to the expression $3c^2 - 10c + 8$?

A) $(3c - 4)(c - 2)$

B) $(3c + 4)(c - 2)$

C) $(3c - 8)(c + 1)$

D) $(3c + 8)(c + 1)$

7

If $(8m - 3) - (-2m + 6) = 0$, what is the value of m ?

A) $m = 1.5$

B) $m = 0.9$

C) $m = 0.5$

D) $m = 0.3$

CONTINUE

8

The formula for determining the angular speed, ω, of an object at an angular acceleration, α, is $\omega = \omega_0 + \alpha t$, where ω_0 is the initial angular speed and t is the time. Which formula represents α in terms of ω, ω_0, and t ?

A) $\alpha = \dfrac{\omega}{\omega_0} + t$

B) $\alpha = \omega - \omega_0 - t$

C) $\alpha = \omega - \omega_0 + t$

D) $\alpha = \dfrac{\omega}{\omega_0} + t$

9

A company makes two different sizes of cylindrical paperweights with identical volumes. If the radius of Paperweight X is one-third the radius of Paperweight Y, then the height of Paperweight X is how many times the height of Paperweight Y ?

A) 9

B) 3

C) $\dfrac{1}{3}$

D) $\dfrac{1}{9}$

10

Cost of Electricity

Electricity charge	Cost
Supply	6 cents per kilowatt hour
Delivery	3 cents per kilowatt hour

Mark's electric bill breakdown is shown in the table above. In addition to his electric bill, Mark's only other apartment expense is $950 a month for rent. The expression $C = (0.06 + 0.03)h + 950$ shows the cost C, in dollars, of living in the apartment for a month as a function of h, the number of kilowatt hours of electricity used in a month. What does the y-intercept of the graph of this equation represent?

A) The cost of electricity supply and delivery per kilowatt hour

B) The cost of electricity supply and rent for a month

C) The cost of rent for a month

D) The cost of rent and electricity per kilowatt hour

CONTINUE

DIRECTIONS

For questions 11–13, solve the problem and enter your answer in the grid, as described below, on the answer sheet.

1. Although not required, it is suggested that you write your answer in the boxes at the top of the columns to help you fill in the circles accurately. You will receive credit only if the circles are filled in correctly.

2. Mark no more than one circle in any column.

3. No question has a negative answer.

4. Some problems may have more than one correct answer. In such cases, grid only one answer.

5. **Mixed numbers** such as $3\frac{1}{2}$ must be gridded as 3.5 or 7/2. (If 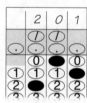 is entered into the grid, it will be interpreted as $\frac{31}{2}$, not as $3\frac{1}{2}$.)

6. **Decimal Answers:** If you obtain a decimal answer with more digits than the grid can accommodate, it may be either rounded or truncated, but it must fill the entire grid.

Answer: $\frac{7}{12}$ Answer: 2.5

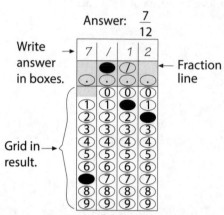 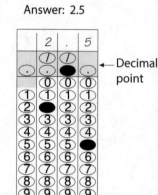

Acceptable ways to grid $\frac{2}{3}$ are:

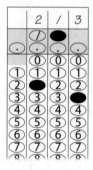  

Answer: 201 – either position is correct

NOTE: You may start your answers in any column, space permitting. Columns you don't need to use should be left blank.

11

$$-8x + 3y = 20$$
$$-4x - 2y = 3$$

The ordered pair (x, y) is a solution to the system of equations above. What is the value of y ?

12

$$y = -3x^2 + x + \frac{1}{2}$$

What is the value of the y-intercept of the equation above when it is graphed in the xy-plane?

13

A class with 9 students went to a local museum. Each student bought a general admission ticket for $10. Each special exhibit ticket at the museum costs the same price, and 2 students bought 4 special exhibit tickets each, while 7 students bought 3 special exhibit tickets each. The total cost for the general admission tickets and special exhibit tickets was $177.00. What was the cost, in dollars, of each special exhibit ticket? (Note: Disregard the $ sign when gridding your answer.)

STOP
If you finish before time is called, you may check your work on this section only.
Do not turn to any other section.

Math Test – Calculator

40 MINUTES, 25 QUESTIONS

Turn to Section 4 of your answer sheet to answer the questions in this section.

DIRECTIONS

For questions 1–21, solve each problem, choose the best answer from the choices provided, and fill in the corresponding circle on your answer sheet. **For questions 22–25**, solve the problem and enter your answer in the grid on the answer sheet. Please refer to the directions before question 22 on how to enter your answers in the grid. You may use any available space in your test booklet for scratch work.

NOTES

1. The use of a calculator **is permitted**.

2. All variables and expressions used represent real numbers unless otherwise indicated.

3. Figures provided in this test are drawn to scale unless otherwise indicated.

4. All figures lie in a plane unless otherwise indicated.

5. Unless otherwise indicated, the domain of a given function f is the set of all real numbers x for which $f(x)$ is a real number.

REFERENCE

$A = \pi r^2$
$C = 2\pi r$

$A = \ell w$

$A = \frac{1}{2}bh$

$c^2 = a^2 + b^2$

Special Right Triangles

$V = \ell wh$

$V = \pi r^2 h$

$V = \frac{4}{3}\pi r^3$

$V = \frac{1}{3}\pi r^2 h$

$V = \frac{1}{3}\ell wh$

The number of degrees of arc in a circle is 360.
The number of radians of arc in a circle is 2π.
The sum of the measures in degrees of the angles of a triangle is 180.

CONTINUE ➤

1

An office supply store sells boxes of paperclips. Each box contains at least 300 but no more than 400 paperclips. Which of the following could be the total number of paperclips in 5 boxes?

A)   850

B)   1,250

C)   1,650

D)   2,050

$5x$

$\times 5$

$300 < X < 400$

$1500 < 5X < 2000$

2

A company conducted a survey in which it asked 500 of its employees whether they were satisfied with their current work schedule. The table below shows the responses from all 500 employees that completed the survey.

	Part-time	Full-time
Satisfied with schedule	126	119
Dissatisfied with schedule	108	?

How many of the full-time employees reported that they were dissatisfied with their work schedules?

A)   147

B)   174

C)   246

D)   354

108
126
119

3

A teacher uses 2 dry erase markers for every student in his class each year. He also needs 1 red pen for every 5 students. If he determines that he will need 7 red pens for the upcoming school year, which of the following could be the number of dry erase markers that he expects to use?

A)   50

B)   60

C)   70

D)   80

$\dfrac{1}{5}$ $\dfrac{7}{x}$

4

The table below shows the maximum and minimum elevations in five counties in Missouri.

Elevation (in meters)

	Clark	Cooper	Putnam	Scotland	St. Charles
Maximum elevation	239	289	329	240	195
Minimum elevation	132	153	196	119	122

What is the mean maximum elevation, in meters, of the five counties shown?

A)   201

B)   201.4

C)   258

D)   258.4

CONTINUE

5

A random sample of 200 widgets was tested from the 5,913 widgets produced by a factory one day. If 41 of the widgets were defective, approximately how many widgets produced in the factory that day would be expected to be defective?

A) 1,200

B) 2,200

C) 3,000

D) 4,700

$$\frac{41}{200} = \frac{X}{5913}$$

6

A city adds a 5% hotel tax to the advertised nightly rate for all hotels booked in the city. If the advertised nightly rate for a certain hotel is $117.50, approximately how much hotel tax will be added to the bill?

A) $5.00

B) $6.00

C) $7.00

D) $8.00

$$\frac{117.50 \cdot 5}{100}$$

7

A teacher asks his students to estimate the weight of the snow on their porches after a light snowfall given the weight of snow per cubic meter. One student's porch is a rectangle measuring 305 centimeters by 425 centimeters and is covered by an even layer of snow 5 millimeters thick. What are the dimensions of the layer of snow (width by length by thickness) in meters? (Note: 1 centimeter = 10 millimeters and 1 meter = 100 centimeters)

A) 3,050 meters by 4,250 meters by 50 meters

B) 3,050 meters by 4,250 meters by 5,000 meters

C) 3.05 meters by 4.25 meters by $\frac{1}{100}$ meters

D) 3.05 meters by 4.25 meters by $\frac{1}{200}$ meters

8

A scientist at a greenhouse studied the relationship between the growth rate of a particular tree species and its current height. The conditions in the greenhouse were kept constant throughout the study period. The results are shown below, along with the graph of the exponential function that best models the data.

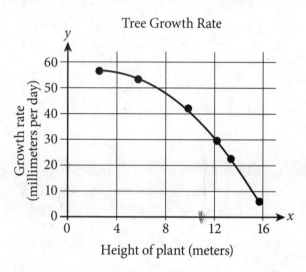

Tree Growth Rate

According to the model, which of the following is the best estimate of the plant's growth rate, in millimeters per day, when the plant was 11 meters tall?

A) 14

B) 15

C) 30

D) 36

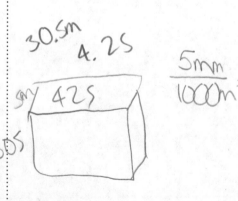

CONTINUE

9

The rates to book a private tour with a company are shown below.

Private Tour Rates
(maximum of 24 participants)

Price of tour ($)	Number of participants
50	up to 2
100	more than 2 and no more than 4
150	more than 4 and no more than 6
200	more than 6 and no more than 12
225	more than 12 and no more than 18
250	more than 18 and no more than 24

Which graph best represents the relationship between the number of participants and the total charge of the tour, in dollars?

step
function

A)

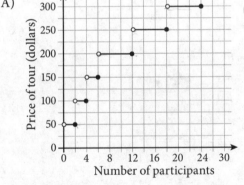

B)

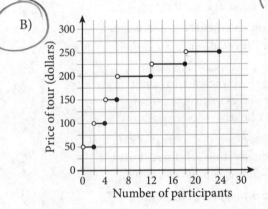

C)

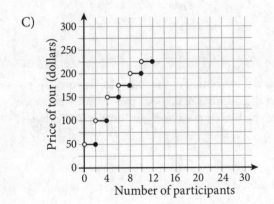

D)

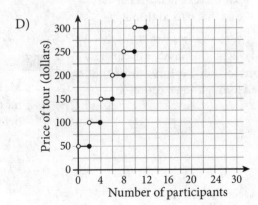

CONTINUE

10

A bakery's specialty flour is a mixture of almond and coconut flour. The ratio of almond flour to coconut flour is 7:38 by volume. If a bakery uses 180 cups of the flour mixture in a day, what is the volume, in cups, of the almond flour used?

A) 28
B) 68
C) 126
D) 152

$180-X$

$$\frac{7}{38} = \frac{X}{(180-X)}$$

$38X = 1260 - 7X$

$45X = 1260 \quad X = 28$

11

The equations below show the total number of cars, t, that have passed through two intersections after d hours of daylight.

         Intersection X: $t = 450d$
         Intersection Y: $t = 150d$

Which of the following statements is an accurate comparison based on the equations?

A) The number of cars that passed through Intersection X per hour increased at a faster rate than the number of cars that passed through Intersection Y per hour.

B) For each hour of daylight, the number of cars that passed through Intersection X is three times the number that passed through Intersection Y.

C) The number of cars that passed through Intersection Y per hour increased at a faster rate than the number of cars that passed through Intersection X per hour.

D) For each hour of daylight, the number of cars that passed through Intersection Y is three times the number that passed through Intersection X.

Questions 12–14 refer to the following information.

Maria plans to purchase a new cell phone for her existing data plan. The cell phone will have a 6.5% sales tax on the purchase price, plus a flat fee of $20 for the phone charger. She has already used 2 Gigabytes of data this month, and her limit is 7 Gigabytes. Maria uses data for 2 hours each day and uses 0.25 Gigabytes for each of those hours. She will use the equation $p = \dfrac{m}{n}$, where m is the number of minutes of power and n is the number of kilowatt-hours of electricity, to determine her charge efficiency, p.

12

Which of the following formulas can Maria use to determine the number of kilowatt-hours of electricity she needs to power her cell phone for a certain number of minutes?

A) $n = pm$

B) $n = \dfrac{m}{p}$

C) $n = \dfrac{p}{m}$

D) $n = p + m$

13

Maria can use which of the following inequalities to model the number of days, d, she can use her phone before she hits or goes over her limit of 7 Gigabytes?

A) $2d + 0.5 \leq 7$

B) $2 + 0.5d \leq 7$

C) $2 \leq 0.5d + 7$

D) $2 \leq 0.5 + 7d$

CONTINUE

14

Including the flat fee for the phone charger and the sales tax, Maria will need to pay a total of $685.72 for the cell phone. How much is the purchase price of the cell phone, to the nearest dollar?

A) $750

B) $659

C) $625

D) $622

6. 665.72

$$1.065(x) = \frac{665.72}{1.065}$$

$$= 625$$

▲

15

A new video game is being tested by a focus group. A group of researchers randomly selected people to evaluate, on a check system, the game they just played. The results of the evaluation are shown in the table below.

Video Game Evaluations

Rating	# of People
✓–	14
✓	29
✓+	13
✓++	18

A total of 240 people played the video game. Based on the results of the evaluations, about how many people who played the video would have evaluated it as a ✓+ or higher?

A) 197

B) 100

C) 42

D) 31

$$\frac{31}{74} \quad \frac{X}{240}$$

16

The following data represents the shoulder heights in meters (m) of 7 elephants that live in a local zoo.

Elephant	Shoulder Height (m)
A	2.04
B	1.83
C	2.13
D	3.14
E	2.45
F	2.68
G	1.90
H	?

An additional elephant is added to the zoo, and its shoulder height is measured. Its shoulder height increases the median value of the group of elephants but decreases the mean value of the group. What is a possible measurement for the shoulder height of the 8th elephant?

A) 1.98 m

B) 2.13 m

C) 2.24 m

D) 2.31 m

1.83, 1.90, 2.04, 2.13, 2.45, 2.68, 3.14

X

$$2.13 < X < 2.31$$

CONTINUE

Questions 17–18 refer to the following information.

Scientists say the ability to run fast helps animals outrun predators and catch prey. The table below shows the distance, in kilometers, covered in 10 minutes (min) of running for several mammals from Africa.

Average Speeds of African Mammals

Animal	Distance covered in 10 min of running
African wild dog	12 km
Cheetah	18 km
Elephant	7 km
Giraffe	9 km
Lion	14 km
Zebra	11 km

17

In a stampede, a lion ran for 20 min, a cheetah ran for 10 min, an African wild dog ran for 10 min, and a zebra ran for 40 min. What is the total distance, in meters, that was covered by the animals?

A)   80 m

B)   102 m

C)   80,000 m

D)   102,000 m

(handwritten: 28, 12, 18, 44, 102)

18

Which of the following mammals covers a distance closest to the combined distance covered by a cheetah running for 15 min and a giraffe running for 5 min ?

A) Zebra running for 30 minutes

B) African wild dog running for 20 minutes

C) Lion running for 50 minutes

D) Elephant running for 60 minutes

(handwritten: 27, 9/10 × 5, 4.5, 31.5)

19

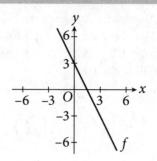

The xy-plane above shows line f. For constants r and s, the equation $y = rx + s$ represents line f. Which of the following sets of inequalities is true about r and s ?

A) $\begin{cases} 0 < r < 3 \\ s < 4 \end{cases}$

B) $\begin{cases} r > 0 \\ s > 2 \end{cases}$

C) $\begin{cases} r < 0 \\ s < 1 \end{cases}$

D) $\begin{cases} -3 < r < 0 \\ s > -1 \end{cases}$

(handwritten: y = mx + b, y = 3)

CONTINUE

20

Ms. Burke is growing tomatoes on a vine. She plants a starter plant with a height of 6 inches and estimates the height of the vine after each day for 6 days, as shown in the table below.

Height of Vine after Each Day of Growth

Day (x)	Height of Vine (y)
1	7.5 in
2	9.0 in
3	10.5 in
4	12.0 in
5	13.5 in
6	15.0 in

If the line passing through the points defined in the table is graphed on an xy-plane, which of the following is the best interpretation of the slope in the context of the problem?

A) The amount that the height of the vine is increasing each day

B) The height of the vine after the seventh day of growth

C) The height of the vine when it was first planted

D) The number of days for which the height of the tomato plant will increase

21

A teacher estimates that 1.5% of the district's students have red hair. Which of the following is the closest to the total number of students with red hair if there are approximately 350 students per school in the 9 different schools in the district?

A) 4,725

B) 525

C) 47

D) 5

$$\frac{3150 \cdot 1.5}{100}$$

CONTINUE

DIRECTIONS

For questions 22–25, solve the problem and enter your answer in the grid, as described below, on the answer sheet.

1. Although not required, it is suggested that you write your answer in the boxes at the top of the columns to help you fill in the circles accurately. You will receive credit only if the circles are filled in correctly.

2. Mark no more than one circle in any column.

3. No question has a negative answer.

4. Some problems may have more than one correct answer. In such cases, grid only one answer.

5. **Mixed numbers** such as $3\frac{1}{2}$ must be gridded as 3.5 or 7/2. (If [3 1 / 2] is entered into the grid, it will be interpreted as $\frac{31}{2}$, not as $3\frac{1}{2}$.)

6. **Decimal Answers:** If you obtain a decimal answer with more digits than the grid can accommodate, it may be either rounded or truncated, but it must fill the entire grid.

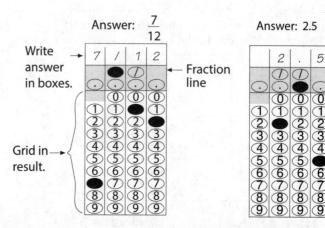

Answer: $\frac{7}{12}$

Write answer in boxes. ← Fraction line

Grid in result.

Answer: 2.5 ← Decimal point

Acceptable ways to grid $\frac{2}{3}$ are:

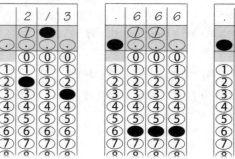

Answer: 201 – either position is correct

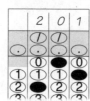 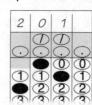

NOTE: You may start your answers in any column, space permitting. Columns you don't need to use should be left blank.

22

A cafe sells drink vouchers for a private event. A voucher for one drink costs $6 and a voucher for two drinks costs $10. A total of 89 drinks were purchased with vouchers, and the voucher sales total was $462. What is the total number of vouchers that were sold?

$6x + y = 89$ $x = -y + 89$

$6x + 10y = 462$

$6(-y + 89) + 10y = 462$

$-6y + 534 + 10y = 462$

$4y = -72$

$y = 49$ $x = -2y + 89$

$x + 2y = 89$

$6x + 10y = 462$

$6(-2y + 89) + 10y = 462$

$-12y + 534 + 10y =$

$-2y = -12$

$y = 36$

$x + 2(36) = 89$ $\boxed{17 + 36 = 53}$

$x + 72 = 89$

$x = 17$

23

$$-3a + 6b = 1.8$$
$$4a - 3b = 1.1$$

The ordered pair (a, b) is a solution to the system of equations above. What is the value of b ?

CONTINUE

Questions 24–25 refer to the following information.

A restaurant surveyed its customers to determine which beverage was most popular with breakfast. Participants were required to choose either coffee or tea. The partially completed table below shows the breakdown by age of a sample of 116 people who responded to a survey on their drink preferences.

Breakdown of Customers' Drink Preferences

		Age range in years				
		18–29	30–44	45–64	65+	Total
Drink preference	Coffee		21		4	
	Tea	17		12		
	Total		55		14	116

24

Among all the people represented in the survey, 25.6% of the people who chose coffee as their preferred beverage were 45–64 years old. What is the total number of people ages 18–29 who voted for either coffee or tea in the survey?

25

What is the total number of people from the sample who chose coffee as their preferred beverage?

▲

STOP
**If you finish before time is called, you may check your work on this section only.
Do not turn to any other section.**

The
Princeton
Review®

PSAT 8/9 PRACTICE ANSWER SHEET

| COMPLETE MARK ● | EXAMPLES OF INCOMPLETE MARKS 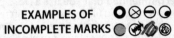 | It is recommended that you use a No. 2 pencil. It is very important that you fill in the entire circle darkly and completely. If you change your response, erase as completely as possible. Incomplete marks or erasures may affect your score. |

■ TEST NUMBER

■ SECTION 1

ENTER TEST NUMBER

For instance, for Practice Test #1, fill in the circle for 0 in the first column and for 1 in the second column.

0 ○ ○
1 ○ ○
2 ○ ○
3 ○ ○
4 ○ ○
5 ○ ○
6 ○ ○
7 ○ ○
8 ○ ○
9 ○ ○

1 A ○ B ○ C ● D ○
2 A ● B ○ C ○ D ○
3 A ○ B ○ C ● D ○
4 A ○ B ○ C ○ D ●
5 A ● B ○ C ○ D ○
6 A ○ B ○ C ○ D ●
7 A ○ B ○ C ○ D ○
8 A ○ B ○ C ○ D ○
9 A ○ B ○ C ○ D ○
10 A ○ B ○ C ○ D ○
11 A ○ B ○ C ○ D ○

12 A ○ B ○ C ○ D ○
13 A ○ B ○ C ○ D ○
14 A ○ B ○ C ○ D ○
15 A ○ B ○ C ○ D ○
16 A ○ B ○ C ○ D ○
17 A ○ B ○ C ○ D ○
18 A ○ B ○ C ○ D ○
19 A ○ B ○ C ○ D ○
20 A ○ B ○ C ○ D ○
21 A ○ B ○ C ○ D ○
22 A ○ B ○ C ○ D ○

23 A ○ B ○ C ○ D ○
24 A ○ B ○ C ○ D ○
25 A ○ B ○ C ○ D ○
26 A ○ B ○ C ○ D ○
27 A ○ B ○ C ○ D ○
28 A ○ B ○ C ○ D ○
29 A ○ B ○ C ○ D ○
30 A ○ B ○ C ○ D ○
31 A ○ B ○ C ○ D ○
32 A ○ B ○ C ○ D ○
33 A ○ B ○ C ○ D ○

34 A ○ B ○ C ○ D ○
35 A ○ B ○ C ○ D ○
36 A ○ B ○ C ○ D ○
37 A ○ B ○ C ○ D ○
38 A ○ B ○ C ○ D ○
39 A ○ B ○ C ○ D ○
40 A ○ B ○ C ○ D ○
41 A ○ B ○ C ○ D ○
42 A ○ B ○ C ○ D ○

The
Princeton
Review®

PSAT 8/9 PRACTICE ANSWER SHEET

COMPLETE MARK ●

EXAMPLES OF
INCOMPLETE MARKS

It is recommended that you use a No. 2 pencil. It is very important that you fill in the entire circle darkly and completely. If you change your response, erase as completely as possible. Incomplete marks or erasures may affect your score.

SECTION 2

	A B C D		A B C D		A B C D		A B C D		A B C D
1	○○○○	9	○○○○	17	○○○○	25	○○○○	33	○○○○
2	○○○○	10	○○○○	18	○○○○	26	○○○○	34	○○○○
3	○○○○	11	○○○○	19	○○○○	27	○○○○	35	○○○○
4	○○○○	12	○○○○	20	○○○○	28	○○○○	36	○○○○
5	○○○○	13	○○○○	21	○○○○	29	○○○○	37	○○○○
6	○○○○	14	○○○○	22	○○○○	30	○○○○	38	○○○○
7	○○○○	15	○○○○	23	○○○○	31	○○○○	39	○○○○
8	○○○○	16	○○○○	24	○○○○	32	○○○○	40	○○○○

PSAT 8/9 PRACTICE ANSWER SHEET

COMPLETE MARK ●

EXAMPLES OF
INCOMPLETE MARKS

It is recommended that you use a No. 2 pencil. It is very
important that you fill in the entire circle darkly and completely.
If you change your response, erase as completely as possible.
Incomplete marks or erasures may affect your score.

■ SECTION 3

1 A B C D ◯◯◯◯   5 A B C D ◯◯◯◯   9 A B C D ◯◯◯◯

2 A B C D ◯◯◯◯   6 A B C D ◯◯◯◯   10 A B C D ◯◯◯◯

3 A B C D ◯◯◯◯   7 A B C D ◯◯◯◯

4 A B C D ◯◯◯◯   8 A B C D ◯◯◯◯

11

	/	◯	◯	
	.	◯	◯	◯	◯
0	◯	◯	◯	◯
1	◯	◯	◯	◯
2	◯	◯	◯	◯
3	◯	◯	◯	◯
4	◯	◯	◯	◯
5	◯	◯	◯	◯
6	◯	◯	◯	◯
7	◯	◯	◯	◯
8	◯	◯	◯	◯
9	◯	◯	◯	◯

12

	/	◯	◯	
	.	◯	◯	◯	◯
0	◯	◯	◯	◯
1	◯	◯	◯	◯
2	◯	◯	◯	◯
3	◯	◯	◯	◯
4	◯	◯	◯	◯
5	◯	◯	◯	◯
6	◯	◯	◯	◯
7	◯	◯	◯	◯
8	◯	◯	◯	◯
9	◯	◯	◯	◯

13

	/	◯	◯	
	.	◯	◯	◯	◯
0	◯	◯	◯	◯
1	◯	◯	◯	◯
2	◯	◯	◯	◯
3	◯	◯	◯	◯
4	◯	◯	◯	◯
5	◯	◯	◯	◯
6	◯	◯	◯	◯
7	◯	◯	◯	◯
8	◯	◯	◯	◯
9	◯	◯	◯	◯

NO CALCULATOR
ALLOWED

PSAT 8/9 PRACTICE ANSWER SHEET

COMPLETE MARK ● EXAMPLES OF INCOMPLETE MARKS

It is recommended that you use a No. 2 pencil. It is very important that you fill in the entire circle darkly and completely. If you change your response, erase as completely as possible. Incomplete marks or erasures may affect your score.

■ SECTION 4

1 Ⓐ Ⓑ Ⓒ Ⓓ
2 Ⓐ Ⓑ Ⓒ Ⓓ
3 Ⓐ Ⓑ Ⓒ Ⓓ
4 Ⓐ Ⓑ Ⓒ Ⓓ
5 Ⓐ Ⓑ Ⓒ Ⓓ
6 Ⓐ Ⓑ Ⓒ Ⓓ

7 Ⓐ Ⓑ Ⓒ Ⓓ
8 Ⓐ Ⓑ Ⓒ Ⓓ
9 Ⓐ Ⓑ Ⓒ Ⓓ
10 Ⓐ Ⓑ Ⓒ Ⓓ
11 Ⓐ Ⓑ Ⓒ Ⓓ

12 Ⓐ Ⓑ Ⓒ Ⓓ
13 Ⓐ Ⓑ Ⓒ Ⓓ
14 Ⓐ Ⓑ Ⓒ Ⓓ
15 Ⓐ Ⓑ Ⓒ Ⓓ
16 Ⓐ Ⓑ Ⓒ Ⓓ

17 Ⓐ Ⓑ Ⓒ Ⓓ
18 Ⓐ Ⓑ Ⓒ Ⓓ
19 Ⓐ Ⓑ Ⓒ Ⓓ
20 Ⓐ Ⓑ Ⓒ Ⓓ
21 Ⓐ Ⓑ Ⓒ Ⓓ

22, 23, 24, 25 (grid-in response areas with digits / . 0 1 2 3 4 5 6 7 8 9)

CALCULATOR ALLOWED

Chapter 4
Practice Test 1:
Answers and
Explanations

PRACTICE TEST 1 ANSWER KEY

Section 1: Reading		Section 2: Writing and Language		Section 3: Math (No Calculator)	Section 4: Math (Calculator)	
1. A	22. A	1. B	21. D	1. B	1. C	14. C
2. C	23. C	2. C	22. A	2. C	2. A	15. B
3. B	24. D	3. C	23. C	3. D	3. C	16. C
4. A	25. B	4. C	24. C	4. A	4. D	17. D
5. C	26. A	5. D	25. B	5. B	5. A	18. A
6. B	27. D	6. B	26. A	6. A	6. B	19. D
7. D	28. A	7. A	27. A	7. B	7. D	20. A
8. C	29. D	8. D	28. D	8. D	8. D	21. C
9. D	30. C	9. D	29. C	9. A	9. B	22. 53
10. C	31. B	10. A	30. D	10. C	10. A	23. $\frac{7}{10}$ or 0.7
11. A	32. C	11. D	31. C	11. 2	11. B	24. 24
12. B	33. C	12. C	32. C	12. $\frac{1}{2}$ or 0.5	12. B	25. 43
13. C	34. B	13. C	33. D	13. 3	13. B	
14. A	35. A	14. A	34. B			
15. D	36. B	15. A	35. D			
16. C	37. B	16. B	36. B			
17. D	38. C	17. B	37. C			
18. C	39. D	18. C	38. D			
19. C	40. A	19. D	39. A			
20. B	41. D	20. B	40. A			
21. B	42. C					

PRACTICE TEST 1 EXPLANATIONS

Section 1—Reading

1. **A** The question asks about *a main theme of the passage*. Since this is a general question, it should be answered after the specific questions. The passage is a story about the narrator and his friend, Hassan. The narrator states in the second paragraph, *Over the years, I had seen a lot of guys run kites. But Hassan was by far the greatest kite runner I'd ever seen,* and the majority of the passage gives a specific example of Hassan's expertise during a kite-fighting tournament. The narrator follows Hassan, even though it appears that Hassan is running the wrong way to catch the kite. At the end of the passage, Hassan catches the kite, which shows that the narrator was right to trust Hassan. Eliminate answers that don't match the prediction. Keep (A) as it matches the prediction. Eliminate (B) because the passage doesn't focus on *hard work*; it focuses on Hassan's talent and on the relationship between Hassan and the narrator. Eliminate (C) because only Hassan is successful in catching the kite; the passage does not mention the other competitors doing their best. Therefore, the passage does not focus on competition bringing out the best in *each competitor*. Choice (D) matches the narrator's initial uncertainty, but since Hassan is successful, the passage indicates that the narrator was right to trust Hassan, rather than to *be cautious*. Eliminate (D). The correct answer is (A).

2. **C** The question asks why the author includes the *second paragraph*. Read the second paragraph as the window. The paragraph states, *But Hassan was by far the greatest kite runner I'd ever seen. It was downright eerie the way he always got to the spot the kite would land before the kite did, as if he had some sort of inner compass.* This emphasizes what the narrator thought about his friend Hassan's skill. Eliminate answers that don't match the prediction. Eliminate (A) because, although the second paragraph indicates that Hassan is *a skilled kite-runner*, it does not mention *how* he *became* skilled. This is a Mostly Right, Slightly Wrong trap answer. Eliminate (B) because there is no mention of *competitiveness* between the characters. This is a Could Be True trap answer that is not supported by direct evidence from the passage. Keep (C) because it matches the prediction; the narrator states his impression that Hassan was a skilled kite-runner. Eliminate (D) because the paragraph only focuses on Hassan and the narrator; it does not describe any *time period*. The correct answer is (C).

3. **B** The question asks for the evidence that best supports the narrator's description of Hassan as *the greatest kite runner I'd ever seen* (lines 13–14). Read the lines for each answer, eliminating any that do not support this description. The lines for (A) state that the narrator *had seen a lot of guys run kites,* but they don't mention Hassan, so eliminate (A). The lines for (B) refer to Hassan, saying, *It was downright eerie the way he always got to the spot the kite would land before the kite did, as if he had some sort of inner compass.* These lines support the description of Hassan as a great kite runner, so keep (B). The lines for (C) state that the narrator fell behind Hassan when they ran, but they don't directly support the idea that Hassan is a great kite runner. Eliminate (C). The lines for (D) describe the approaching kite runners, but they don't mention Hassan, so eliminate (D). The correct answer is (B).

4. **A**   The question asks what the phrase *"inner compass" most strongly suggests* about *Hassan*. Use the given line reference to find the window. The passage states *It was downright eerie the way he always got to the spot the kite would land before the kite did, as if he had some sort of inner compass*, meaning that Hassan is naturally very good at finding kites. Eliminate answers that don't match the prediction. Keep (A) because it matches the prediction. Eliminate (B) because there is no indication that Hassan is in a *strange city*. In fact, the passage implies that the children know this city very well. This is a Mostly Right, Slightly Wrong trap answer. Choice (C) can be eliminated because, while Hassan seems to be guided in the direction of the kite by an inner compass, the passage does not mention *morals*. This is a Right Words, Wrong Meaning trap answer based on another meaning of *inner compass* that is not supported by the passage. Eliminate (D) because there is no evidence that Hassan is *cheating*. The correct answer is (A).

5. **C**   The question asks what the word *ragged* most nearly means in line 22. Go back to the text, find the word *ragged*, and cross it out. Then read the window carefully, using context clues to determine another word that would fit in the text. The text says, *"Hassan! Wait!" I yelled, my breathing hot and ragged.* The narrator is running after Hassan, who is *faster*, so the narrator is struggling to breathe normally. Therefore, *ragged* must mean something like "uneven." *Fast* does not match "uneven," so eliminate (A). This is a Could Be True trap answer; it is likely that the narrator's breath is also *fast*, since he is running, but this is not the meaning of *ragged*. *Loud* does not match "uneven," so eliminate (B). *Rough* matches "uneven," so keep (C). *Fevered* does not match "uneven," so eliminate (D). This is a Right Answer, Wrong Question trap answer; *fevered* could match *hot*, but it is not the meaning of *ragged*. The correct answer is (C).

6. **B**   The question asks what *Hassan's actions suggest* about him after he and the narrator *reach the middle school*. Notice that this is the first question in a paired set, so it can be done in tandem with Q7. Look at the answer choices for Q7 first. The lines for (7A) come from the first paragraph, before the boys reach the middle school. Therefore, these lines do not answer Q6, so eliminate (7A). The lines for (7B) describe the narrator's actions rather than Hassan's actions. These lines do not answer Q6, so eliminate (7B). The lines for (7C) are spoken by the narrator; since these lines do not describe Hassan's actions, they do not answer Q6. Eliminate (7C). The lines for (7D) say, *Hassan popped a mulberry in his mouth. "It's coming," he said.* Check to see whether these lines support any of the answers for Q6. They support (6B): Hassan shows his confidence by sitting calmly and eating while he waits for the kite, and by stating that the kite is coming. Draw a line connecting (7D) and (6B). Without any support in the answers from Q7, (6A), (6C), and (6D) can be eliminated. The correct answers are (6B) and (7D).

7. **D**   (See explanation above.)

8. **C**   The question asks what *sound* is heard *while the kite is falling*. Since there is no line reference, use lead words and the order of the questions to find the window for the question. The answers for questions 6 and 7 came from lines 50–51, so the window for Q8 is most likely after those lines. Beginning with line 52, look for information about the kite falling and a sound. Lines 55–57 state, *I looked up,*

saw the kite plummeting toward us. I heard footfalls, shouts, an approaching melee of kite runners. The sounds being described come from the approaching group of competitors. Eliminate answers that don't match the prediction. Eliminate (A) as the paragraph does not mention the *wind*. Eliminate (B): although Hassan calls out to the narrator earlier in the passage, he does not call out to the narrator while the kite is falling. This is a Right Answer, Wrong Question trap answer. Keep (C) as it matches the prediction. Choice (D) can be eliminated because the sound of *parents cheering* is mentioned in the first paragraph, but it does not occur while the kite is falling. This is another Right Answer, Wrong Question trap answer. The correct answer is (C).

9. **D** The question asks about the *main idea of the passage*. Because this is a general question, it should be done after the specific questions. The first paragraph introduces *Pokémon Go* and says that *the phenomenon has made its way through civilization and is now venturing into uncharted territory: national parks.* The sixth paragraph captures the main idea of the passage, stating that *Pokémon Go may become a new way to explore historic parks.* Choice (A) is a Right Answer, Wrong Question trap answer; although the passage does mention that *injuries abound* when playing the game, this is not the main idea of the passage. Eliminate (A). Eliminate (B) because it does not mention Pokémon Go. Although (C) mentions both *Pokémon Go* and *national parks*, this is Right Words, Wrong Meaning trap answer. One of the park employees quoted in the passage says that games such as Pokémon Go *are a new and emerging opportunity to bring new audiences to the park*, but the passage doesn't indicate that Pokémon Go players are *more likely* than others to visit national parks. Eliminate (C). Keep (D) because it matches the prediction. The correct answer is (D).

10. **C** The question asks what the word *create* most nearly means in line 33. Go back to the text, find the word *create*, and cross it out. Then read the window carefully, using context clues to determine another word that would fit in the text. The text says, *"One of our goals as part of the National Park Service Centennial is to connect with and create the next generation of park visitors, supporters, and advocates."* Therefore, *create* must mean something like "develop." Choice (A) is a Could Be True trap answer; *design* can mean "to draw or plan out," which is an alternate meaning of *create* that is not supported by the passage. Eliminate (A). Eliminate (B) because *birth* means "give life to," which does not match "develop." Keep (C) because *foster* matches "develop." *Help* does not match "develop," so eliminate (D). The correct answer is (C).

11. **A** The question asks what the word *emerging* most nearly means in line 36. Go back to the text, find the word *emerging*, and cross it out. Then read the window carefully, using context clues to determine another word that would fit in the text. The text says, *"Games that use geolocation are a new and emerging opportunity to bring new audiences to the park."* Therefore, *emerging* must mean something like "growing." *Developing* matches "growing," so keep (A). *Appearing* means "becoming visible," which does not match "growing." Eliminate (B). *Becoming* does not match "growing," so eliminate (C). Note that (B) and (C) are Could Be True trap answers based on other meanings of *emerging* that are not supported by the text. *Unexpected* means "surprising," which does not match "growing." Eliminate (D). The correct answer is (A).

12. **B**   The question asks what assertion the example in lines 39–42 supports. This is the first question in a paired set, but it is easy to find, so it can be done on its own. Use the given line reference to find the window. The lines state, *Great Smoky Mountains's Mountain Farm Museum has three Pokéstops. When found, historical text will pop up on screen, and players can tap an icon to learn more before returning to the game.* The previous sentence states that *Pokémon Go also has an educational component to it.* Therefore, the Mountain Farm Museum's Pokéstops are examples of Pokémon Go's educational components. Eliminate answers that don't match the prediction. Eliminate (A) because there is no mention of *injury* in the window. Keep (B) because informing *Pokémon Go players about the national parks* matches the prediction. Eliminate (C) because there is no mention of the *National Park Service Centennial* in the window. Eliminate (D) because there is no indication that visitors *demanded* Pokémon Go. The correct answer is (B).

13. **C**   The question is the best evidence question in a paired set. Because Q12 was easy to find, simply look at the lines used to answer the previous question. Lines 38–42—*Pokémon Go also has an educational component to it. Great Smoky Mountains's Mountain Farm Museum has three Pokéstops. When found, historical text will pop up on screen, and players can tap an icon to learn more before returning to the game*—were used to answer Q12. Of these lines, only lines 38–39 are given as an answer choice. The correct answer is (C).

14. **A**   The question asks what *Lynda Doucette indicates.* Notice that this is the first question in a paired set, so it can be done in tandem with Q15. Look at the answers for Q15 first. The lines of (15A) say that Lynda Doucette claims *the park's landscape obstructs cell service* but that *she and her colleagues have found at least five Pokéstops.* Check the answers for Q14 to see whether any of the answers are supported by these lines. These lines do not support any of the answer choices in Q14; eliminate (15A). The lines in (15B) state, *"It gets people out there,"* Doucette says. *"I think it's an opportunity to bring a new audience to a site."* These lines do not support any of the answer choices in Q14; eliminate (15B). The lines in (15C) state, *But as play increases, injuries abound. Already, players have been hurt after falling or walking into obstacles while cruising for critters.* Although these lines may seem to match (14D), they were not spoken by Lynda Doucette, so they do not answer Q14. Eliminate (15C). The lines in (15D) state, *"I don't anticipate that we're going to have any new rules implemented,"* Doucette says. *"It's the same safety concerns we've had before this game."* These lines match (14A); since Doucette mentions the *same safety concerns*, there are no *unique safety concerns* for Pokémon Go players. Draw a line connecting (14A) and (15D). Without any support in the answers from Q15, (14B), (14C), and (14D) can be eliminated. The correct answers are (14A) and (15D).

15. **D**   (See explanation above.)

16. **C**   The question asks which park had fewer visits than *Olympic National Park* in *2018*, according to the graph. First locate the number of visits to Olympic National Park in 2018. The right side of the graph shows that Olympic National Park had 3,104,455 visits in 2018. There is only one park that had fewer visits in 2018: Glacier National Park. The correct answer is (C).

17. **D**   The question asks which statement best matches the structure of the passage. Since this is a general

question, it should be answered after the specific questions. The passage begins by stating, *Coral reefs are among the most valuable natural assets on Earth* and then discusses the role that *herbivorous fish* play in maintaining coral reefs. Eliminate answers that don't match the prediction. Though the authors do discuss *various types of herbivorous fish*, they do not discuss how these types *interact* with each other. Eliminate (A). Though the text mentions *herbivorous fish* several times, the passage is not about the *history of research* on *herbivorous fish*. Eliminate (B). No specific *event that occurs on coral reefs* is discussed in depth in the passage. Eliminate (C). Keep (D) because it refers to both *herbivorous fish* and *coral reefs* and matches the prediction. The correct answer is (D).

18. **C** The question asks for the *authors' perspective on studying coral reefs*. Since there is no line reference, use lead words and the order of the questions to find the window. There are no line references prior to this question, but Q19 asks about line 5, so the window for Q18 is likely in the first paragraph. Scan the first paragraph, looking for the lead words *coral reefs*. The passage begins by stating, *Coral reefs are among the most valuable natural assets on Earth*. The correct answer should reflect the authors' belief in the importance of coral reefs. Eliminate answers that don't match the prediction. The passage says that *seaweeds and algal turfs* grow on coral reefs and that herbivorous fish eat them, but it does not indicate that the authors find it *confusing* that there are *varying amounts of seaweed and algal turfs*. Eliminate (A). The authors mention that *populations of herbivorous fish vary widely* and explore the reasons behind the variations, but the passage does not say that the topic is *difficult to understand*. Eliminate (B). Choices (A) and (B) are Mostly Right, Slightly Wrong trap answers. Choice (C) is supported because the text describes coral reefs as *valuable* and mentions the *importance of coral reef conservation*. Keep (C). While the authors do discuss human impacts on coral reefs, no mention is made of any controversy. Eliminate (D). The correct answer is (C).

19. **C** The question asks what the word *shocks* most nearly means in line 5. Go back to the text, find the word *shocks*, and cross it out. Carefully read the surrounding text to determine another word that would fit in the blank based on the context in the passage. The text states that *reefs face many stresses and shocks* and then provides several examples of those *shocks*: *overfishing, habitat damage, and pollution*. Therefore, *shocks* must mean something like "problems" or "disruptions." *Surprises* does not match "problems," so eliminate (A). *Jolts* does not match "problems." Eliminate (B). *Disturbances* matches "problems," so keep (C). *Reactions* does not match "problems," so eliminate (D). The correct answer is (C).

20. **B** This question asks why *conservation efforts should take local conditions into account*, based on evidence about *populations of herbivorous fish*. This is the first question in a paired set, but it is easy to find, so it can be done on its own. Since there is no line reference, use lead words and the order of the questions to find the window. Q18 and Q19 ask about the first paragraph, so the window for Q20 most likely comes after the first paragraph. Beginning with the second paragraph, scan the passage looking for the lead words *local conditions*, which appear in line 29. Earlier in that paragraph, the authors state, *we found that populations of herbivorous fish vary widely from site to site, and are strongly influenced by factors including temperature and island type*. Thus, local conditions are important because they can determine the *populations of herbivorous fish*. Eliminate answers that don't match the prediction.

Choice (A) is a Could Be True trap answer, but no *competing species* are mentioned in this paragraph, so eliminate (A). Choice (B) is well supported by the prediction, so keep it. Choice (C) is a Right Words, Wrong Meaning trap answer. Though the authors mention *herbivorous fish* in this window, the text directly contradicts (C), as it indicates that *herbivorous fish* are *strongly influenced by factors including temperature*. Eliminate (C). No *other important species* are mentioned in this paragraph, so eliminate (D). The correct answer is (B).

21. **B**   The question is the best evidence question in a paired set. Because Q20 was easy to find, simply look at the lines used to answer the previous question. The prediction for Q20 was found in lines 24–27, which state, *we found that populations of herbivorous fish vary widely from site to site, and are strongly influenced by factors including temperature and island type.* These lines match those in (B). The correct answer is (B).

22. **A**   The question asks what the word *drivers* suggests about the fish population. Use given line reference to find the window. In the window, the authors state that *it is hard to separate human impacts from the natural biophysical and environmental drivers of these fish populations.* Therefore, the authors imply that the fish population is impacted by both human and natural factors. Eliminate answers that don't match the prediction. Choice (A) says that *human and natural factors affect the fish population.* This matches the prediction, so keep (A). Choice (B) is a Mostly Right, Slightly Wrong trap answer, as the *feeding habits of fish* are not mentioned in the window. Eliminate (B). Choice (C) is a Right Words, Wrong Meaning trap answer. Though the words *fishing* and *fish populations* appear in the passage, there are no *new locations around the globe* mentioned in the window. Eliminate (C). Choice (D) is a Right Words, Wrong Meaning trap answer. The text mentions *human impacts* and states that those impacts are hard to *separate* from other factors that affect *fish populations*. This does not mean that human activity has not caused a significant change in *fish populations*, but that it is hard to determine the source of the change. Eliminate (D). The correct answer is (A).

23. **C**   The question is a best evidence question that asks for evidence that supports the claim that *different types of herbivorous fish perform different roles in the reef environment.* Use the line references given in the answer choices to find a statement that supports this claim. The correct answer must discuss both *different types of fish* and *different roles.* Choice (A) does not mention *types* of fish, so eliminate it. Choice (B) states that *all herbivorous fish are not equal,* but this information does not specify in what way they aren't equal and does not relate to the fish's *roles.* Eliminate (B). Choice (C) mentions specific types of herbivorous fish (*browsers, detritivores, and scrapers*) and their roles, so keep (C). Choice (D) mentions only one type of fish, so eliminate it. The correct answer is (C).

24. **D**   The question asks which group *includes the greatest biomass of herbivorous fish.* Work through each answer choice using the figures. Figure 2 shows a biomass of about 1.8 for *detritivores at a water temperature of 28 degrees Celsius.* Figure 1 shows a biomass close to 1.5 for *parrotfishes when there are 0 humans per hectare of reef.* Figure 1 shows a biomass close to 0 for *browsers and parrotfishes when there are 40 humans per hectare of reef.* Figure 2 shows a biomass of about 3 for *browsers when the water temperature is 20 degrees Celsius.* Since *browsers when the water temperature is 20 degrees Celsius* have the highest biomass among the answer choices, keep (D) and eliminate (A), (B), and (C). The correct answer is (D).

25. **B** The question asks *which idea from the passage is supported by the information in the graphs*. Work through each answer choice using the figures. Eliminate (A), as *different types of seaweed* are not mentioned in either figure. Choice (B) states, *Certain types of herbivorous fish are affected by the presence of humans*. Human presence is measured on the horizontal axis of figure 1, and the graph shows that as the number of humans increases, the number of browsers and parrotfishes generally declines. The idea in (B) also appears in the passage, which mentions *fishing* as causing *widespread reductions in herbivorous fish populations*. Keep (B). Eliminate (C) because neither figure measures *different functional roles in coral reefs*. The figures do not measure the relationship between *conservation* and *fish populations*, so eliminate (D). The correct answer is (B).

26. **A** The question asks for the *main purpose of the passage*. Since this is a general question, it should be answered after the specific questions. The blurb states that Nehru delivered this speech to India's Parliament. Throughout the speech, Nehru talks about the *responsibility that rests upon* the Parliament and the need to *work hard* to *give reality to our dreams* for India. Therefore, the speech is intended to encourage the members of Parliament to work hard, to fulfill their responsibilities, and to help India succeed. Eliminate answers that don't match the prediction. Keep (A) because it matches the prediction. Eliminate (B) because the speech discusses the need for Parliament to create new opportunities, rather than for *Indian citizens* to *take advantage* of new opportunities. Choice (C) is a Right Answer, Wrong Question trap answer—it includes a detail from the passage, but it doesn't answer the question that was asked. In the second paragraph, Nehru does say that *our hearts are heavy with the memory of* the *sorrow* that people suffered before gaining independence. However, this is only mentioned once in the passage, so comforting *those who lost a great deal* is not the main purpose of the passage. Eliminate (C). Eliminate (D) because Nehru does not *seek advice* from the Parliament; instead he tells them what he thinks is most important. The correct answer is (A).

27. **D** The question asks for a summary of the passage. Since this is a general question, it should be answered after the specific questions. The blurb indicates that Nehru delivered this speech to India's Parliament when India was about to become independent from the United Kingdom. In the first paragraph, Nehru states, *The achievement we celebrate today is but a step, an opening of opportunity, to the greater triumphs and achievements that await us. Are we brave enough and wise enough to grasp this opportunity and accept the challenge of the future?* Throughout the speech, Nehru talks about the *hard work* that needs to be done *to give reality to our dreams*. Therefore, the speech celebrates independence but also conveys that there is more work to be done. Eliminate answers that don't match the prediction. Eliminate (A) because Nehru does not focus on encouraging *the common people* to *organize*; instead, he focuses on the Parliament's responsibility to create opportunity for India's people. Eliminate (B) because the passage focuses on India at a particular moment in history, not on *the nations of the world throughout history*. Although Nehru mentions that nations must work together, this is one detail in the speech, and therefore it does not summarize the passage, making it a Right Answer, Wrong Question trap answer. Eliminate (C) because the tone of the passage is hopeful. Although sorrow is mentioned in one paragraph, Nehru does not indicate that the Indian people *will be sorrowful and burdened until they realize their dreams*. Keep (D) because it matches the prediction. The correct answer is (D).

28. **A** The question asks what *Nehru* wants to convey with *the statement in lines 4–6.* Use the line reference to find the window. This sentence states that India *has never lost sight* of its goals or *forgotten the ideals* which gave it strength, through both *good and ill fortune.* Nehru uses this statement to convey that India has been true to its ideals and goals in both good and bad circumstances. Eliminate answers that don't match the prediction. Choice (A) matches the prediction, so keep it. Eliminate (B) because the lines in the question do not make any prediction for the future; later in the paragraph, Nehru indicates that India will succeed, but that idea is not conveyed by these lines. Therefore, (B) a Right Answer, Wrong Question trap answer that is based on a fact from the passage but does not answer the question that was asked. Eliminate (C) because the lines in the question do not mention any of India's leaders. Choice (C) is a Could Be True trap answer that is not directly supported by the text. Eliminate (D) because in these lines, Nehru does not suggest what India's people *must* do; instead, he describes what they have already done. This is a Mostly Right, Slightly Wrong trap answer. The correct answer is (A).

29. **D** The question asks why Nehru uses the words *birth* and *pains.* Use the given line reference to find the window. In lines 16–17, Nehru uses a metaphor of giving birth to refer to the difficulties that the Indian people faced before they achieved independence. Like giving birth, the struggle for independence was painful, but the struggle produced something worthwhile. Eliminate answers that don't match the prediction. Choice (A) says that sad memories *will continue even in happier times*, but Nehru does not say that the memories will continue in the future; he says that some of those sorrowful memories *continue even now.* Choice (A) is a Right Words, Wrong Meaning trap answer, so eliminate it. Although Nehru indicates that freedom is a positive outcome, he does not mention joy in the lines that the question asks about. Furthermore, (B) does not mention the struggles of the past, so it does not match the prediction. Eliminate (B). Eliminate (C) because Nehru does not indicate that there will be an *easy road ahead.* Keep (D) because it matches the prediction. The correct answer is (D).

30. **C** The question asks what Nehru suggests that the *members of Parliament* must do to help India succeed. Notice that this is the first question in a paired set, so it can be done in tandem with Q31. Look at the answers for Q31 first. The lines for (31A) do not mention anything that members of Parliament must do. These lines do not address Q30, so eliminate (31A). The lines for (31B) say, *That future is not one of ease or resting but of incessant striving so that we may fulfill the pledges we have so often taken and the one we shall take today.* Nehru's speech is directed to the members of India's Parliament, and in this sentence, he tells them that they must work hard to fulfill the promises they have made. Check the answers for Q30 to see whether any of the answers are supported by these lines. This information supports (30C), so draw a line connecting (31B) with (30C). The lines for (31C) do not mention anything that members of Parliament must do. These lines do not address Q30, so eliminate (31C). The lines for (31D) say that India promises to *cooperate* with the *peoples of the world* to support *peace, freedom and democracy.* This information does not support any of the answers to Q30: although (30D) mentions keeping *promises*, they are promises that the *common people* have made *to each other*, which does not match the lines for (31D). Eliminate (30D). Without any support in the answers from Q31, (30A), (30B), and (30D) can be eliminated. The correct answers are (30C) and (31B).

31. **B** (See explanation above.)

32. **C** The question asks for *Nehru's perspective on opportunity*. Since there is no line reference, use lead words and the order of the questions to find the window. The answer to Q31 came from lines 21–23, so the window for Q32 is most likely after those lines. Scan the passage beginning with line 24, looking for the lead word *opportunity*. Lines 24–26 state, *The service of India…means the ending of…inequality of opportunity*. Nehru is speaking to the members of the Indian Parliament, so this statement indicates that he believes the government should support equal opportunity for India's people. Eliminate answers that don't match the prediction. Eliminate (A) because it contradicts the prediction, saying that *there is no need to work for greater* opportunity. Eliminate (B) because Nehru does not discuss balancing *opportunities for personal prosperity* with *opportunities for national prosperity*. Keep (C) because it matches the prediction. Eliminate (D) because Nehru does not contrast the importance of *economic opportunity* and *religious equality*. The correct answer is (C).

33. **C** The question asks what the word *narrow* most nearly means in line 68. Go back to the text, find the word *narrow*, and cross it out. Then read the window carefully, using context clues to determine another word that would fit in the text. The text says, *We cannot encourage…narrow-mindedness, for no nation can be great whose people are narrow in thought or in action*. Therefore, *narrow* must mean something like "restricted," and must refer to thoughts and actions. *Thin* does not match "restricted," so eliminate (A). *Fine* does not match "restricted," so eliminate (B). *Limited* matches "restricted," so keep (C). Although a space that is *tight* might also be described as "restricted," this refers to physical space, not to thoughts and actions, so eliminate (D). Note that (A), (B), and (D) are Could Be True trap answers based on other meanings of *narrow* that are not supported by the text. The correct answer is (C).

34. **B** The question asks what Nehru suggests is most important to support India in reaching its potential. Since there is no line reference, use the order of the questions to find the window. Q33 asked about line 68, so the window for Q34 is most likely after that line. Scan the final paragraph for information about what Nehru thinks is important to support India. Lines 72–75 say, *And to India…we pay our reverent homage and we bind ourselves afresh to her service*. Nehru thinks that is important to respect and serve India (*reverent* means "highly respectful" and *homage* means "show of respect"). Eliminate answers that don't match the prediction. Nehru does not say that *evaluating good and ill fortune* is important; the words *good and ill fortune* appear in the first paragraph, but there is no mention of *evaluating* them to support India. Eliminate (A). Keep (B) because it matches the prediction. Choice (C) is a Right Words, Wrong Meaning trap answer: in the first paragraph, Nehru mentions *ideals*, but says that they have *never* been forgotten. Therefore, *remembering forgotten ideals* does not match the text. Eliminate (C). In the final paragraph, Nehru mentions other *nations*, but he does not say that India should seek their *advice*. Therefore, (D) is another Right Words, Wrong Meaning trap answer; eliminate (D). The correct answer is (B).

35. **A** The question asks what *can be reasonably inferred about neutrinos* from Passage 1. Notice that this is the first question in a paired set, so it can be done in tandem with Q36. Look at the answer choices for Q36 first. The lines for (36A) say that neutrinos *were predicted to be completely massless*, but *surprisingly do have some mass*. Check the answers for Q35 to see whether any of the answers are supported by these lines. These lines do not support any of the answers for Q35, so eliminate (36A).

The lines for (36B) indicate that *the maximum weight* of a neutrino was estimated to be *at least six million times lighter than an electron*. It is not possible to feel the weight of an electron, let alone an item lighter than an electron, so (35A) may be inferred from (36B). Draw a line connecting (36B) and (35A). The lines for (36C) say that *scientists can infer the mass of a neutrino* by *measuring the energy of the electron*. Both (36C) and (35D) discuss the size of a particle and its relation to other particles. However, the lines for (36C) discuss how the mass of a neutrino depends on the energy of the electron, whereas (35D) suggests that the charge of other particles depends on the size of the neutrino. Eliminate (36C). The lines for (36D) say that all ways of measuring mass will be used in finding a finite answer about the neutrino's mass. These lines do not support any of the answers for Q35, so eliminate (36D). Without any support in the answers from Q36, (35B), (35C), and (35D) can be eliminated. The correct answers are (35A) and (36B).

36. **B**   (See explanation above.)

37. **B**   The question asks why the author uses the word *weirdest* in line 1. Use the given line reference to find the window. The first paragraph of Passage 1 says that neutrinos *are nearly massless*, and it discusses how a prior belief about the weight of neutrinos was *surprisingly* overturned. The paragraph suggests that not much is known about neutrinos, as the true weight of neutrinos *has remained a mystery*. Therefore, the correct answer should indicate that neutrinos are perplexing to scientists. Eliminate answers that don't match the prediction. Though the paragraph discusses previous observations, the word *weirdest* is not used to describe these observations. Eliminate (A) and (D). The word *weirdest* is used to point out the *puzzling* nature of *neutrinos*. Keep (B). Choice (C) is a Mostly Right, Slightly Wrong trap answer: the word *unusual* could match the word *weirdest*, but (C) uses *unusual* to refer to *recent experiments*, not neutrinos. Eliminate (C). The correct answer is (B).

38. **C**   The question asks what the word *robust* most nearly means in line 42. Go back to the text, find the word *robust*, and cross it out. Then read the window carefully, using context clues to determine another word that would fit in the text. The text says that *combing all the possible ways of measuring the neutrino mass* will allow scientists to *have a finite and robust answer*. Therefore, *robust* must mean something like "dependable" or "consistent." *Exact* means "precise," which does not match "dependable," so eliminate (A). *Healthy* does not match "dependable," so eliminate (B). *Reliable* matches "dependable," so keep (C). *Vigorous* means "energetic" or "strong" and does not match "dependable," so eliminate (D). Note that (B) and (D) are Could Be True trap answers based on other meanings of *robust* that are not supported by the text. The correct answer is (C).

39. **D**   The question asks about the purpose of the *last paragraph of Passage 2*. Read the last paragraph of Passage 2 as the window. The paragraph discusses planned improvements to KATRIN and the measurements that may be possible as a result of the improvements: *During the next five years, Drexlin's collaboration plans to make continuous improvements to KATRIN's sensitivity that could enable it to make an actual measurement of a neutrino's mass—or to narrow the range of the estimate as far as the machine's sensitivity will allow* (lines 81–86). Eliminate answers that don't match the prediction. The paragraph does not discuss *the claim that scientists have studied particles for many years*. Eliminate

(A). The paragraph does not *explain the methods* used to *measure neutrinos*, so eliminate (B). The paragraph does not *celebrate* achievements; it discusses potential future achievements, so eliminate (C). The paragraph does discuss *future research possibilities*, so keep (D). The correct answer is (D).

40. **A** The question asks for the *main purpose* of both passages. Because this is a question about both passages, it should be done after all the questions that ask about each passage individually. Passage 1 discusses a discovery that challenged a previous assumption about neutrinos and details future projects that will try to confirm this discovery. Passage 2 discusses one such project, the *KATRIN experiment,* and a discovery about neutrinos made from this experiment. Choice (A) matches the main focus of both passages, which is to discuss *discoveries about one type of particle,* the neutrino. Keep (A). Neither passage discusses how researchers developed the *tools* needed to make the calculations, so eliminate (B). Choice (C) is a Mostly Right, Slightly Wrong trap answer; a neutrino is a *subatomic particle,* but it is only one type of subatomic particle. Neither passage summarizes *what physicists have learned* about *subatomic particles* in general. Eliminate (C). Both passages indicate that scientists want to make more accurate measurements of the neutrino's mass, but neither author makes an argument intended to *persuade scientists*. Eliminate (D). The correct answer is (A).

41. **D** The question asks for a statement that *the authors of Passage 1 and Passage 2* would agree on. Because this is a question about both passages, it should be done after the questions that ask about each passage individually. Notice that this is the first question in a paired set, so it can be done in tandem with Q42. Look at the answer choices for Q42 first. The lines for (42A) read, *An experiment in Germany has made the most precise measurement yet of the maximum mass of neutrinos*. Check the answers for Q41 to see if any of the answers are supported by these lines. These lines do not support any of the answers for Q41, so eliminate (42A). The lines for (42B) indicate that the new measurement is an *improvement* over previous measurements. These lines do not support any of the answers for Q41, so eliminate (42B). The lines for (42C) discuss the evolving states that a subatomic particle may assume as it decays before a neutrino is produced. This matches the idea that *subatomic particles do not always keep the same form*. Draw a line connecting (42C) and (41D). The lines for (42D) state that *KATRIN cannot detect the neutrinos directly*. Choice (41B) is a Right Words, Wrong Meaning trap answer related to these lines: KATRIN uses indirect measurements, but this does not indicate that indirect measurements will *replace direct observation*. Eliminate (42D) because these lines do not support any of the answers for Q41. Without any support in the answers from Q42, (41A), (41B), and (41C) can be eliminated. Because this pair is the only match, there is no need to find evidence in Passage 1. However, (41D) is supported in line 32 of Passage 1, which states that *a neutron transforms into a proton*. The correct answers are (41D) and (42C).

42. **C** (See explanation above.)

Section 2—Writing and Language

1. **B**   Punctuation is changing in the answer choices, so this question is testing STOP, HALF-STOP, and GO punctuation. However, notice that punctuation is changing around three items in a list, so the question is also testing comma rules. In a list of three or more items, there needs to be a comma after each item in the list. Choice (A) has an extra comma after the word *and*, which is not correct, so eliminate (A). Choice (B) correctly uses a comma after every item in the list. Keep (B). Choices (C) and (D) each use a semicolon instead of a comma to separate two items in the list, which is not correct. Eliminate (C) and (D). The correct answer is (B).

2. **C**   The number of words is changing in the answer choices, so this question could be testing concision. Choices (A), (B), and (D) each include the phrase *diamonds, rubies, sapphires, and compass*, so determine whether this phrase is necessary. All of these items are mentioned in the previous sentence, and the word *also* implies that that the knowledge was carried along with those items, so there is no need to repeat the names of the items here. Eliminate (A), (B), and (D). The correct answer is (C).

3. **C**   Punctuation is changing in the answer choices, so this question is testing STOP, HALF-STOP, and GO punctuation. Use the Vertical Line Test and identify the ideas as complete or incomplete. Draw the vertical line between the words *gained* and *from*. The first part of the sentence, *Polo also carried knowledge he had gained*, is a complete idea. The second part, *from his journey east*, is an incomplete idea. To connect a complete idea to an incomplete idea, HALF-STOP or GO punctuation is needed. Eliminate (A) and (B) because a semicolon and a period are both STOP punctuation. Keep (C) because no punctuation is GO punctuation. The addition of the word *it* in (D) changes the second part of the sentence to a complete idea, *it was from his journey east*. Each part of the sentence is now a complete idea, so STOP punctuation is needed. Since a comma is GO punctuation, eliminate (D). The correct answer is (C).

4. **C**   Note the question! The question asks whether a sentence should be added, so it's testing consistency. If the content of the new sentence is consistent with the ideas surrounding it, then it should be added. The paragraph discusses Marco Polo's return from China and what he brought back. The new sentence discusses a belief held by *Europeans*, so it is not consistent with the ideas in the text; the sentence should not be added. Eliminate (A) and (B). Keep (C) because it accurately states that the new sentence *interrupts the discussion of Marco Polo's journey*. Eliminate (D) because the *information* was not *previously stated*. The correct answer is (C).

5. **D**   The vocabulary and number of words are changing in the answer choices, so this question is testing precision of word choice and could be testing concision. The previous sentence states that *Polo became appointed as a diplomat*; it is redundant to restate *as a diplomat* because the word *this* clearly refers back to what he did as a diplomat, so eliminate (A) and (C). Between *life* and *role*, *role* is more precise and correctly refers to his appointment as a diplomat in the previous sentence. Eliminate (B). The correct answer is (D).

6. **B**   Note the question! The question asks whether a sentence should be revised, so it's testing consistency. If the content of the revised sentence is consistent with the ideas surrounding it, then it should be revised. The original sentence says *He encountered many things that were unknown in Europe.* The proposed revision includes the specific things that Marco Polo encountered, so the sentence should be revised to make it more precise; eliminate (C) and (D). The revision doesn't mention Polo's *everyday life in Asia*, so eliminate (A). The revision does give details about *what Marco Polo learned in his travels.* The correct answer is (B).

7. **A**   Verbs are changing in the answer choices, so this question is testing consistency of verbs. A verb must be consistent with its subject and with the other verbs in the sentence. The subject of the verb is *explanation*, which is singular. To be consistent, the underlined verb must also be singular. Eliminate (B) and (D) because *were* and *are* are plural. The other verb in the sentence is *was*, which is in the past tense. To be consistent, the underlined verb must also be in the past tense. Eliminate (C) because it is not in the past tense. The correct answer is (A).

8. **D**   Note the question! The question asks where sentence 3 should be placed, so it's testing consistency of ideas. The sentence must be consistent with the ideas that come both before and after it. Sentence 3 says that *Polo's explanation of paper money…was new and intriguing,* so it must come after some mention of *paper money*. Sentence 5 discusses *paper currency*. Therefore, sentence 3 should follow sentence 5. The correct answer is (D).

9. **D**   Note the question! The question asks which choice *would most effectively introduce the topic of the paragraph*, so it's testing consistency of ideas. Determine the subject of the paragraph and find the answer that is consistent with that idea. The paragraph discusses Polo's original manuscript and says *it may never be known exactly what Polo's original manuscript said.* Eliminate (A) and (B) because *Christopher Columbus* and the *Age of Discovery* are not mentioned in the paragraph. Eliminate (C) because the paragraph doesn't mention *historians* questioning the accuracy of Polo's manuscript. Keep (D) because it is consistent with the content of the paragraph. The correct answer is (D).

10. **A**   Punctuation is changing in the answer choices, so this question is testing STOP, HALF-STOP, and GO punctuation. Use the Vertical Line Test and identify the ideas as complete or incomplete. Draw the vertical line between the words *including* and *cartography*. The first part of the sentence, *While it may never be known exactly what Polo's original manuscript said, his influence lives on in many areas, including,* is an incomplete idea. The second part, *cartography, currency, and exploration*, is an incomplete idea. To connect an incomplete idea to an incomplete idea, GO punctuation is needed. Keep (A) because no punctuation is GO punctuation. Eliminate (B) and (C) because a single dash and a colon are HALF-STOP punctuation. Eliminate (D) because a semicolon is STOP punctuation. The correct answer is (A).

11. **D**   Punctuation is changing in the answer choices, so this question is testing STOP, HALF-STOP, and GO punctuation. Use the Vertical Line Test and identify the ideas as complete or incomplete. Draw the vertical line through the FANBOYS word *and* between the words *learning* and *the*. The first part of the sentence, *Research has shown that both terrestrial and aquatic animals practice spatial learning,*

is a complete idea. The second part, *the ability to navigate a physical environment*, is an incomplete idea. To connect a complete idea to an incomplete idea, HALF-STOP or GO punctuation is needed. Eliminate (A) and (B) because a comma with FANBOYS and a period are both STOP punctuation. Although no punctuation is GO punctuation, the two ideas need to be separated because the second part is an explanation of the first part; eliminate (C). Keep (D) because a single dash is HALF-STOP punctuation. The correct answer is (D).

12. **C**   Note the question! The question asks which choice *provides the best transition to the next paragraph*, so it's testing consistency of ideas. Determine the subject of the paragraph and find the answer that is consistent with that idea. The paragraph discusses *a study* on *how members of an aquatic species navigate* an *underwater environment*. Eliminate (A) because the study is only on *an aquatic species* and does not include any *terrestrial species*. Eliminate (B) because the study is on only one *aquatic species*, not multiple. Keep (C) because it is consistent with the paragraph. Eliminate (D) because the study is on *how* the crabs navigate, and not *why they need* those abilities. The correct answer is (C).

13. **C**   Pronouns and apostrophes are changing in the answer choices, so this question is testing consistency of pronouns and apostrophes. In this sentence, the *underwater environment* belongs to *members of an aquatic species*, so a possessive pronoun is needed. A pronoun with an apostrophe is a contraction. *They're* means "they are." It is not correct to say that "they are" underwater environment; eliminate (A) and (B). Keep (C) because it uses the correct possessive pronoun to show that the underwater environment belongs to the crabs. Eliminate (D) because *there* is not a possessive pronoun. The correct answer is (C).

14. **A**   Note the question! The question asks whether a quotation should be removed, so it's testing consistency. If the content of the quotation is consistent with the ideas surrounding it, then it should be kept. The paragraph discusses a study about the spatial abilities of shore crabs. The quotation gives a reason for the study, saying *we haven't really looked for them in their aquatic counterparts*. Since the quotation is consistent with the rest of the paragraph, it should be kept; eliminate (C) and (D). Keep (A) because it correctly says that the quotation *gives a reason* for the study. Eliminate (B) because the quotation does not discuss the study's *scientific approach*. The correct answer is (A).

15. **A**   The word after *crabs* is changing in the answer choices, so this question is testing precision and concision. First determine whether any of the words after *crabs* is necessary. The non-underlined portion of the sentence includes the word *suspect* and the phrase *may have*, so there is no need to further emphasize that Pope's statement (*crabs may have...abilities*) is a theory. Eliminate (B), (C), and (D) because *perchance*, *perhaps*, and *possibly* are all redundant. The correct answer is (A).

16. **B**   Vocabulary is changing in the answer choices, so this question is testing precision of word choice. Look for a phrase with a definition that is consistent with the other ideas in the paragraph. The paragraph is about the study of the crabs. The previous sentence mentions the time frame *four-week period*. Since the first part of the sentence with the underlined portion describes an event that happened after the event in the previous sentence, the correct phrase must also refer to a time period. Eliminate (A) and (D) because *weaks* means "feeble" and is not a time period. Keep (B) because *two*

weeks describes a time period. Eliminate (C) because *too* means "also" or "excessive." The correct answer is (B).

17. **B**   Pronouns are changing in the answer choices, so this question is testing consistency of pronouns. A pronoun must be consistent in number with the noun it refers to. The underlined pronoun refers to the noun *crabs*, which is plural. To be consistent, the underlined pronoun must also be plural. Eliminate (A) because *you* is not consistent with *crabs*. Keep (B) because *they* is plural. Eliminate (C) and (D) because *he or she* and *it* are both singular. The correct answer is (B).

18. **C**   Note the question! The question asks where sentence 1 should be placed, so it's testing consistency of ideas. The sentence must be consistent with the ideas that come both before and after it. Sentence 1 says that *At the end of this period, scientists had observed a decrease in both the time it took each of the 12 crabs to complete the maze and the number of wrong turns each crab took*, so it must come after some mention of a *period* of time. Sentence 3 mentions *a four-week period*. Therefore, sentence 1 should follow sentence 3. The correct answer is (C).

19. **D**   Vocabulary is changing in the answer choices, so this question is testing precision of word choice. Look for a phrase with a definition and tone that are consistent with the other ideas in the sentence. The sentence suggests that *Pope* "wants to do" *further research*. Choice (A) is too strong for the tone of the passage, as nothing suggests that Pope is *desperate*, so eliminate (A). Choice (B) uses the awkward phrase *dreams with hope*, which does not match the straightforward, factual tone of the passage, so eliminate (B). Choice (C) is also not consistent with the passage's factual tone, so eliminate (C). Choice (D) is precise and consistent with the passage's tone. The correct answer is (D).

20. **B**   Words are changing in the answer choices, so this question is testing consistency and precision of word choice. Look for a phrase that is consistent with the other ideas in the sentence. The previous sentence does not set up a contrast, so eliminate (A). Keep (B) because it clearly sets up the rest of the sentence, which summarizes the main idea of the passage. Both (C) and (D) imply that the crabs' abilities are in some way caused by the research, which is not correct, so eliminate (C) and (D). The correct answer is (B).

21. **D**   Vocabulary is changing in the answer choices, so this question is testing precision of word choice. Look for a word with a definition that is consistent with the other ideas in the sentence. The sentence says that robotic surgery *allows the doctor to perform* procedures without making *significant incisions*. Procedures that would otherwise require *significant incisions* are complicated, so the correct word should mean "complicated." *Puzzling* is similar in meaning to "complicated," so keep (A). *Twisted* means "distorted," which doesn't match "complicated," so eliminate (B). *Mysterious* means "secretive," which doesn't match "complicated," so eliminate (C). *Complex* means "complicated," so keep (D). Although *puzzling* has some support, it implies that the procedures are confusing to the doctors, which is not necessarily true. Eliminate (A). Choice (D) makes the meaning of the sentence most precise. The correct answer is (D).

22. **A**   Apostrophes are changing in the answer choices, so the question is testing apostrophe usage. When used with a noun, on the PSAT, an apostrophe indicates possession. In this sentence, the *bodies* belong to *patients*, so an apostrophe is needed after *patients*, and because *patients* is plural, the apostrophe should be placed after the *s*. Keep (A) because it supplies the apostrophe after the *s* in patients. Eliminate (B), (C), and (D) because none of these uses the correct apostrophe after *patients*. The correct answer is (A).

23. **C**   Note the question! The question asks how to effectively combine the underlined sentences, so it's testing precision and concision. The phrase after *industry* changes in the answer choices, so determine the function of this phrase. The phrase must connect two sentences, so determine the relationship between the sentences. Sentence 1 says that *surgical robots have changed the medical industry.* Sentence 2 explains how they have changed the medical industry. Therefore, the underlined portion must give a clue that the information that follows explains a point from sentence 1. Eliminate (A) because the word *though* indicates that the information that is to follow will contrast sentence 1. Eliminate (B) because *which* suggests that surgical robots changing the medical industry caused doctors to be able to make precise cuts, which reverses the correct order of ideas. Keep (C) because *by* indicates that the information that follows will explain how surgical robots changed the medical industry. Eliminate (D) because *that* simply implies that the medical industry allows doctors to make precise cuts—this may be true, but it does not explain how surgical robots changed the industry. The correct answer is (C).

24. **C**   Verbs are changing in the answer choices, so this question is testing consistency of verbs. A verb must be consistent with its subject and with the other verbs in the sentence. The subject of the verb is *physician*, which is singular. To be consistent, the underlined verb must also be singular. Eliminate (A) and (D) because *have been* and *were* are plural. Verbs must also be consistent with other verbs in the sentence. The other verb in the sentence, before the underlined portion, is *makes*, which is in the present tense. To be consistent, the underlined verb must also be in the present tense. Eliminate (B) because *was* is past tense. Keep (C) because it is present tense. The correct answer is (C).

25. **B**   Note the question! The question asks *which choice most accurately represents the data in the chart*, so it's testing consistency. Read the labels on the chart carefully, and look for an answer that is consistent with the information given in the chart. Notice that all four answer choices involve the number *86*, so look for this number on the chart and determine its meaning. The chart shows 86% for *faculty-led time with robot*, and the title indicates that the percentages are the portion of *medical programs* that *train doctors* using these techniques. Eliminate (A) because it does not relate to *faculty-led time*. The chart says that 86 percent of medical programs use *faculty-led time with a robot* to train students, so (B) is consistent with the chart. Keep (B). The chart does not show how much *time* students spent with robots, so (C) is not consistent with the chart. Eliminate (C). Choice (D) implies *case observation* rather than *faculty-led time with robot*, which was used by 80% of programs, not 86%. Eliminate (D). The correct answer is (B).

26. **A**   Note the question! The question asks *which choice most accurately and precisely provides specific data from the chart*, so it's testing consistency. Read the labels on the chart carefully, and look for an answer that is consistent with the information given in the chart. The chart says that *51 percent of programs* used videos to train students, so (A) is consistent with the chart. Keep (A). Since the bars represent percentages, not the number of programs, it is not true that *51 programs* used videos to train students. Eliminate (B). It is true that *some of the participants* in the survey (the medical programs) used videos to train students, so keep (C). Likewise, it is also true that *additional programs* used videos, to add on to the methods mentioned in the previous sentence. While (A), (C), and (D) are all true, the question is asking for *specific data*. Choice (A) provides a specific percentage, so eliminate (C) and (D). The correct answer is (A).

27. **A**   Commas are changing in the answer choices, so this question is testing the four ways to use a comma. Commas are changing around the phrase *to an effective local surgeon*, so determine whether this phrase is necessary. The phrase identifies the people that *an isolated or impoverished region* might not have access to, so it is necessary to the meaning of the sentence. The phrase should not be surrounded by commas. However, the sentence is constructed with an incomplete idea followed by a complete idea, and a comma is needed between the two ideas to separate them. So, there should not be a comma before the phrase, but there should be a comma after it. Keep (A) because it does not place a comma before the phrase, but it does place a comma after the phrase. Eliminate (B) because it places a comma before and after the phrase. Eliminate (C) because it does not place a comma after the phrase. Eliminate (D) because it places a comma before the phrase. The answer correct is (A).

28. **D**   Transitions are changing in the answer choices, so this question is testing consistency of ideas. A transition must be consistent with the relationship between the ideas it connects. The sentence before the transition states that *A 2017 study...showed a 95 percent overall success rate* for robotic surgeries, and the sentence that starts with the transition states that the same study showed that no patients had complications from the surgeries mentioned in the previous sentence. These ideas agree, so a same-direction transition is needed. *Surprisingly* implies that the second sentence will provide information that is unexpected to follow the first sentence. Since both ideas are positive, this is not the correct direction. Eliminate (A). The two sentences agree, so eliminate (B), which contains an opposite-direction transition. *As previously stated* indicates that the positive recoveries of patients was previously mentioned. This is not true, so eliminate (C). The second sentence provides an additional outcome of the study mentioned in the first sentence, so *additionally* is an appropriate link between the two ideas. Keep (D). The correct answer is (D).

29. **C**   Transitions are changing in the answer choices, so this question is testing consistency of ideas. A transition must be consistent with the relationship between the ideas it connects. The sentence before the transition states that *Surgical robots can help doctors to make precise movements in complex procedures*, and the sentence that starts with the transition states that surgical robots *also allow doctors to operate* remotely. These two sentences each discuss a benefit of surgical robots, so the correct transition must indicate that the second sentence is an additional benefit. *For this reason* implies that the first sentence provides a reason that doctors may operate remotely. This is not true, so eliminate

(A). The two sentences agree, so eliminate (B), which contains an opposite-direction transition. *As another benefit* indicates that the second sentence will contain an additional benefit of robotic surgery. This is true, so keep (C). *Thus* implies that the second sentence is a conclusion that follows from the first sentence. This is not true, so eliminate (D). The correct answer is (C).

30. **D**   Prepositions are changing in the answer choices, so this question is testing idioms. Look at the phrase before the preposition to determine the correct idiom. The first half of the sentence says that some patients *need surgery right away*, and the word *Since* implies that the information after the comma will provide a conclusion that relates to the first half. The second half of the sentence implies that surgical robotics can save the lives of those who need surgery right away but don't have access to an on-site doctor. Therefore, surgical robotics connects people through the use of life-saving technology. Eliminate (A) because *while* makes the sentence incomplete. Choice (B) implies that people connect the field of surgical robotics, which is the opposite of what the sentence should say. Eliminate (B). Eliminate (C) because the phrase *connecting with people with…technology* is not correct. Choice (D) suggests that surgical robotics can connect *people with life-saving technology*. This is true, and it is the correct meaning of the sentence in context. The correct answer is (D).

31. **C**   Punctuation is changing in the answer choices, so this question is testing STOP, HALF-STOP, and GO punctuation. Use the Vertical Line Test and identify the ideas as complete or incomplete. Draw the vertical line between the words *gathering* and *on*. The first part of the sentence, *The crowd was gathering*, is a complete idea. The second part, *on September 3, 1922, as Bessie Coleman looked up to see a clear sky, ideal conditions for her air show*, is an incomplete idea. To connect a complete idea to an incomplete idea, HALF-STOP or GO punctuation is needed. All the answer choices are either HALF-STOP or GO punctuation, so look for another way to eliminate choices. Although a comma is GO punctuation, there is no reason to use a comma after *gathering*. Eliminate (A) and (D). A colon implies that the following information is either a list or an explanation of a prior idea. Since neither happens in this sentence, there is no reason to use a colon after *gathering*. Eliminate (B). The correct answer is (C).

32. **C**   Transitions are changing in the answer choices, so this question is testing consistency of ideas. A transition must be consistent with the relationship between the ideas it connects. The sentence before the transition states that *Bessie had fallen in love with flying* years before the air show *while watching newsreels about World War I*, and the sentence that starts with the transition discusses how aviation technology changed during a time of war. Since both sentences indicate actions that occurred continuously during the war, the transition must indicate a general period of time. *At this point* and *At this time* both indicate a specific time, not a general period, so eliminate (A) and (B). To choose between (C) and (D), consider the idiom being used. *Time of war* is the correct idiom in this context, so keep (C) and eliminate (D). The correct answer is (C).

33. **D**   Pronouns are changing in the answer choices, so this question is testing consistency of pronouns. A pronoun must be consistent in number with the noun it refers to. The underlined pronoun refers to the noun *aspiring aviators*, which is plural. To be consistent, the underlined pronoun must also be

plural. Eliminate (B) and (C) because *she* and *he* are singular pronouns. The pronouns *you* and *they* can be used in plural contexts, so consider the other pronouns in the sentence. The sentence uses *they* elsewhere to refer to aspiring aviators, so the underlined pronoun must be consistent. Eliminate (A). The correct answer is (D).

34. **B** Commas are changing in the answer choices, so this question is testing the four ways to use a comma. Commas change around the phrase *who would train Bessie*, so determine if the phrase is necessary. The phrase is necessary information, since it explains why the instructors were important, so it should not have commas around it. Choices (A), (C), and (D) all include commas, so eliminate them. The correct answer is (B).

35. **D** Note the question! The question asks which choice would *explain why Bessie might be cautious*, so it's testing consistency. Eliminate answers that are inconsistent with the purpose stated in the question. The paragraph discusses Bessie's experience in flight school, and the sentence before question 35 states that *Bessie knew that aviation training was dangerous*. Look for an answer that explains how Bessie might have known it was *dangerous*. Eliminate (A) because the length of her training does not relate to the dangers of aviation training. Eliminate (B) because it discusses danger in the present day, not in Bessie's time. Eliminate (C) because there is no indication that Bessie thought of danger while imagining herself in the pilot's seat. Keep (D) because watching *a fellow classmate die in a crash* supports the idea that aviation training was dangerous. The correct answer is (D).

36. **B** Note the question! The question asks where sentence 2 should be placed, so it's testing consistency of ideas. The sentence must be consistent with the ideas that come both before and after it. Sentence 2 says that Bessie was, once again, *unable to find an instructor in any American school*, so it must come after some mention of a decision to return to school. Sentence 3 states that Bessie *decided to pursue advanced aviation training*. Therefore, sentence 2 should follow sentence 3. The correct answer is (B).

37. **C** Note the question! The question asks whether a sentence should be added, so it's testing consistency. If the content of the new sentence is consistent with the ideas surrounding it, then it should be added. The paragraph discusses Bessie's career-defining air show at Curtiss Field. The new sentence discusses *safety concerns about stunt flying* after World War II and a contemporary effect of these consequences, so it is not consistent with the ideas in the text; the sentence should not be added. Eliminate (A) and (B). Keep (C) because it accurately states that the new sentence is *irrelevant*. Eliminate (D) because the paragraph does not focus on *explaining airshows*. The correct answer is (C).

38. **D** The wording changes in the answer choices, so this question is testing consistency. There is also the option to DELETE; consider this choice carefully as it is often the correct answer. Determine whether the underlined phrase is necessary. The paragraph discusses Bessie's career-defining air show at Curtiss Field. The first part of the sentence that contains the underlined phrase says that *The crowd cheered loudly*. Choices (A), (B), and (C) all give reasons that the crowd may have cheered for Bessie, but all of those reasons are implied by the statement that the audience *cheered loudly*. Eliminate (A), (B), and (C) because they are overly wordy. The correct answer is (D).

39. **A**   Vocabulary is changing in the answer choices, so this question is testing precision of word choice. Look for a word with a definition that is consistent with the other ideas in the sentence. The sentence says that Bessie toured the country, *showcasing a range of* impressive *aerial maneuvers*, so the correct word should mean "exciting." *Electrifying* means "thrilling," which matches "exciting." Keep (A). *Pleasing* means "making happy," which is similar to "exciting" but does not convey the same energy. Eliminate (B). *Occupying* means "keeping busy," which does not match "exciting." Eliminate (C). *Growing* means "making larger," which does not match "exciting." Eliminate (D). The correct answer is (A).

40. **A**   Note the question! The question asks which choice best *emphasizes the idea of Bessie Coleman as a significant aviator*, so it's testing consistency of ideas. Keep (A) because the idea that *"Queen Bess" continues to be an inspiration* to people matches the idea that she was a significant aviator. Eliminate (B) because Coleman's memories do not suggest her significance. Eliminate (C) because it focuses on the *start* of her career rather than the importance of her influence. Eliminate (D) because it focuses on one detail from the text rather than Coleman's overall significance. The correct answer is (A).

Section 3—Math (No Calculator)

1. **B**   The question asks for a system of equations that represents a specific situation. Translate the question in bite-sized pieces and eliminate after each piece. One piece of information says *the store sold 52 pieces of softball equipment*, so one of the equations must equal 52. Eliminate (A) and (D), as neither choice shows an equation equaling 52. Compare the remaining answer choices. The difference between (B) and (C) is the right side of the second equation. Since the question states that gloves (g) cost \$20 and bats (b) cost \$50, one of the equations shows $50b$ and $20g$ being added together to equal the total money made by the store. Eliminate (C), as it does not show $50b + 20g$ as equal to the total of 1,700. The correct answer is (B).

2. **C**   The question asks for the value of a that satisfies an equation. There are specific values in the answers, so plug in the answers. Begin by labeling the answers as a, and start with (B), 24. Plug this value into the equation to see if it makes the equation true. The equation becomes $\frac{8}{24} = \frac{2}{12}$ or $\frac{1}{3} = \frac{1}{6}$. This is not true, so eliminate (B). Since (B) is too small, (A) can also be eliminated. Plug (C), 48, into the equation. The equation becomes $\frac{8}{48} = \frac{2}{12}$ or $\frac{1}{6} = \frac{1}{6}$. This is true, so stop here. Another way to approach this is by solving the equation for the value of a. To solve for a, cross-multiply to get (8)(12) = 2a or 96 = 2a. Divide both sides by 2 to get 48 = a. Either way, the correct answer is (C).

3. **D**   The question asks for an equation that represents the relationship between two variables. When given a table of values and asked for the correct equation, plug values from the table into the answer choices to see which one works. According to the table, $f(x) = 2$ when $x = 0$. Choice (A) becomes $2 = 4(0) - 2$, or $2 = -2$. This is not true, so eliminate (A). Choice (B) becomes $2 = -2(0) + 2$, or $2 = 2$. This is true, so keep (B) for now, but check the remaining answers just in case. Choice (C) becomes

2 = –3(0) + 1, or 2 = 1. This is not true, so eliminate (C). Choice (D) becomes 2 = –4(0) +2, or 2 = 2. This is true, so keep (D) for now. Since two answers match the target value, choose a new set of values from the table to plug into the remaining answer choices. According to the table, $f(x) = -2$ when $x = 1$. Choice (B) becomes –2 = –2(1) + 2, or –2 = 0. This is not true, so eliminate (B). Choice (D) becomes –2 = –4(1) + 2, or –2 = –2, which is true. The correct answer is (D).

4. **A** The question asks for an equation that represents a line. To find the best equation, compare features of the line to the answer choices. The graph for this line has a y-intercept of –5 and a positive slope. Eliminate answer choices that do not match this information. The equations are written in slope-intercept form, $y = mx + b$, where m represents the slope and b represents the y-intercept. Choices (B) and (D) have negative slopes, so eliminate (B) and (D). Compare the remaining answer choices. Both (A) and (C) have y-intercepts of –5 and positive slopes, so find the slope of the line using two points on the line, such as (6, –1) and (3, –3). Slope is calculated using the equation $slope = \dfrac{y_2 - y_1}{x_2 - x_1}$. The equation becomes $\dfrac{-3-(-1)}{3-6} = \dfrac{-2}{-3} = \dfrac{2}{3}$. Choice (C) has a slope of $\dfrac{3}{2}$, so eliminate (C). Another option would be to pick a point on the graph such as (6, –1) and plug it into the given equations to see if they are true. Either way, the correct answer is (A).

5. **B** The question asks for an equivalent form of an expression. There are variables in the answer choices, so plug in. Make $t = 1$ and $v = 2$. The expression becomes –9[3(1) – 3(2)] + [9(1) – 13(2)] = –9(3 – 6) + (9 – 26) = –9(–3) – 17 = 27 – 17 = 10. This is the target value; circle it. Now plug $t = 1$ and $v = 2$ into the answer choices to see which one matches the target value. Choice (A) becomes –18(1) – 40(2) = –18 – 80 = –98. This does not match the target value, so eliminate (A). Choice (B) becomes –18(1) + 14(2) = –18 + 28 = 10. This matches the target value, so keep (B), but check the remaining answers, just in case. Choice (C) becomes 36(1) + 14(2) = 36 + 28 = 64. Eliminate (C). Choice (D) becomes 36(1) – 40(2) = 36 – 80 = –44. Eliminate (D). The correct answer is (B).

6. **A** The question asks for an equivalent form of an expression. There is a variable in the answer choices, so plug in. Make $c = 2$. The expression becomes $3(2)^2 - 10(2) + 8 = 3(4) - 20 + 8 = 12 - 20 + 8 = 0$. This is the target value; circle it. Now plug $c = 2$ into the answer choices to see which one matches the target value. Choice (A) becomes [3(2) – 4][(2) – 2] = (2)(0) = 0. This matches the target value, so keep (A) for now, but check the remaining answers just in case. Choice (B) becomes [3(2) + 4][(2) – 2] = (10)(0) = 0. Keep (B) for now. Choice (C) becomes [3(2) – 8][(2) + 1] = (–2)(3) = –6. This is does not match the target value, so eliminate (C). Choice (D) becomes [3(2) + 8][(2) + 1] = (14)(3) = 42. Eliminate (D). Since two answers match the target value, choose a new value to plug in to the remaining answer choices. Make $c = 3$. The expression becomes $3(3)^2 - 10(3) + 8 = 3(9) - 30 + 8 = 27 - 30 + 8 = 5$. This is the new target value; circle it. Choice (A) becomes [3(3) – 4][(3) – 2] = (5)(1) = 5. This matches the new target, so keep (A) for now. Choice (B) becomes [3(3) + 4][(3) – 2] = (13)(1) = 13. Eliminate (B). The correct answer is (A).

7. **B**   The question asks for the value of m that satisfies an equation. Since the question asks for a specific value and the answers contain numbers, Plugging In the Answers could work. However, the answers are in decimal form, so it may get confusing without a calculator. Try to simplify the equation instead. Start by distributing the negative sign and combining like terms. The equation becomes $8m - 3 + 2m - 6 = 10m - 9 = 0$. Add 9 to both sides of the equation to get $10m = 9$, then divide both sides by 10 to get $m = \dfrac{9}{10} = 0.9$. The correct answer is (B).

8. **D**   The question asks for an equation in terms of a specific variable. Although there are variables in the answer choices, plugging in on this question would be difficult because of the number of different variables. Instead, solve for α. To begin to isolate α, subtract ω_0 from both sides of the equation to get $\omega - \omega_0 = \alpha t$. Divide both sides by t to get $\alpha = \dfrac{\omega - \omega_0}{t}$. The correct answer is (D).

9. **A**   The question asks for the relationship between the heights of two cylinders of identical volume. The question involves a relationship between unknown numbers, so plug in. The question states the *radius of Paperweight X is one-third the radius of Paperweight Y*, so use $r_X = 3$ for Paperweight X and $r_Y = 9$ for the Paperweight Y. The formula for the volume of a cylinder is $V = \pi r^2 h$, so plug in the values to determine the volume of each cylinder. The volume of the Paperweight X is $V = \pi(3)^2 h_X = 9\pi h_X$. The volume of Paperweight Y is $V = \pi(9)^2 h_Y = 81\pi h_Y$. Since the volumes are equal, set the equations equal to get $9\pi h_X = 81\pi h_Y$. Divide both sides by 9π to get $h_X = 9h_Y$. Paperweight X's height will be 9 times that of Paperweight Y. The correct answer is (A).

10. **C**   The question asks about the graph of the data representing a certain situation. Label the parts of the equation to determine what they represent. In this question, C represents the cost of living in the apartment for a month and h represents the number of kilowatt hours of electricity used in a month. The y-intercept of a graph is defined as a point where the graph intersects the y-axis, so the y-intercept must relate to cost of living in the apartment. Eliminate (A), since it does not mention the cost of rent. The equation is in $y = mx + b$ form, where b is the y-intercept of a graph, so here the y-intercept is 950. The question states the *only other apartment expense is $950 a month for rent*. Therefore, the y-intercept represents the cost of rent. The correct answer is (C).

11. **2**   The question asks for the value of a variable in a system of equations. The point of intersection will be the x and y solutions to the system, so solve the system of equations using stacking and adding. To make the x terms disappear, multiply the second equation by -2. The second equation becomes $-2(-4x - 2y) = -2$ (3) or $8x + 4y = -6$. Now stack the equations and add them together.

$$\begin{array}{r} -8x + 3y = 20 \\ +\ 8x + 4y = -6 \\ \hline 7y = 14 \end{array}$$

Divide both sides of the resulting equation by 7 to get $y = 2$. The correct answer is 2.

12. $\frac{1}{2}$ or 0.5   The question asks for the value of y-intercept of an equation. The y-intercept of a graph is defined as a point where the graph intersects the y-axis, or when $x = 0$. To find the y-coordinate at that point, plug $x = 0$ into the equation. The equation becomes $y = -3(0)^2 + (0) + \frac{1}{2}$, which simplifies to $-3(0) + \frac{1}{2}$, or $\frac{1}{2}$. The correct answer is $\frac{1}{2}$ or 0.5.

13. **3**   The question asks for the cost a special exhibit ticket when given information about the total cost of a trip to a museum. Translate the English to math in bite-sized pieces. The price of a general admission ticket is $10. There were 9 students on the trip, so the cost of general admission can be represented as 90. The price of a special exhibit ticket can be represented as s. The question states that *7 students bought 3 special exhibit tickets each*, which can be represented as $21s$. It also states that *2 students bought 4 special exhibit tickets each*, which can be represented as $8s$. The total cost was $177.00, so the information can be written as $177 = 90 + 21s + 8s$ or $177 = 90 + 29s$. Subtract 90 from both sides of the equation to get $87 = 29s$, then divide both sides by 29 to get $s = \frac{87}{29} = 3$. The correct answer is 3.

Section 4—Math (Calculator)

1. **C**   The question asks for the number of paperclips that could be in 5 boxes. Since there is a range for the number of paperclips in one box, find the minimum and maximum number that could be in 5 boxes. If each box contains the minimum of 300 paperclips, 5 boxes would contain $5(300) = 1,500$ paperclips. Eliminate (A) and (B), as these numbers are too small. If each box contains the maximum of 400 paperclips, 5 boxes would contain $5(400) = 2,000$ paperclips. Eliminate (D), as this number is too large. The correct answer is (C).

2. **A**   The question asks for the number of full-time employees that were dissatisfied with their work schedules. Looking at the chart, the space under the column "Full-time" in the row "Dissatisfied" is the only box that is not filled in. Call this number x. Read the information above the chart to determine how many employees were surveyed. The question states that 500 employees were surveyed, so the numbers in the chart add up to 500, or $126 + 119 + 108 + x = 500$. Simplify to $353 + x = 500$, then subtract 353 from both sides to get $x = 147$. The correct answer is (A).

3. **C**   The question asks for the number of dry erase markers the teacher expects to use for a certain number of students. Begin by reading the question to find information about the number of red pens. The question states that the teacher uses *1 red pen for every 5 students*. Set up a proportion to determine how many students the teacher has if he needs 7 red pens, being sure to match up units: $\frac{1 \text{ red pen}}{5 \text{ students}} = \frac{7 \text{ red pens}}{x \text{ students}}$. Cross-multiply to get $x = 35$ students. If the teacher uses 2 dry erase markers for each of the 35 students, he will use $2(35) = 70$ dry erase markers. The correct answer is (C).

4. **D**   The question asks about the mean (average) of a set of numbers in a chart. Read the chart carefully to find the correct numbers, which are in the *maximum elevation* row. Use the formula $T = AN$, where T is the total, A is the average, and N is the number of things. The *total* is 239 + 289 + 329 + 240 + 195 = 1,292, and the *number of things* is 5. The equation becomes 1,292 = A(5). Divide both sides by 5 to get $A = 258.4$. The correct answer is (D).

5. **A**   The question asks about the number of defective widgets based on information about a random sample of the total produced. Since the widgets were randomly selected, the incidence of those defective in the sample should match that of the total produced. Start by ballparking. Less than half the widgets were defective, so the answer must be less than half of 5,913. Eliminate (D), which is too large. To extrapolate the sample results, set up a proportion. In this case, the proportion is based on the number of defective widgets out of the total of each group: $\dfrac{41}{200} = \dfrac{x}{5,913}$. Cross-multiply to get $200x = 242,433$. Divide both sides by 200 to get $x = 1,212.165$, or approximately 1,200. The correct answer is (A).

6. **B**   The question asks for the tax added to a bill based on a percentage. Translate the question in bite-sized pieces. Percent means "out of 100," so 5% can be written as $\dfrac{5}{100}$. When a percent is taken of a value, that percent is multiplied by the value, so this becomes $\dfrac{5}{100}(117.5) = \$5.875$. This is closest to $6.00. The correct answer is (B).

7. **D**   The question asks for measurements and gives conflicting units. Start by ballparking. The given measurements are in *centimeters* and *millimeters*, which are smaller than *meters*. Therefore, the number of meters for each measurement will be smaller than the number of centimeters and millimeters. Eliminate (A) and (B), which have very large measurements. Compare the remaining answers. The only difference is the third measurement. Start by converting the 5 millimeters to centimeters. The question states that *1 centimeter = 10 millimeters*. Set up a proportion to determine how many centimeters are in 5 millimeters, being sure to match up units: $\dfrac{10 \text{ millimeters}}{1 \text{ centimeter}} = \dfrac{5 \text{ millimeters}}{x \text{ centimeters}}$. Cross-multiply to get $10x = 5$. Divide both sides by 10 to get $x = 0.5$ centimeters. Next, convert 0.5 centimeters to meters. The question states that *1 meter = 100 centimeters*. Set up a proportion to determine how many meters are in 0.5 centimeters, being sure to match up units: $\dfrac{100 \text{ centimeters}}{1 \text{ meter}} = \dfrac{0.5 \text{ centimeters}}{x \text{ meters}}$. Cross-multiply to get $100x = 0.5$. Divide both sides by 100 to get $x = 0.005$ meters. As a fraction, this is $\dfrac{1}{200}$. The correct answer is (D).

8. **D** The question asks for a certain value on a graph. *Height* is listed along the horizontal axis, so find 11 on that axis. It will be between the lines for 8 and 12, closer to the 12. From this point, trace up to find the intersection with the line of best fit, using the answer sheet as a straight edge if necessary. It is between the horizontal gridlines for 30 and 40 on the vertical *Growth rate* axis. Only the value in (D) falls between 30 and 40. The correct answer is (D).

9. **B** The question asks for the graph that best represents data in a table. Pick a piece of information from the table and use it to eliminate graphs in the answer choices. The graphs all look similar for small numbers of participants, so try a large number. If there are 20 participants, the price of the tour is $250. The numbers for *Tour participants* are listed along the horizontal axis in each answer, so find 20 on that axis. From this point, trace up to find the intersection with the graph, using the answer sheet as a straight edge if necessary. For (A), it is on the gridline for $300. This does not match the target value of $250, so eliminate (A). For (B), it is on the gridline for $250, so keep (B), but check the remaining answers just in case. For (C) and (D), there is no price indicated for 20 tour participants, so eliminate (C) and (D). The correct answer is (B).

10. **A** The question asks for a value based on a ratio. The question states *the ratio of almond flour to coconut flour is 7:38*. To solve a ratio question, determine the number of parts in each group, then determine the number of groups in the whole. To do this, add the ratio numbers to get the number of parts: $7 + 38 = 45$. To find the number of groups of 45 that are needed to get to the whole of 180, set up an equation: $45x = 180$. Divide both sides by 45 to get $x = 4$. Use the ratio number for almond flour parts and the number of groups in the whole to calculate the actual volume of almond flour: $7(4) = 28$ cups. The correct answer is (A).

11. **B** The question asks for an accurate comparison based on a system of equations. Start by reading the full question, which gives equations for the number of cars passing through two intersections. Then label the parts of the equations with the information given. The question states that t is the total number of cars passing through the intersection and d is hours of daylight. Next, use Process of Elimination to get rid of answer choices that are not consistent with the labels. Choice (A) refers to the number of cars per hour increasing at a certain rate. To check this, plug in some numbers for d. Plug in $d = 1$, $d = 2$, and $d = 3$ to see what happens over time.

	$d = 1$	$d = 2$	$d = 3$
For Intersection X:	$t = 450(1) = 450$	$450(2) = 900$	$450(3) = 1,350$
For Intersection Y:	$t = 150(1) = 150$	$150(2) = 300$	$150(3) = 450$

Each hour, the number of cars passing through Intersection X increases by 450, and the number of cars passing through Intersection Y increases by 150. Therefore, for either intersection, the rate is constant and not increasing at all for either intersection. Eliminate (A) and (C), since both refer to an increasing rate. Compare the remaining answers. The only difference is whether the number of cars passing through Intersection X or Intersection Y is greater. Choice (D) says that the number of cars passing through Intersection Y is greater, which is not true. Intersection X has greater numbers at all values of d, so eliminate (D). The correct answer is (B).

12. **B**   The question asks for an equation in terms of a specific variable. Although there are variables in the answer choices, plugging in on this question would be difficult given the number of variables. Instead, solve for n. To begin to isolate n, multiply both sides of the equation by n to get $np = m$. Divide both sides by p to get $n = \dfrac{m}{p}$. The correct answer is (B).

13. **B**   The question asks for an inequality that models a specific situation. Translate the English to math in bite-sized pieces. The days are represented as d. The inequality must show the number of days *before she hits or goes over her limit or 7 Gigabytes*. This means that the expression containing d must be less than or equal to 7, which is represented as "≤ 7." Eliminate (C) and (D), as the expression for days is not less than or equal to 7. The question asks about data use of *2 hours each day* and *0.25 Gigabytes for each of those hours*, so Maria uses 0.25(2) = 0.5 Gigabytes of data each day, represented as 0.5d. Eliminate (A), as it does not show 0.5 Gigabytes used each day. The correct answer is (B).

14. **C**   The question asks for the purchase price of the cell phone to the nearest dollar. Start by ballparking. The purchase price does not include the tax or the flat fee for the phone charger, so the purchase price must be less than the actual total paid. Eliminate (A), as it is not less than the total of $685.72 paid for the cell phone. Since the question asks for a specific value and the answers contain numbers in decreasing order, plug in the answers. Begin by labeling the answers as "purchase price" and start with (C), $625. The question states that *the cell phone will have a 6.5% sales tax on the purchase price*. "Percent" means divide by 100. Then multiply the result by the value of which the percent is taken. This becomes 0.065($625) = $40.625. Add this to $625 to get $665.63. The question also states that a *flat fee of $20* is added for the phone charger, so this becomes $665.63 + $20 = $685.63. This nearly matches the value given in the question, which asks for the price *to the nearest dollar*, so stop here. The correct answer is (C).

15. **B**   The question asks for an estimate of the number of people in a group who would have rated a game at a certain level or higher based on an evaluation completed by a portion of the group. Since the people were randomly selected, the results found in the evaluation should match that of the larger group. To extrapolate the evaluation results, set up a proportion being sure to match up units. In this case, the proportion is based on the ratings of a video game given by members of the group. The total number of people that completed the survey was 14 + 29 + 13 + 18 = 74. Of those, 13 people rating the video game ✓+ and 18 people rating the video game ✓++, so the number of people who rated it with a ✓+ or higher was 13 + 18 = 31. The proportion becomes $\dfrac{31}{74} = \dfrac{x}{240}$. Cross-multiply to get $74x = 7{,}440$. Divide both sides by 74 to get $x = 100.54$. The question asks for an approximation, so round this to 100. The correct answer is (B).

16. **C**   The question asks for a new data point based on how it changes the mean and median of a set of data. The median is easier to determine, so start by finding the median of the existing data. The median of a list of numbers is the middle number when all values are arranged in order. The shoulder heights are not listed in order, so start by listing the shoulder heights from shortest to tallest. Elephant B has the shortest shoulder height of 1.83 meters. Elephant G has the 2nd shortest shoulder height of 1.90 meters, and Elephant A has the 3rd shortest shoulder height of 2.04 meters. Elephant C, Elephant E, Elephant

F, and Elephant D have shoulder heights of 2.13, 2.45, 2.68, and 3.14 meters, respectively. Therefore, the median shoulder height of the original 7 elephants is 2.13 meters. The question states that Elephant H's shoulder height *increases the median value of the group of elephants*. Eliminate (A) which is smaller than 2.13 meters and would decrease the median value. Eliminate (B) which matches the median and therefore would not increase it. The question also refers to a change in the mean or average value, so calculate the average shoulder height. Use the formula $T = AN$, where T is the total, A is the average, and N is the number of things. The *total* is 1.83 + 1.90 + 2.04 + 2.13 + 2.45 + 2.68 + 3.14 = 16.17, and the *number of things* is 7. The equation becomes 16.17 = A(7). Divide both sides by 7 to get A = 2.31. The question states that Elephant H's shoulder height *decreases the mean value of the group*. Eliminate (D), as this value is equal to the mean and would keep the mean the same. The correct answer is (C).

17. **D**   The question asks for the total distance in meters covered by four animals over specified periods of time given the distance they can cover in kilometers in 10 minutes of running. Use Bite-Sized Pieces and Process of Elimination to tackle this question. The distance covered by the cheetah and the African wild dog can be read directly from the table, since the table's data is based on an interval of 10 minutes. According to the table, the cheetah covers 18 km in 10 minutes, and the African wild dog covers 12 km in 10 minutes. Use proportions to determine the other two distances. Begin by setting up a proportion to calculate the distance covered by the lion in 20 minutes, being sure to match up units: $\frac{14 \text{ km}}{10 \text{ min}} = \frac{x \text{ km}}{20 \text{ min}}$. Cross-multiply to get $10x = 280$, then divide both sides by 10 to get $x = 28$ km. Repeat the process to determine the distances for the zebra. The zebra ran for 40 minutes: $\frac{11 \text{ km}}{10 \text{ min}} = \frac{x \text{ km}}{40 \text{ min}}$. Cross-multiply to get $10x = 440$, or $x = 44$ km. The total distance covered by the four animals in the specified time periods is 28 km + 18 km + 12 km + 44 km = 102 km. The question asks for an answer in meters, so set up a proportion to convert the units, being sure to match up units: $\frac{1 \text{ km}}{1,000 \text{ m}} = \frac{102 \text{ km}}{x \text{ m}}$. Cross-multiply to get $x = 102,000$ m. The correct answer is (D).

18. **A**   The question asks for the animal running for a specified period of time that covers a distance that is equivalent to the sum of two other animals' distances over specified periods of time. Use Bite-Sized Pieces and Process of Elimination to tackle this question. Begin by calculating the *distance covered by a cheetah running for 15 min and a giraffe running for 5 min*. Set up a proportion to determine the distance covered by a cheetah in 15 minutes, being sure to match up units: $\frac{18 \text{ km}}{10 \text{ min}} = \frac{x \text{ km}}{15 \text{ min}}$. Cross-multiply to get $10x = 270$, then divide both sides by 10 to get $x = 27$ km. Repeat the process to determine the distance covered by a giraffe in 5 minutes: $\frac{9 \text{ km}}{10 \text{ min}} = \frac{x \text{ km}}{5 \text{ min}}$, which becomes

$10x = 45$, or $x = 4.5$ km. The total distance covered by a cheetah and a giraffe in the specified time periods is 27 km + 4.5 km = 31.5 km. Use a proportion to calculate the distance covered by each animal in each answer choice, and eliminate answer choices that are not close to this value. Choice (A) becomes $\dfrac{11 \text{ km}}{10 \text{ min}} = \dfrac{x \text{ km}}{30 \text{ min}}$, then $10x = 330$, or $x = 33$ km. Keep (A) for now, as it is very close to the target value of 31.5, but check the remaining answer choices to see if one is closer. Choice (B) becomes $\dfrac{12 \text{ km}}{10 \text{ min}} = \dfrac{x \text{ km}}{20 \text{ min}}$, then $10x = 240$, or $x = 24$ km. Eliminate (B), as it is not closer to 31.5 km than (A). Choice (C) becomes $\dfrac{14 \text{ km}}{10 \text{ min}} = \dfrac{x \text{ km}}{50 \text{ min}}$, then $10x = 700$ km, or $x = 70$ km. Eliminate (C). Choice (D) becomes $\dfrac{7 \text{ km}}{10 \text{ min}} = \dfrac{x \text{ km}}{60 \text{ min}}$, then $10x = 420$ km, or $x = 42$ km. Eliminate (D). The correct answer is (A).

19. **D** The question asks for a set of inequalities that are true for the slope and the y-intercept of a line on a graph. To find the correct set of inequalities, compare features of the graph to the answer choices. The equation is given in slope-intercept form, so r is the slope of the line and s is the y-intercept. The graph for this question has a y-intercept of 3 and a negative slope. Eliminate answer choices that do not match this information. Choices (A) and (B) say r, the slope, is positive. Eliminate (A) and (B), since they are not consistent with the graph's negative slope. Choice (C) says s, the y-intercept, is less than 1. Eliminate (C) since this is not consistent with the graph's y-intercept of 3. The correct answer is (D).

20. **A** The question asks for the best interpretation of the slope of a line representing a set of data. In this question, y represents the height of a vine, and x represents the number of days since the vine was planted. The slope of a graph is defined as the change in y over the change in x, so the slope must relate to height as it increases over time. Eliminate (B) and (C), as they reference the height on specific days. Eliminate (D), as x itself represents days, so the slope cannot also be the number of days. Another way to approach this is to plug and play to see what gives a value that matches the value of the slope. Slope is calculated using the equation slope $= \dfrac{y_2 - y_1}{x_2 - x_1}$. Calculate the slope of the line using two points, such as (1, 7.5) and (2, 9.0). The slope formula becomes $\dfrac{9 - 7.5}{2 - 1} = \dfrac{1.5}{1} = 1.5$. Choice (A) refers to *the amount that the height of the vine is increasing each day*. Each day, the vine's height increases by 1.5 inches. Keep (A), but check the remaining answer choices just in case. Choice (B) refers to *the height of the vine after the seventh day of growth*. The vine grows 1.5 inches each day, so the vine will be 15.0 + 1.5 = 16.5 inches on the seventh day. Eliminate (B), as this does not match the value of 1.5 inches. Choice (C) refers to *the height of the vine when it was first planted*. The question states that the starter plant had *a height of 6 inches*. Since the vine's height when planted is not 1.5

inches, eliminate (C). Choice (D) refers to the number of days the plant will keep growing, but no information is given about how long the plant will grow. Either way, the correct answer is (A).

21. **C** The question asks for *the total number of students with red hair* in a school district based on a percentage. There are *approximately 350 students per school in the 9 different schools*, so there are approximately 9(350) = 3,150 total students in the district. The question states *1.5% of the district's students have red hair*. "Percent" means divide by 100. Then multiply the result by the value of which the percent is taken. This becomes 0.015(3,150) = 47.25 students have red hair in the district. The correct answer is (C).

22. **53** The question asks for the total number of vouchers sold based on the cost of each voucher, the total voucher sales, and the total number of drinks sold. Translate the question in bite-sized pieces and write a system of equations for the situation. Use x to represent the number of vouchers sold for 1 drink and y to represent the number of vouchers sold for 2 drinks. One piece of information says that *a voucher for 1 drink costs $6*, so the sales for vouchers for 1 drink would be represented as $6x$. The question states that *a voucher for 2 drinks costs $10*, so the sales for vouchers for 2 drinks would be represented as $10y$. The question also states that *the voucher sales total was $462*, so $6x + 10y = 462$. The question states that *89 drinks were purchased with vouchers*. Each voucher represented as x is for 1 drink and each voucher represented as y is for 2 drinks, so the equation to represent the total number of drinks is $x + 2y = 89$. Solve the system of equations by stacking. Multiply the second equation by -6 and add it to the first equation to eliminate the x variable.

$$
\begin{array}{ll}
6x + 10y = 462 & \quad 6x + 10y = 462 \\
-6(x + 2y = 89) & \quad \underline{-6x - 12y = -534} \\
& \qquad\qquad -2y = -72
\end{array}
$$

The result is $-2y = -72$. Divide both sides by -2 to get $y = 36$. Plug y back into either equation to solve for x. The second equation becomes $x + 2(36) = 89$, or $x + 72 = 89$. Subtract 72 from both sides to get $x = 17$. The total number of vouchers sold, or $x + y$, is $17 + 36 = 53$. The correct answer is 53.

23. $\dfrac{7}{10}$ **or 0.7** The question asks for the value of a variable in a system of equations. Solve the system of equations using stacking. When stacking the system of equations, multiply the second equation by 2 and add it to the first equation to eliminate the b variable.

$$
\begin{array}{ll}
-3a + 6b = 1.8 & \quad -3a + 6b = 1.8 \\
+2(4a - 3b = 1.1) & \quad \underline{+ 8a - 6b = 2.2} \\
& \quad\; 5a = 4.0
\end{array}
$$

The new equation becomes $5a = 4$. Divide both sides by 5 to get $a = 0.8$. Plug a back into either equation to solve for b. The first equation becomes $-3(0.8) + 6b = 1.8$, or $-2.4 + 6b = 1.8$. Add 2.4 to both sides to get $6b = 4.2$. Divide both sides by 6 to get $b = 0.7$. The correct answer is 0.7 or $\dfrac{7}{10}$.

24. **24** The question asks for the number of people ages 18–29 who participated in a survey. This question is much longer and more complicated than Q25, so start with that question, filling in the table with one piece of information at a time. The information determined in Q25 is bolded in the table below.

		Age range in years				
		18–29	30–44	45–64	65+	Total
Drink preference	Coffee		21		4	**43**
	Tea	17	**34**	12	**10**	73
	Total		55		14	116

This question states that *25.6% of the people who chose coffee as their preferred beverage were 45–64 years old*. The total number of people who prefer coffee is 43, so 0.256(43) = 11 people ages 45–64 prefer coffee. There were 12 people ages 45–64 who prefer tea, so 11 + 12 = 23 people ages 45–64 surveyed in total. These numbers are bolded in the table below.

		Age range in years				
		18–29	30–44	45–64	65+	Total
Drink preference	Coffee		21	**11**	4	**43**
	Tea	17	**34**	12	**10**	73
	Total		55	**23**	14	116

The total number of people surveyed is 116, so 116 – 14 – 23 – 55 = 24 people ages 18–29 surveyed in total. The completed table is shown below.

		Age range in years				
		18–29	30–44	45–64	65+	Total
Drink preference	Coffee		21	**11**	4	**43**
	Tea	17	**34**	12	**10**	73
	Total	**24**	55	**23**	14	116

The correct answer is 24.

25. **43** The question asks for the total number of people surveyed who prefer coffee. Start by filling in the table one piece of information at a time. There were 55 people ages 30–44 surveyed and 21 of those prefer coffee, so 55 – 21 = 34 people ages 30–44 prefer tea. There were 14 people ages 65+ surveyed and 4 of those prefer coffee, so 14 – 4 = 10 people ages 65+ prefer tea. These numbers are bolded in the table below.

		Age range in years				
		18–29	30–44	45–64	65+	Total
Drink preference	Coffee		21		4	
	Tea	17	**34**	12	**10**	
	Total		55		14	116

The total number of people who prefer tea is 17 + 34 + 12 + 10 = 73. The total people surveyed is 116, so 116 – 73 = 43 total people prefer coffee. These numbers are bolded in the table below.

		Age range in years				
		18–29	30–44	45–64	65+	Total
Drink preference	Coffee		21		4	**43**
	Tea	17	**34**	12	**10**	**73**
	Total		55		14	116

The correct answer is 43.

RAW SCORE CONVERSION TABLE | SECTION AND TEST SCORES

Raw Score (# of correct answers)	Reading Test Score	Writing and Language Test Score	Math Section Score	Raw Score (# of correct answers)	Reading Test Score	Writing and Language Test Score	Math Section Score
0	6	6	120	22	22	22	500
1	7	7	150	23	22	23	510
2	9	8	180	24	23	23	520
3	10	10	210	25	23	24	530
4	11	11	240	26	24	25	540
5	12	12	270	27	25	25	560
6	13	13	290	28	25	26	570
7	14	13	310	29	26	26	580
8	15	14	330	30	27	27	590
9	16	15	340	31	27	28	610
10	16	15	360	32	28	28	620
11	17	16	670	33	29	29	640
12	17	16	380	34	30	30	660
13	17	17	400	35	30	31	680
14	18	17	410	36	31	32	690
15	18	18	420	37	32	33	710
16	19	18	440	38	33	34	720
17	19	19	450	39	34	35	
18	20	19	460	40	35	36	
19	20	20	470	41	35		
20	21	21	480	42	36		
21	21	21	490				

CONVERSION EQUATION | SECTION AND TEST SCORES

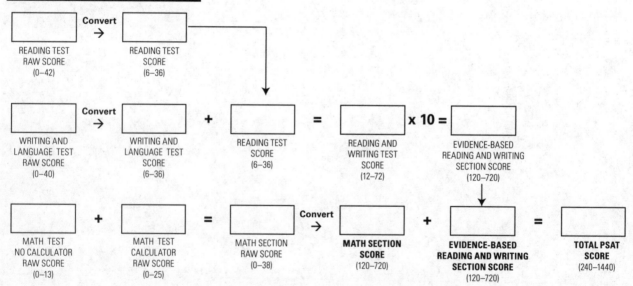

Part III
PSAT 8/9 Prep

5   Reading Comprehension
6   Introduction to Writing and Language Strategy
7   Punctuation
8   Words
9   Questions
10 Math Basics
11 Math Techniques
12 Advanced Math

Chapter 5
Reading Comprehension

Half of your Evidence-Based Reading and Writing score comes from the Reading Test, a 55-minute test that requires you to answer 42 questions spread out over five passages. The questions will ask you to do everything from determining the meaning of words in context, to deciding an author's purpose for providing a detail, to finding the main idea of an entire passage, to pinpointing information on a graph. Each passage ranges from 500 to 700 words and has 8 or 9 questions. Time will be tight on this test. The purpose of this chapter is to introduce you to a basic approach that will streamline how you take the test and allow you to focus on only what you need to get your points.

PSAT 8/9 READING: CRACKING THE PASSAGES

Answering passage-based reading questions is exactly like taking an open-book test: all of the information that you could be asked about is right in front of you, so you never have to worry about any history, literature, or chemistry that you may (or may not) have learned in school. Of course, you will use the passage to answer the questions, but you will not need to read the passage from beginning to end, master all its details, and then carefully select the one choice that answers the question perfectly. What you need is a way to get in and get out of this section with as little stress and as many points as possible.

If someone asked you in what year Louis Pasteur invented pasteurization, would you read the Wikipedia entry on Pasteur from the beginning until you found the answer? Or would you quickly scan through it looking for words like "invented" and "pasteurization"—or better yet, look for the numbers that represent a year, which are easy to spot? We're sure his childhood was fascinating, but your job is to answer a specific question, not read an entire text. This is exactly how to approach passage-based reading questions on the PSAT 8/9.

Your Mission:

Process five passages and answer 8 or 9 questions for each passage (or pair of passages). Get as many points as you can.

Okay…so how do you get those points? Let's start with the instructions for the Reading Test.

DIRECTIONS

Each passage or pair of passages below is followed by a number of questions. After reading each passage or pair, choose the best answer to each question based on what is stated or implied in the passage or passages and in any accompanying graphics (such as a table or graph).

Notice that the directions clearly tell you that the correct answer is based on "what is stated or implied in the passage." This is great news! You do not have to rely on your outside knowledge here. All the College Board cares about is whether you can read a text and understand it well enough to answer some questions about it. Unlike in the Math or the Writing and Language Tests, there are no formulas to memorize, no comma rules to learn. You just need to know how to efficiently process the text, the questions, and the answer choices in order to maximize your score. A mantra you can use here: Don't think! Just read!

Another benefit of this open-book test format: you can (and should!) flip back and forth between the passage and the questions so that you are reading only what you need in order to answer a given question.

Your POOD and Your Reading Test

You will get all five of the Reading passages at the same time, so use that to your advantage. Take a quick look through the entire section and figure out the best order for you to do the passages in. Depending on your target score, you may be able to temporarily skip (don't forget LOTD!) an entire passage or two, so figure out which passages are hardest, and save them for last (or for never).

How do you decide which ones to do and which ones to skip? Consider these concepts:

- **Type of passage:** You'll have one literature passage, two science passages, and two history/social studies passages. If you like to read fiction, the literature passage may be a good place for you to start. If you like to read nonfiction, the science or history/social studies might be a better starting place for you.

- **Topic of passage:** The blurb will give you some basic information about the passage that can help you decide whether to do the passage or skip it.

- **Types of questions:** Do the questions have a good number of Line References and Lead Words? Will you be able to find what you're looking for relatively quickly, or will you have to spend more time wading through the passage to find what you need?

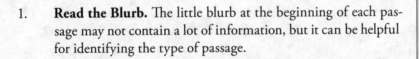

Don't forget: On any questions or passages that you skip, always fill in your LOTD!

Basic Approach for the Reading Test

Follow these steps for every Reading passage. We'll go over these in greater detail in the next few pages.

1. **Read the Blurb.** The little blurb at the beginning of each passage may not contain a lot of information, but it can be helpful for identifying the type of passage.

2. **Select and Understand a Question.** For the most part, do the questions in order, saving the general questions for last and using your LOTD on any questions you want to skip.

3. **Read What You Need.** Don't read the whole passage! Use Line References, Lead Words, and the natural order of the questions to find the reference for the question, and then carefully read a window of about 10–12 lines (usually about 5 or 6 lines above and below the Line Reference/Lead Word) to find the answer to the question.

Where the Money Is

A reporter once asked notorious thief Willie Sutton why he robbed banks. Legend has it that his answer was, "Because that's where the money is." While reading comprehension is safer and slightly more productive than larceny, the same principle applies. Concentrate on the questions and answer choices because that's where the points are. The passage is just a place for the College Board to stash facts and details. You'll find them when you need to. What's the point of memorizing all 67 pesky details about plankton if the College Board asks you about only 9?

4. **Predict the Correct Answer.** Your prediction should come straight from the text. Don't analyze or paraphrase. Often, you'll be able to find something in the text that you can actually underline to predict the answer.

5. **POE.** Eliminate anything that isn't consistent with your prediction. Don't necessarily try to find the right answer immediately, because there is a good chance you won't see anything that you like. If you can eliminate answers that you know are wrong, though, you'll be closer to the right answer. If you can't eliminate three answers with your prediction, use the POE criteria (which we'll talk about in a few pages).

Let's see these steps in action!

A sample passage and questions appear on the next few pages. Don't start working the passage right away. In fact…you can't! The answer choices are missing. Just go ahead to page 113, where we will begin going through the steps of the Basic Approach, using the upcoming passage and questions.

SAMPLE PASSAGE AND QUESTIONS

Here is an example of what a reading comprehension passage and questions look like. We will use this passage to illustrate the reading Basic Approach throughout this chapter. You don't need to do the questions now, but you might want to paperclip this page so it's easy to flip back to later.

This passage is adapted from Agustín Fuentes, "Are We Really as Awful as We Act Online?" ©2018 by National Geographic Society.

Is this aggression on social media giving us a glimpse of human nature, one in which we are, at our core, nasty, belligerent beasts? No. It's
Line true that hate crimes are on the rise, political
5 divisions are at record heights, and the level of vitriol in the public sphere, especially online, is substantial. But that's not because social media has unleashed a brutish human nature. In my work as an evolutionary anthropologist, I've spent
10 years researching and writing about how, over the past two million years, our lineage transformed from groups of apelike beings armed with sticks and stones to the creators of cars, rockets, great artworks, nations, and global economic systems.

15 How did we do this? Our brains got bigger, and our capacities for cooperation exploded. We're wired to work together, to forge diverse social relationships, and to creatively problem-solve together. I would argue that the increase
20 in online aggression is due to an explosive combination of this human evolutionary social skill set, the social media boom, and the specific political and economic context in which we find ourselves—a combination that's opened up a
25 space for more and more people to fan the flames of aggression and insult online.

We've all heard the diet-conscious axiom "You are what you eat." But when it comes to our behavior, a more apt variation is "You are whom
30 you meet." How we perceive, experience, and act in the world is intensely shaped by who and what surround us on a daily basis—our families, communities, institutions, beliefs, and role models. This process has deep evolutionary roots
35 and gives humans what we call a shared reality. The connection between minds and experiences enables us to share space and work together effectively, more so than most other beings. It's in part how we've become such a successful species.

40 But the "who" that constitutes "whom we meet" in this system has been changing. Today the who can include more virtual, social media

friends than physical ones; more information absorbed via Twitter, Facebook, and Instagram
45 than in physical social experiences; and more pronouncements from ad-sponsored 24-hour news outlets than from conversations with other human beings. Historically, we have maintained harmony by displaying compassion
50 and geniality, and by fostering connectedness when we get together. Anonymity and the lack of face-to-face interaction on social media platforms remove a crucial part of the equation of human sociality—and that opens the door to
55 more frequent, and severe, displays of aggression. Being an antagonizer, especially to those you don't have to confront face-to-face, is easier now than it's ever been. If there are no repercussions for it, that encourages the growth of aggression,
60 incivility, and just plain meanness on social media platforms.

Since we'll continue to be influenced by whom we meet virtually, the next question is: Whom do we *want* to meet? What kind of society do we
65 want to shape and be shaped by? That is, how do we modify the whom by which our brains and bodies are being molded—and thereby reduce the aggression?

Humans are evolutionarily successful because
70 our big brains have allowed us to bond together and cooperate in more complex and diverse manners than any other animal. The capacity to observe how the world operates, to imagine how it might improve, and to turn that vision into reality
75 (or at least make the attempt) is the hallmark of humanity. And therein lies the solution to the problem. We are equipped with the skill set both to quell aggression and to encourage cohesion.

For countless millennia people have acted
80 collectively to punish and shame aggressive antisocial actions such as bullying or abuse. On social media, where the troll is remote and anonymous, even the best-intentioned individual challenge may devolve into a shouting match.
85 But confronting the bully with a group action—a reasoned, communal response rather than a knee-jerk, solo gesture—can be more effective at shutting down aggression.

These are the questions for the passage. We've removed the answer choices because, for now, we just want you to see the different question types the PSAT 8/9 will ask. Don't worry about answering these here.

9

The primary purpose of the passage is to

10

The author indicates that the reason humans have been able to create inventions such as cars and rockets is that

11

Which choice provides the best evidence for the answer to the previous question?

12

The phrase "You are whom you meet" (lines 29–30) most strongly suggests that

13

As used in line 44, "absorbed" most nearly means

14

The author most likely mentions Facebook, Instagram, and Twitter as examples of

15

Based on information in the passage, it can reasonably be inferred that aggression

16

Which choice provides the best evidence for the answer to the previous question?

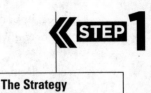

Step 1: Read the Blurb

You should always begin by reading the blurb (the introductory material above the passage). The blurb gives you the title of the piece, as well as the author and the publication date. Typically the blurb won't have much more information than that, but it'll be enough to let you know whether the passage is literature, history/social studies, or science. It will also give you a sense of what the passage will be about and can help you make a POOD decision about when to do the passage.

The Strategy
1. Read the Blurb

Read the blurb at the beginning of the passage on page 111. Based on the blurb, is the passage literature, history/social studies, or science? What will the passage be about?

_____history/social studie_____

_____

Step 2: Select and Understand a Question

Select...

Notice that the steps of the Basic Approach have you jumping straight from the blurb to the questions. There is no "Read the Passage" step. You get points for answering questions, not for reading the passage, so we're going to go straight to the questions.

The Strategy
1. Read the Blurb
2. Select and Understand a Question

On a test you take in school, you probably do the questions in order. That seems logical and straightforward. However, doing the questions in order on a Reading passage can set you up for a serious time issue. The College Board says the order of the questions is "as natural as possible, with general questions about central ideas, themes, point of view, overall text structure, and the like coming early in the sequence, followed by more localized questions about details, words in context, evidence, and the like." So to sum it up, the general questions come first, followed by the specific questions.

That question structure works great in an English class, when you have plenty of time to read and digest the text on your own. When you're trying to get through five passages in less than an hour, you don't have time for that. Instead of starting with the general questions and then answering the specific questions, we're going to flip that and do the specific questions first.

Look back at the questions on page 112.

What does the first question ask you about?

In order to answer that question, you'd have to read what part of the passage?

And what we don't want to do is read the whole passage! So skip that first question. You'll come back to it, but not until you've done the specific questions. Once you go through and answer all (or most) of the specific questions, you'll have a really good idea what the test-writers think is important. You'll also have read most of the passage, so answering the general questions at the end will be easier than it would be if you had started with them.

Remember we mentioned earlier that the questions are in "natural" order? The specific questions are written roughly in the same order in which they appear in the passage. So work through them as they're given, and you'll work through the passage from beginning to end. Do not get stuck on a hard question, though. If you find yourself stumped, use your LOTD and move on to the next question. You can always come back if you have time.

Based on that logic, let's skip the first question and move on to the second question.

...and Understand

Once you've selected a question, you need to make sure you understand what it's asking. Reading questions are often not in question format. Instead, they will make statements such as, "The author's primary reason for mentioning the gadfly is to," and then the answer choices will follow. Make sure that you understand the question by turning it into a question—that is, back into a sentence that ends with a question mark and begins with What/Why/How?

> **Rephrase the Question...**
> ...so that it asks:
> What?
> Why?
> How?

10

The author indicates that the reason humans have been able to create inventions such as cars and rockets is that

What is this question asking?

Notice the phrase *the author indicates that*. This phrase lets you know that the question can be rephrased as a "what" question. That "what" question is, "What is the reason humans have been able to create inventions such as cars and rockets?" Notice that the question asks what the *author* indicates. This lets you know that you don't have to come up with the answer on your own. You just need to find what the author actually said about humans creating cars and rockets and use that information to answer the question.

Step 3: Read What You Need

Line References and Lead Words

Many questions will refer you to a specific set of lines or to a particular paragraph. A set of lines that a question refers to is called a Line Reference. Other questions may not give you a Line Reference but may ask about specific names, quotes, or phrases from the text. We'll call those words from the text Lead Words. Capitalized words, italicized words, and words that only appear in one place in a passage are good Lead Words because they are easy to find. It's important to remember that a Line Reference or Lead Word shows you where the *question* is in the passage, but you'll have to read more than that single line in order to find the *answer* in the passage.

If you read a window of about five lines above and five lines below each Line Reference or Lead Word, you should find the information you need. It's important to note that while you do not need to read more than these 10–12 lines of text, you usually cannot get away with reading less. If you read only the lines from the Line Reference, you will very likely not find the information you need to answer the question. Read carefully! You should be able to put your finger on the particular phrase, sentence, or set of lines that answers your question.

> The Strategy
> 1. Read the Blurb
> 2. Select and Understand a Question
> 3. Read What You Need

> Read a window of about 5 lines above and 5 lines below the Line Reference to get the context for the question.

> **5 Above, 5 Below**
> 5 is the magic number when it comes to Line Reference questions. Read about 5 lines above the Line Reference and then about 5 lines below it to get all of the information you need in order to answer the question correctly.

10

The author indicates that the reason humans have been able to create inventions such as cars and rockets is that

What are the Lead Words in this question?

What lines will you need to read to find the answer?

The best Lead Words for this question are *cars* and *rockets* because these words actually appear in the passage, and they will probably only be mentioned in one place. Remember that specific questions are written roughly in the order that they appear in the passage. Since question 10 is the first specific question, the window is probably near the beginning of the passage. Scan the first paragraph, looking for the Lead Words *cars* and *rockets*. These Lead Words appear in line 13. Once you use the Lead Words to find the reference, draw a bracket around a window of about 5 lines above and 5 lines below the reference to remind you which lines you need to read. The more you can get out of your brain and onto the page, the better off you'll be. In this case, the end of the first paragraph and the first three sentences of the second paragraph would be a good window.

Now it's time to read.

 **Step 4: Predict the Answer**

The College Board does their best to distract you by creating tempting—but wrong—answers. However, if you know what you're looking for in advance, you will be less likely to fall for a trap answer. Before you even glance at the answer choices, take the time to think about what specific, stated information in your window supplies the answer to the question. Be careful not to paraphrase too far from the text or try to analyze what you're reading. Remember that what might be a good "English class" answer may lead you in the wrong direction on the PSAT 8/9! Stick with the text.

> **The Strategy**
> 1. Read the Blurb
> 2. Select and Under-
>   stand a Question
> 3. Read What You Need
> 4. Predict the Answer

As you read the window, look for specific lines or phrases that answer the question. Often what you're looking for will be in a sentence before or after the Line Reference or Lead Word, so it's crucial that you read the full window.

Once you've found text to answer the question, underline it if you can! Otherwise, jot down a prediction for the answer, sticking as close to the text as possible.

Let's keep looking at question 10, this time with the window.

10

The author indicates that the reason humans have been able to create inventions such as cars and rockets is that

Here's your window from the passage. Even though you're reading only a chunk of the text, make sure you read it carefully. See whether you can find something in this chunk of text that answers the question. Underline your prediction if you can.

> In my
> work as an evolutionary anthropologist, I've spent
> 10 years researching and writing about how, over the
> past two million years, our lineage transformed
> from groups of apelike beings armed with sticks
> and stones to the creators of cars, rockets, great
> artworks, nations, and global economic systems.
> 15   How did we do this? Our brains got bigger,
> and our capacities for cooperation exploded.
> We're wired to work together, to forge diverse
> social relationships, and to creatively problem-
> solve together.

Did you underline *Our brains got bigger, and our capacities for cooperation exploded?* The passage gives you evidence that the author thinks that bigger brains and an increasing capacity for cooperation allowed humans to create cars, rockets, and other innovations.

Step 5: Use Process of Elimination

A multiple-choice test is a cool thing because you have all the right answers on the page in front of you. All you have to do is eliminate anything that isn't correct. Sometimes, especially on Reading, it's easier to find wrong answers that aren't supported by the passage rather than trying to find the right answer that might not look the way you think it should.

Process of Elimination, or POE, involves two steps. The first step will be the question, "What can I eliminate that doesn't match—or is inconsistent with—my prediction?" For many of the easy and medium questions, this step will be enough to get down to the right answer.

<table>
<tr><th colspan="2">The Strategy</th></tr>
<tr><td colspan="2">1. Read the Blurb</td></tr>
<tr><td colspan="2">2. Select and Understand a Question</td></tr>
<tr><td colspan="2">3. Read What You Need</td></tr>
<tr><td colspan="2">4. Predict Your Answer</td></tr>
<tr><td colspan="2">5. Use Process of Elimination</td></tr>
</table>

10

The author indicates that the reason humans have been able to create inventions such as cars and rockets is that

Remember, in the previous step, you used the text to predict that bigger brains and an increasing capacity for cooperation allowed humans to create cars, rockets, and other innovations. Start by eliminating anything that does not match your prediction.

	Keep?	Eliminate?
A) we are motivated by a tendency to be aggressively competitive.		
B) we have gradually overcome our brutish human nature.		
C) online communication has allowed us to problem-solve together.		
D) our ability to collaborate grew as we evolved.		

Did you eliminate (A) and (B) right away? Neither choice involves either bigger brains or increasing cooperation. That was fast! Now you're down to two answer choices that use words or ideas from your prediction. Look for the differences between the two answers and use the text to eliminate the incorrect one. Choice (C) says that *online communication* has led to cooperative problem-solving. Does that match the text in the window from the passage? No. The lines in the window don't mention *online communication*, so eliminate (C). Choice (D) says that *our ability to collaborate grew as we evolved*. Does this match the text in the window? Yes. The phrase *our ability to collaborate grew* matches the idea that *our capacities for cooperation exploded*, and the word *evolved* matches the idea that humans *transformed* over the course of two million years. The correct answer needs to match the prediction, but it does not have to use exactly the same words used in the passage. The correct answer is (D).

POE Criteria

On most of the easy and medium questions, you'll be able to eliminate three of the four answers simply by using your prediction. On other questions, usually the harder questions, your prediction will help you get rid of one or two answers, and then you'll need to consider the remaining answers a little more carefully. If you're down to two answers, and they both seem to make sense, you're probably down to the right answer and the trap answer. Luckily, there are some common traps that the College Board will set for you, and knowing them can help you figure out which is the trap answer and which is the right answer. Here are a few of those traps:

- **Mostly Right, Slightly Wrong**: These answers look just about perfect except for a word or two that doesn't match what's in the text.

- **Could Be True**: These answers might initially look good because they make sense or seem logical. You might be able to support these answers in an English class, but they lack the concrete support from the text to make them correct PSAT 8/9 answers.

- **Right Words, Wrong Meaning**: These answer choices have individual words that look exactly like what you saw in the passage, but the words are put together in such a way that they don't actually match the meaning that is in the passage.

- **Right Answer, Wrong Question**: These answer choices include details that are mentioned in the passage, but they don't answer the question that was asked.

QUESTION TYPES AND FORMATS

Now that you know the steps of the Basic Approach, let's consider the different types of questions you'll be answering. It's not important that you can identify the question types by the names we give them. But it is extremely important that you can read a question and know how to respond. Is the question asking you WHAT the author says, WHAT the author means, WHAT a particular word means, WHAT evidence supports a point, etc.? The next section of this chapter will help you decode those question types and formats. The final section will help you make sense of WHY or HOW an author does something, as well as the General WHAT questions.

WHAT Question Types
- Detail
- Infer/Imply/Suggest
- Vocabulary-in-Context
- Best Evidence

DETAIL (*WHAT?*)

When you see a question that contains a phrase such as *according to the passage* or *the author indicates*, your job is fairly simple. Get to that part of the text, find the detail that tells you WHAT the passage or the author is saying, and then use POE to get rid of wrong answers.

Carefully read the window and do not simply rely on your memory. The question writers are really good at tricking people who use their memories rather than their eyes.

A few pages ago, we discussed this question:

10

The author indicates that the reason humans have been able to create inventions such as cars and rockets is that

A) we are motivated by a tendency to be aggressively competitive.

B) we have gradually overcome our brutish human nature.

C) online communication has allowed us to problem-solve together.

D) our ability to collaborate grew as we evolved.

Question 10 is a Detail question. Recall how we solved it by going back to the text, finding relevant evidence, predicting an answer, and then using POE to eliminate answers that didn't match the prediction. If you rely on this process, you will improve your performance with Detail questions.

INFER/IMPLY/SUGGEST (*WHAT?*)

When you see a question that contains the words infer, imply, or suggest, be extra careful. In real life, those words often signify a question asking your interpretation. You may think that the test-writers want you to do some English-class-level reading between the lines. In actuality, though, they don't. It's still just a straight reading comprehension question. There may be a tiny bit of reading between the lines, because the answer may not be as directly stated in the text as it will with a detail question, but there will still be plenty of evidence in the text to support the correct answer.

12

The phrase "You are whom you meet" most strongly suggests that

A) we are only affected by people we meet in person.

B) most nonhuman animals are not evolutionarily successful.

C) the people we regularly interact with influence our behavior.

D) we are most effective when we share our working space with others.

Here's How to Crack It

The question asks what is suggested by the phrase *"You are whom you meet."* Use Lead Words and the order of the questions to find the window for the question. The window for question 10 was in lines 8–19. Since the questions are in order, the window for this question probably starts after the window for question 10. Starting with line 19, scan the passage for the Lead Words *"You are whom you meet."* Lines 28–34 state, *But when it comes to our behavior, a more apt variation is "You are whom you meet." How we perceive, experience, and act in the world is intensely shaped by who and what surround us on a daily basis—our families, communities, institutions, beliefs, and role models.* Underline the second of these two sentences, and eliminate answers that do not match the prediction.

Choice (A) is a Mostly Right, Slightly Wrong trap answer. The text does indicate that we are affected by people we meet, but it does not say that we are *only* affected by people we meet *in person*. Eliminate (A).

Choice (B) says that *most nonhuman animals are not evolutionarily successful.* The text says that humans can work together *more so than most other beings*, and that the ability to work together is part of *how we've become such a successful species.* However, it does not indicate that most animals other than humans *are not evolutionarily successful.* Eliminate (B).

Choice (C) says that *the people we regularly interact with influence our behavior.* This matches the prediction that the people who *surround us on a daily basis* shape the way we *act in the world.* Keep (C).

Choice (D) says that *we are most effective when we share our working space with others.* Although the passage suggests that the ability to work together is part of *how we've become such a successful species*, it does not state that sharing *working space* makes us *most effective.* Choice (D) is a Right Words, Wrong Meaning trap answer. Eliminate (D).

Remember: don't create your own interpretation just because a question uses the word *suggests.* Instead, read and underline a prediction from the passage, and eliminate answers that don't match the prediction.

VOCABULARY-IN-CONTEXT (*WHAT?*)

Another way that the College Board will test your reading comprehension is with Vocabulary-in-Context (VIC) questions. The most important thing to remember is that these are IN CONTEXT! Gone are the days of "SAT Vocabulary" when you had to memorize lists of obscure words like impecunious and perspicacious. Now the test-writers want to see that you can understand what a word means based on context. You'll see words that look familiar but may be used in ways that are a little less familiar. Do not try to answer these questions simply by defining the word in your head and looking for that definition. You have to go back to the text and look at the context for the word.

13

As used in line 44, "absorbed" most nearly means

A) shared.

B) soaked.

C) tolerated.

D) learned.

Here's How to Crack It

The question asks, "What does the word *absorbed* mean as it is used in line 44?" With Vocabulary-in-Context questions, you don't need to read a full 10–12 lines. Typically, a few lines before and a few lines after will give you what you need. Go to line 44 and find the word *absorbed*. Cross it out. When you read a bit before and after the word, say lines 41–48, the text says, *Today the who can include more virtual, social media friends than physical ones; more information ~~absorbed~~ via Twitter, Facebook, and Instagram than in physical social experiences; and more pronouncements from ad-sponsored 24-hour news outlets than from conversations with other human beings.* Now read the sentence and put in a different word or phrase that means the same thing as *absorbed*. Did you use a word like "gained"? Compare your prediction to the answer choices, and you can quickly eliminate (A), (B), and (C).

Do not give into the temptation to simply answer the question without looking at the text. Did you notice that at least two of the wrong answer choices do legitimately mean *absorbed*? If you don't go back to the text, you can easily fall for such a wrong answer. But if you make a prediction based on what the text actually says, you will avoid these tricky answers.

BEST EVIDENCE QUESTIONS (*WHAT?*)

Remember the full name of the "verbal" score for the PSAT 8/9? It's the "Evidence-Based Reading and Writing" score. Throughout this chapter, you've been using evidence to answer all of these questions, so this question type won't come as a complete surprise. In fact, once you get comfortable with the best way to manage evidence questions, you'll be glad to see them. In some cases, you can do the work for one question and get points for two!

Best Evidence: Easy-to-Find Paired Questions

We discussed question 10 earlier. Here it is again:

10

The author indicates that the reason humans have been able to create inventions such as cars and rockets is that

The correct answer was (D): *our ability to collaborate grew as we evolved*. Recall that we based this answer on the part of the text that said that as humans evolved, *our capacities for cooperation exploded*.

Take a look at the question that follows:

11

Which choice provides the best evidence for the answer to the previous question?

A) Lines 7–8 ("But that's…nature")

B) Lines 15–16 ("Our brains…exploded")

C) Lines 19–24 ("I would…ourselves")

D) Lines 40–41 ("But the…changing")

Here's How to Crack It

What to do? Since the text you already used to answer question 10 (*our capacities for cooperation exploded*) was in lines 15–16, simply pick (B) and move on! Buy one, get one free.

We're not kidding: easy-to-find best evidence questions are like free points. Get them all!

Best Evidence: Harder-to-Find Paired Questions

Sometimes, though, the best evidence question follows a question that is harder to find in the passage. The first question may have no Line References or Lead Words, and the order of the questions might leave you with a long section of the passage to search. You might think that you have to answer the first question by reading a long section of the passage and then answer the evidence question based on that exhaustive research. But luckily, there's a time-saving and accuracy-improving alternative: a strategy that we call Parallel POE.

Using Parallel POE, you'll be able to work through both questions in a paired set at the same time! When you find yourself faced with a set of paired questions, you can start with the second question (the "best evidence" question) if (1) you aren't sure where to look for the answer to the first question, or (2) the first question is a general question that asks about the passage as a whole. Because the second question in the pair asks which lines provide the best evidence for the previous question, the correct answer to the first question has to be in one of the four sets of lines given in the second question. You can use those lines to help you work through the answers for the previous question. Let's take a look.

Best Evidence
Not sure where to find the answer? Let the "best evidence" lines help!

15

Based on information in the passage, it can reasonably be inferred that aggression

A) is reduced more effectively by a community response than by a response from one person.

B) increases when a culture begins to place less value on good manners.

C) has been a fundamental part of human nature throughout our evolution.

D) is more harmful to human society than is any other problem that we face today.

16

Which choice provides the best evidence for the answer to the previous question?

A) Lines 58–61 ("If there…platforms")

B) Lines 65–68 ("That is…aggression")

C) Lines 69–72 ("Humans are…animal")

D) Lines 85–88 ("But confronting…aggression")

Here's How to Crack It

Aggression is discussed throughout the whole passage, and question 13 asked about line 44. Half of the passage comes after line 44. So, even after using Lead Words and the order of the questions to narrow down the search, you're left with a long section of the passage. What to do? Here's where Parallel POE comes in. Notice that question 16 gives you the only possible lines for your evidence. Choice (16A) references lines 58–61, (16B) references lines 65–68, (16C) references lines 69–72, and (16D) references lines 85–88. So what would you rather do: read the entire second half of the passage hoping you might find an answer somewhere or read these tiny chunks one at a time to see if they answer the question? We hope you answered, "tiny chunks!"

Think again about how paired questions operate. The correct answer to the first question must be supported by an answer to the best evidence question, and the correct answer to the best evidence question must support an answer to the first question. In other words, if there is a best evidence answer that doesn't support an answer to the first question, it is wrong. Period. Like-wise, if there is an answer to the first question that isn't supported by a best evidence answer, it too is wrong. Period.

Let's use this to our advantage! Start making connections between the two answer sets. If a best evidence answer supports a first question answer, physically draw a line connecting them. Any best evidence answer that isn't connected to an answer in the first question can be eliminated. Likewise, any best evidence answer that doesn't address the first question can be eliminated.

Let's take a look at how this first Parallel POE pass would look. (The paired questions have been arranged in two columns for your convenience. This does not represent what you will see on the official test.)

15. Based on information in the passage, it can reasonably be inferred that aggression	16. Which choice provides the best evidence for the previous question?
A) is reduced more effectively by a community response than by a response from one person.	A) Lines 58–61 ("If there…platforms")
B) increases when a culture begins to place less value on good manners.	B) Lines 65–68 ("That is…aggression")
C) has been a fundamental part of human nature throughout our evolution.	C) Lines 69–72 ("Humans are…animal")
D) is more harmful to human society than any other problem that we face today.	D) Lines 85–88 ("But confronting… aggression")

Question 15 asks what can be inferred about *aggression*. Start with the line references in the answers for question 16.

The lines in (16A) say, *If there are no repercussions for it, that encourages the growth of aggression, incivility, and just plain meanness on social media platforms.* Does this evidence support any of the answers for question 15? Choice (15B) looks possible, so draw a line physically connecting (16A) with (15B).

The lines in (16B) say, *That is, how do we modify the whom by which our brains and bodies are being molded—and thereby reduce the aggression?* Does this evidence support any of the answers for question 15? Nope. So eliminate (16B) and move on.

The lines in (16C) say, *Humans are evolutionarily successful because our big brains have allowed us to bond together and cooperate in more complex and diverse manners than any other animal.* These lines do not provide an answer to question 15 because they are not about *aggression*. Therefore, they cannot provide the best evidence to answer question 15, so eliminate (16C).

The lines in (16D) say, *But confronting the bully with a group action—a reasoned, communal response rather than a knee-jerk, solo gesture—can be more effective at shutting down aggression.* Does this evidence support any of the answers for question 15? Yes. It supports (15A), so draw a line physically connecting (16D) with (15A).

Look at your progress so far: (15C) and (15D) have no support from question 16, so go ahead and eliminate (15C) and (15D). No matter how good they may sound, they CANNOT be right if there is no evidence supporting them from the best evidence question.

Your work should look something like this at this point:

15. Based on information in the passage, it can reasonably be inferred that aggression	16. Which choice provides the best evidence for the previous question?
A) is reduced more effectively by a community response than by a response from one person.	A) Lines 58–61 ("If there…platforms")
B) increases when a culture begins to place less value on good manners.	B) Lines 65–68 ("That is…aggression")
C) has been a fundamental part of human nature throughout our evolution.	C) Lines 69–72 ("Humans are…animal")
D) is more harmful to human society than any other problem that we face today.	D) Lines 85–88 ("But confronting… aggression")

Now you're down to a very nice 50/50 split. Go back to the question. Of the two pairs, which one best answers the question and matches the text of the passage? At this point, you may need to read a wider window around the remaining line references in question 16 and do some translating of the text to make sure you understand each answer. The window around the lines in (16A) says, *Anonymity and the lack of face-to-face interaction on social media platforms…opens the door to more frequent, and severe, displays of aggression. Being an antagonizer, especially to those you don't have to confront face-to-face, is easier now than it's ever been. If there are no repercussions for it, that encourages the growth of aggression, incivility, and just plain meanness on social media platforms.* In other words, the text indicates that the lack of face-to-face interaction and the lack of repercussions (consequences) for antagonizers (bullies) causes an increase in aggression. The text does not mention a *culture* placing *less value on good manners*, so these lines do not fully support (15B). Eliminate (16A) and (15B). Choose the remaining answers, (15A) and (16D), and get two points.

Parallel POE

Since you can't draw a full table on the actual exam, try making notations as shown in question 15; that is, create a column to the left of the best evidence answer choices listing out the choices to the previous question.

There is a list of common question wording in the Chapter Summary on page 142. Use this list as you practice to help you identify the question types.

On the actual test, it would be too complicated for you to draw a full table like the one above, but all you need to do is create a column to the left of the best evidence answer choices for the answers to the previous question. Basically, it should look something like this:

Q15   16

Which choice provides the best evidence for the previous question?

A   A) Lines 58–61 ("If there…platforms")

B   B) Lines 65–68 ("That is…aggression")

C   C) Lines 69–72 ("Humans are…animal")

D   D) Lines 85–88 ("But confronting…aggression")

Best Evidence: Single Questions

You will also see some Best Evidence questions that are not paired with another question. When you see a single Best Evidence question, look at the lines given in each answer choice, and eliminate answers that don't provide evidence for the claim in the question. You will see an example of a single Best Evidence question in the next section.

Sample Passage and Questions

Here is another example of a Reading Passage and questions. We will use this passage to let you independently practice the Basic Approach on the WHAT questions you already know how to do (Detail, Infer, Vocabulary-in-Context, Best Evidence) and to model for you how to manage the WHY and HOW questions, as well as the Charts and Graphs questions and General questions.

Questions 35-42 are based on the following passage and supplementary material.

This passage is adapted from Virginia Hughes, "Why Does Music Feel So Good?" ©2013 by *National Geographic*.

Music moves people of all cultures, in a way that doesn't seem to happen with other animals. Nobody really understands why listening to
Line music can trigger such profoundly rewarding
5 experiences. Valorie Salimpoor and other neuroscientists are trying to figure it out with the help of brain scanners.

In today's issue of *Science*, Salimpoor's group reports that when you listen to a song for the first
10 time, the strength of certain neural connections can predict how much you like the music, and that these preferences are guided by what you've heard and enjoyed in the past.

A few years ago, Salimpoor and neuroscientist
15 Robert Zatorre performed another type of brain scanning experiment in which participants listened to music that gave them goosebumps or chills. The researchers then injected them with a radioactive tracer that binds to the receptors
20 of dopamine, a chemical that's involved in motivation and reward. With this technique, called positron emission tomography or PET, the researchers showed that 15 minutes after participants listened to their favorite song, their
25 brains flooded with dopamine.

The dopamine system is old, evolutionarily speaking, and is active in many animals during sex and eating. "But animals don't get intense pleasures to music," Salimpoor says. "So we knew
30 there had to be a lot more to it."

In the new experiment, the researchers used functional magnetic resonance imaging (fMRI) to track real-time brain activity as participants listened to the first 30 seconds of 60 unfamiliar
35 songs. To quantify how much they liked the music, participants were given the chance to buy the full version of each song using a computer program resembling iTunes. The program was set up like an auction, so participants would choose how

40 much they were willing to spend on the song, with bids ranging from $0 to $2.

Salimpoor began by giving 126 volunteers comprehensive surveys about their musical preferences. "We asked them to list all of the
45 music they listen to, everything they like, everything they've ever bought," Salimpoor says. She ultimately scanned 19 volunteers who had indicated similar preferences.

To create the list of unfamiliar songs,
50 Salimpoor first looked at songs and artists that showed up on many of the volunteers' surveys. She plugged those choices into musical recommendation programs, such as Pandora and iTunes, to find similar but less well-known
55 selections. She also asked people who worked at local music stores what new songs they'd recommend in those genres.

The brain scans highlighted the nucleus accumbens, often referred to as the brain's
60 'pleasure center', a deep region of the brain that connects to dopamine neurons. It turns out that connections between the nucleus accumbens and several other brain areas could predict how much a participant was willing to spend on a given song.

65 So why is it that one person might spend $2 on a song while another pans it? Salimpoor says it all depends on past musical experiences. "Depending on what styles you're used to — Eastern, Western, jazz, heavy metal, pop — all of these
70 have very different rules they follow, and they're all implicitly recorded in your brain," she says. "Whether you realize it or not, every time you're listening to music, you're constantly activating these templates that you have."

75 Using those musical memory templates, the nucleus accumbens then acts as a prediction machine, she says. It predicts the reward that you'll feel from a given piece of music based on similar types of music you've heard before. If you
80 like it better than predicted, it registers as intense pleasure. If you feel worse than predicted, you feel bored or disappointed.

Music, Salimpoor says, is an intellectual reward. "It's really an exercise for your whole brain."

Brain Activity Changes Corresponding to Bid Value (Nucleus Accumbens)

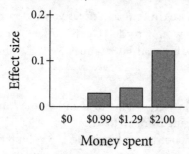

34

Which choice best describes the overall structure of the passage?

A) The author presents an effect of music, discusses literature written about the effect, and explains how the effect can be reproduced.

B) The author presents an outdated belief, summarizes an experiment that seemed to support the belief, and describes a new experiment that contradicts the belief.

C) The author presents a question, discusses a study related to the question, and describes findings that may help researchers develop an answer to the question.

D) The author presents a common musical experience, examines the experience in different cultures, and explains why many people have similar experiences.

35

As used in line 1, "moves" most nearly means

A) carries.

B) persuades.

C) transports.

D) affects.

36

The passage most strongly suggests that research has not yet determined

A) the best application for positron emission tomography.

B) the effects of previous experience on musical preference.

C) which brain regions are associated with feelings of boredom.

D) why music is capable of creating a sense of pleasure.

37

Which choice provides the best evidence for the answer to the previous question?

A) Lines 3–5 ("Nobody really…experiences")

B) Lines 12–13 ("these preferences…past")

C) Lines 21–25 ("With this…dopamine")

D) Lines 79–82 ("If you…disappointed")

38

In the context of the passage, what is the main purpose of the sentence in lines 28-30?

A) To explain the role of dopamine in the evolution of animal behavior

B) To suggest the reason that Salimpoor's team conducted the study described in the next paragraph

C) To point out the shortcomings of Salimpoor's early research into brain chemistry

D) To predict the outcome of future studies about brain activity and music

39

Based on the passage, which additional information, if true, would challenge the conclusions Salimpoor drew from the study that was set up like an auction?

A) People's decisions about how much they are willing to spend on a song are primarily based on their beliefs about their friends' preferences rather than on their own enjoyment of the music.

B) Some people who work at national chain music stores are just as knowledgeable about music as people who work at local music stores are.

C) People experience increased activity in the nucleus accumbens when viewing paintings that they describe as beautiful.

D) Dopamine may not flood a person's brain until several minutes after the person experiences something pleasant.

40

According to the passage, Salimpoor visited local music stores after collecting surveys of volunteers' music preferences in order to

A) seek information about what causes people to prefer certain musical genres.

B) compare the music available online with music available in stores.

C) select songs that the study participants had not heard previously.

D) determine which songs the staff had recommended to the study participants.

41

Which choice best supports the idea that human responses to music can be tracked by measuring specific types of brain activity?

A) Lines 61–64 ("It turns…song")

B) Lines 65–67 ("So why…experiences")

C) Lines 67–71 ("Depending…says")

D) Lines 72–74 ("Whether you…have")

42

According to the figure, which of the following correctly describes the effect size for songs on which $1.29 was spent?

A) 0

B) Greater than 0 but less than 0.1

C) Greater than 0.1 but less than 0.2

D) Greater than 0.2

Do you recognize the formats of questions 35, 36, 37, 40 and 41? Q35 is a Vocabulary-in-Context question, Q36 is an Infer question, Q40 is a Detail question, and Q37 and Q41 are Best Evidence questions (Q37 is paired with Q36, and Q41 is a single Best Evidence question). Try answering these on your own, using the strategies we've been discussing. Answers can be found in Part IV.

That leaves us with a few other mysterious question types. In the following pages, we will demystify them for you.

PURPOSE QUESTIONS (*WHY?*)

Take a look at question 38, and think about how it's different from the WHAT questions we've been talking about.

38

In the context of the passage, what is the main purpose of the sentence in lines 28–30?

Notice that it's not asking you WHAT the sentence says. It is asking about the sentence's *purpose*. The *purpose* for something is the reason it is there. How would you talk about that? You would explain WHY it is there, right? Yes! So when you see questions with phrases like "what is the purpose" or "in order to," just translate them into questions starting with WHY.

Question 38 is really asking WHY the author included the sentence in lines 28–30. Doesn't that feel easier to deal with than the way it was originally worded? We think so too.

Think for a moment about how authors make and support their points: they give details or examples to help convey a certain theme or to provide evidence for a claim. When the College Board asks why the author includes certain words, sentences, or paragraphs, you have to look for the larger idea the author is supporting with a particular detail. You won't have to guess the author's purpose—there will be evidence in the passage of the point the author is making. You do need to read a window around the line reference in order to identify the author's point. In other words, the Basic Approach for a WHY question is similar to the approach for a WHAT question, but the prediction will be based on how the detail in the question relates to the surrounding text.

To work question 38, begin by carefully reading a window around the line reference. Lines 21–25 describe the results of an experiment: *15 minutes after participants listened to their favorite song, their brains flooded with dopamine.* The sentence that question 38 asks about is a quote by Salimpoor about the experiment's results. She says, *"But animals don't get intense pleasures to music...So we knew there had to be a lot more to it."* The next paragraph describes a *new experiment* that Salimpoor and her team conducted to learn more about the *brain activity* that occurs when people listen to music.

Remember, the question asks *WHY* the author includes the information in lines 28–30. In lines 28–30, Salimpoor indicates that the researchers knew there was more to learn, and the next paragraph describes a new experiment they conducted. Therefore, the purpose of the sentence in lines 28–30 is to suggest what prompted Salimpoor and her team to conduct the new experiment. Let's compare that prediction with the answer choices.

A) To explain the role of dopamine in the evolution of animal behavior

B) To suggest the reason that Salimpoor's team conducted the study described in the next paragraph

C) To point out the shortcomings of Salimpoor's early research into brain chemistry

D) To predict the outcome of future studies about brain activity and music

This sentence does not *explain the role of dopamine in the evolution of animal behavior*, so eliminate (A).

The author's intention is not to *point out the shortcomings of Salimpoor's early research*—nothing in the surrounding text suggests that the author is critical of Salimpoor. Eliminate (C).

The sentence does not *predict the outcome of future studies*, so eliminate (D).

Choice (B) is consistent with the prediction, and it's the correct answer. But do the words in the answer sound much like what you read in the passage? Not really—the answer choice doesn't include the words *animals*, *brain activity*, or *music*. On certain WHY and HOW questions, instead of naming the actual people or topics from the passage, the College Board uses general language to make it tougher to pick out the correct answer. (They would probably describe the plot of a movie like this: "A character was introduced, a problem arose, possible solutions were explored and rejected, and a resolution emerged from an unexpected alliance with a former antagonist.") Don't dismiss these answers because they don't contain words that remind you of the passage. Instead, if you see "a theory," ask yourself: was a theory discussed? If you see "a disagreement," try to identify whether there was such a disagreement in the text. Try to match the general words from the answer choices back to the specific words in the text.

STRUCTURE AND ARGUMENT QUESTIONS (*HOW?*)

Take a look at question 39, and think about how it's different from the WHAT and WHY questions we've talked about.

39

Based on the passage, which additional information, if true, would challenge the conclusions Salimpoor drew from the study that was set up like an auction?

Notice that this question is not asking you WHAT the author is saying, nor is it asking you WHY the author says certain things. It's asking you HOW you could weaken the researcher's conclusions.

Begin by finding the window so that you can Read What You Need from the passage. Use lead words and the order of the questions to find the window. Question 38 asked about lines 28–30, so begin with those lines and scan for the lead words *set up like an auction*.

The paragraph describes a study in which participants listened to *unfamiliar songs*. *To quantify how much they liked the music, participants were given the chance to buy the full version of each song using a computer program resembling iTunes. The program was set up like an auction, so participants would choose how much they were willing to spend on the song, with bids ranging from $0 to $2.*

Notice that the question asks for *additional information*. The answers for some HOW questions may not come directly from the text, so you may not be able to predict exactly what the correct answer will *say*. However, the answers will still be supported by the text, and you can predict what the correct answer needs to *do*. The answer for question 39 needs to cast doubt on something that was important to Salimpoor's study. Use Process of Elimination to eliminate answers that don't relate to the study described in this paragraph, as well as answers that do not weaken the study.

A) People's decisions about how much they are willing to spend on a song are primarily based on their beliefs about their friends' preferences rather than on their own enjoyment of the music.

B) Some people who work at national chain music stores are just as knowledgeable about music as people who work at local music stores are.

C) People experience increased activity in the nucleus accumbens when viewing paintings that they describe as beautiful.

D) Dopamine may not flood a person's brain until several minutes after the person experiences something pleasant.

Choice (A) says that people don't decide how much money to spend on a song based on their own enjoyment of the music. The passage says that the study was set up like an auction to *quantify* (measure) how much the participants *liked the music*. If it's true that people do not decide how much money to spend on a song based on their own enjoyment of the music, then the experiment would not have shown what the researchers thought it showed. That would weaken the conclusions that they drew from the study, so keep (A).

Choice (B) says that some employees of *national chain music stores are just as knowledgeable about music as* employees of *local music stores are*. The researchers found some of the music used in the study by talking to people who worked in local music stores. But the fact that people at other stores are also knowledgeable about music would not mean that local music store employees were not knowledgeable, so this information does not weaken the conclusions of the study. Eliminate (B).

Choice (C) says that people *experience increased activity in the nucleus accumbens* when they look at beautiful paintings. The study showed that people experience increased activity in the nucleus accumbens when they listen to music they enjoy. Since looking at beautiful paintings is also probably enjoyable, this information might actually support the study's conclusions, and the question asks for something that weakens them. Eliminate (C).

Choice (D) says that dopamine *may not flood a person's brain until several minutes after* a pleasant experience. The earlier study that Salimpoor did found that *dopamine* flooded the brain 15 minutes after the person listened to a song that gave them goosebumps or chills. However, the study that this question asks about wasn't about the amount of time it takes dopamine to flood the brain, so this information doesn't affect the study's conclusions. Eliminate (D).

The correct answer is (A).

CHARTS AND GRAPHS

Charts, graphs, and diagrams are not limited to the Math Test! You will see a variety of graphics in the Reading Test and even in the Writing and Language Test. (More on the Writing and Language Test later.) The good news is that the graphics you'll be dealing with in the Reading Test are very straightforward and do not require any computations. All you need to do is make sure you can put your pencil on the place in the graphic that supports the answer. Let's take a look at an example.

Step 1: Read the Graphic

Carefully look at the title, labels, and units. In this figure, we have a bar graph showing the size of the participants' brain activity changes (in the brain region called the nucleus accumbens) corresponding to the amount of money they were willing to spend on particular songs.

Step 2: Read the Question

> 42
>
> According to the figure, which of the following correctly describes the effect size for songs on which $1.29 was spent?

Since the question asks for a description based on the figure, your job will be to carefully look up the correct information in the graph and eliminate answers that are not consistent with that information. Make sure you can put your pencil on the data you're using to keep or eliminate certain answers.

The horizontal axis shows "Money spent," and the third bar is for the bid value of $1.29. The vertical axis shows "Effect size," and the bar for $1.29 comes a little less than halfway to the mark for an effect size of 0.1.

Step 3: Read the Answers

A) 0

B) Greater than 0 but less than 0.1

C) Greater than 0.1 but less than 0.2

D) Greater than 0.2

Choice (B) is consistent with the graph, since the effect size for the $1.29 bar is greater than 0 but less than 0.1. Keep (B). Eliminate (A), (C), and (D) because they are not consistent with the information in the graph. Notice that (A) and (C) are Right Answer, Wrong Question trap answers: (A) describes the effect size for bids of $0, and (C) describes the effect size for bids of $2. The correct answer is (B).

GENERAL QUESTIONS

For many of the Reading passages, the very first question will ask a question about the passage as a whole. It might ask about the main idea or primary purpose, the narrative point of view, or the structure of the passage. In other words, General questions can be what, why, or how questions.

Remember the Select a Question step? General questions are not good to do first because you haven't read the passage yet, but once you've answered the other questions, you'll have a good idea of the general themes of the text. So, it's best to do General questions last.

Let's take a look at question 34.

34

Which choice best describes the overall structure of the passage?

Because this question asks about the *overall structure of the passage*, there's no one place you can look for the answer. General questions don't have specific windows in the passage to read. It's okay, though: after answering all of the specific questions, you're quite familiar with the passage. Not only that, but you also have a good sense of what the test-writers found most interesting about the passage. If there are answer choices that have nothing to do with either the questions or the answers you've seen repeatedly, eliminate them and instead choose the one that is consistent with those questions and answers. For question 34, consider what the passage begins with (neuroscientists are trying to figure out why music creates such rewarding experiences for people), what is described in the middle of the passage (a study done by the neuroscientists to help them figure it out), and how the passage ends (an explanation for what the neuroscientists found during their study). Eliminate any answer that is inconsistent with those major pieces of the structure.

Let's take a look at the answer choices:

A) The author presents an effect of music, discusses literature written about the effect, and explains how the effect can be reproduced.

B) The author presents an outdated belief, summarizes an experiment that seemed to support the belief, and describes a new experiment that contradicts the belief.

C) The author presents a question, discusses a study related to the question, and describes findings that may help researchers develop an answer to the question.

D) The author presents a common musical experience, examines the experience in different cultures, and explains why many people have similar experiences.

Remember what we said earlier about answers that use general language. Try to match the general language in these answers back to the specifics discussed in the passage, and eliminate what does not match.

The first part of (A) is consistent with the idea that music creates a rewarding experience for people, but the middle part of (A) doesn't match the passage. The text describes a study, not *literature* written about the effect of music. The passage also doesn't explain how to *reproduce* the effect of music, so eliminate (A).

Choice (B) mentions an *outdated belief*. Can you find any evidence in the passage of a belief that has changed? No. Eliminate (B).

The first part of (C) is consistent with the idea that neuroscientists are trying to find out why music creates such rewarding experiences for people. The middle part of (C) is consistent with the study described in the passage, and the last part is consistent with the explanation for what the neuroscientists found during their study. Keep (C).

The first part of (D) is consistent with the idea that music *moves people of all cultures*. However, the passage does not examine a musical *experience in different cultures*, so eliminate (D).

The correct answer is (C).

DUAL PASSAGES

One of your Science or History/Social Studies passages will be a set of dual passages. There will be two shorter passages about one topic. Although the two passages will be about the same topic, there will also be differences that you'll need to pay attention to. Rather than attempting to read and understand both passages at the same time, just follow the Basic Approach and focus on one passage at a time.

The questions for Passage 1 will come before the questions for Passage 2. The questions about both passages will follow the questions for Passage 2.

Two-Passage Questions

For questions that ask you to compare or contrast both passages, it's helpful to consider one passage at a time rather than trying to juggle both passages at the same time. First, find the answer for the first passage (or the second passage if that one is easier) and use POE to narrow down the answer choices. Then find the answer in the other passage and use POE to arrive at the correct answer. This will save time and keep you from confusing the two passages when you're evaluating the answer choices. Always keep in mind that the same POE criteria apply, no matter how two-passage questions are presented.

- If a question is about what is supported by both passages, make sure that you find specific support in both passages, and be wary of all the usual trap answers.

- If a question is about an issue on which the authors of the two passages disagree or on how the passages relate to one another, make sure you find support in each passage for the author's particular opinion.

- If the question asks how one author would respond to the other passage, find out what was said in that other passage, and then find out exactly what the author you are asked about said on that exact topic.

The bottom line is that if you are organized and remember your basic reading comprehension strategy, you'll see that two-passage questions are no harder than single-passage questions! In the following drill, you'll have a chance to try a set of dual passages. Answers and explanations can be found in Part IV.

Dual Passage Drill

Answers and explanations can be found in Part IV.

Passage 1 is adapted from a speech delivered on April 23, 1971, by Mark O. Hatfield, "Democracy's Stake in Voluntary Armed Forces." Passage 2 is adapted from a speech delivered on June 4, 1971, by Lloyd M. Bentsen, "The Military Selective Service Act." Hatfield served as a United States senator from 1967 to 1997. Bentsen served as a United States senator from 1971 to 1993. These speeches were given as part of an ongoing debate in the Senate about whether to extend or end the military draft (a system of required, rather than voluntary, military service).

Passage 1

Mr. President, Senate action draws nearer on the question of military conscription and an all-volunteer armed force. I cannot stress too
Line strongly the profound weakening of our social
5 fiber, the undermining of the individual's faith in his Government and his hope for his future, the military draft inculcates.

Mr. Nixon's blue-ribbon Commission on an All-Volunteer Armed Force unanimously found
10 the concept of voluntary recruitment to be within practical reach. They declared such a method to be more acceptable and more consistent with historic American practice and tradition than the method of involuntary service to which we have become
15 habituated since World War II.

They estimated that a modest increase in pay for men in the lower ranks would sufficiently increase voluntary recruitment and reenlistments to supply manpower; and they argued that such salary scales
20 for servicemen are deserved and overdue, since today draftees and volunteers alike are paid salaries woefully below the level of compensation for civilian jobs which require comparable skills.

It is time to end the draft. National necessity
25 does not require conscription. Personal freedom demands that it be terminated.

It is time to stop sending to prison an increasing flow of our best young men, men deeply opposed to an unnecessary draft. Only a handful can
30 meet the rigorous definition of the conscientious objector, the objector to all war. But other men are entitled to have their principled objections and scruples respected, especially when the nation can so easily afford to raise its army by voluntary
35 means.

History has shown that Americans will freely sacrifice their lives when they are morally convinced that such a course is necessary and right. Now is the time to bring the American system into
40 line with our professed ideals of individual freedom and personal choice. We must end the draft now!

Passage 2

Mr. President, there has been debate in this body for some weeks now on the need for the military draft. There have been arguments
45 advanced that it should be terminated by the end of this month, that such a termination would end the war in Vietnam, that such a termination would reassert congressional authority over military policies and that such a termination would restore
50 confidence of the young in the Government.

There have been arguments advanced in favor of its extension. Basically, the argument is that without the draft, our commitments as a nation and as a world leader cannot be fulfilled. If I
55 believed for one moment that the military could meet their manpower needs fully solely through volunteer enlistments, I would be in the forefront leading the charge for a volunteer army. I favor a volunteer army. And we can have such a volunteer
60 military force.

Because I do believe the volunteer army is a goal we can reach, I believe that the termination of the draft on July 1, or within the next year, would be folly and do great damage to the ultimate adoption
65 of a sound volunteer army concept. Killing the draft would be disastrous to the planning by the Army which has as its goal the volunteer army. The military must have the time to test various ideas, to work toward the volunteer army.

70 The argument that an immediate cut-off of the authority to draft manpower for military purposes would force the immediate adoption of the volunteer Army has been rejected at every point of its consideration of this legislation. I hope—and I
75 predict—that it will be rejected again by the Senate today. We must not succumb to ends without means. Strip away all of the strong feelings, all of the emotion, and all of the motives, understandable and desirable as these may be, and the hard fact
80 remains: the military cannot, at the present time, without this legislation and without this draft meet its manpower needs solely through volunteer enlistments.

26

In Passage 1, the speaker most clearly implies that one reason that the military draft is harmful to American society is that it may

A) give citizens a false sense of hope.

B) reduce the public's trust in the government.

C) draw criticism from the nation's allies.

D) encourage men to find safety in other countries.

27

Which choice best describes the main shift in focus that occurs within lines 8-35 ("Mr. Nixon's...means") of Passage 1?

A) The passage provides an overview of careers in the military and then shifts to a discussion of the current use of the draft.

B) The passage describes equipment used by the United States during World War II and then shifts to a discussion of how that equipment could be used today.

C) The passage outlines all of the Senate's past actions related to volunteer armed forces and then shifts to a discussion of the Senate's actions on other legislation.

D) The passage praises the idea of a volunteer army and then shifts to a discussion of arguments against the military draft.

28

Based on Passage 1, raising wages for some members of the armed forces would result in which of the following?

A) It would satisfy the demands of draftees and inspire them to serve for longer.

B) It would frustrate military recruits by changing the primary motivation for military service.

C) It would leave civilians feeling underappreciated and prompt them to join the military.

D) It would encourage an adequate number of people to volunteer for the armed forces.

29

Which choice provides the best evidence for the answer to the previous question?

A) Lines 11–15 ("They declared...War II")

B) Lines 16–19 ("They estimated...manpower")

C) Lines 19–23 ("and they...skills")

D) Lines 39–41 ("Now is...now")

30

As used in line 30, "rigorous" most nearly means

A) strict.

B) harsh.

C) excessive.

D) unlikely.

31

As used in line 52, "extension" most nearly means

A) reaching.

B) addition.

C) being enlarged.

D) being continued.

32

Both speakers would most likely agree with which view of the military draft in the United States?

A) It gives the President too much power.

B) It is necessary for one more year.

C) It is not an ideal recruitment method.

D) It can replace a volunteer army.

33

Based on Passage 2, which point of view would the speaker most likely have of people who agree with Passage 1's central claim?

A) He would think that they are overestimating the amount of manpower a volunteer army could provide in the near future.

B) He would think that they are overly optimistic that the war in Vietnam will end within a year.

C) He would think that they are too focused on citizens' confidence in the government.

D) He would think that they are uninformed about the history of the military draft in the United States.

34

Which choice from Passage 2 provides the best evidence for the answer to the previous question?

A) Lines 44–50 ("There have…Government")

B) Lines 54–58 ("If I…army")

C) Lines 65–69 ("Killing the…army")

D) Lines 70–74 ("The argument…legislation")

Summary

- The Reading Test on the PSAT 8/9 makes up 50 percent of your Evidence-Based Reading and Writing score.

- Reading questions are not presented in order of difficulty, but the specific questions are written roughly in the order they appear in the passage.

- Use your POOD to pick up the points you can get, and don't forget LOTD on the rest!

- Reading is an open-book test! Use that to your advantage by focusing only on the text you need to get each point.

- Translate each question back into a what, why, or how question before you start reading your window. See the table below for a guide to translating the question types.

- Use Line References, Lead Words, and the natural order of the specific questions to help you find the answer in the passage. Always start reading a few lines above the Line Reference or the Lead Words and read until you have the answer.

- Use the text to predict the answer to the question before you look at the answer choices.

- Use POE to eliminate answers that don't match your prediction.

- If you have more than one answer left after you eliminate the ones that don't match your prediction, compare the remaining answers to see if any of them:

  - are mostly right but slightly wrong

  - could be true but are not supported by the text

  - have the right words but the wrong meaning

  - have the right answer to the wrong question

o   For Paired Sets, make sure you're following the right strategy.

- Easy-to-find Paired Questions simply require you to follow the Basic Approach, making sure you've underlined the evidence for your prediction in the text.

- Harder-to-find Paired Questions will be much more straightforward if you use Parallel POE to consider the "best evidence" in tandem with the previous question.

o   For Dual Passages, do questions about the first passage first, questions about the second passage second, and dual questions last. Remember that even with dual questions, you must find support in the passages.

o   Save Main Idea or General Questions until the end of the passage. POE will be much more efficient once you've completed all the other questions.

o   Don't get bogged down by hard or time-consuming questions! If you find yourself stuck or running short on time, use LOTD and move on!

Common Question Wording	
What Questions	according to the passage, based on the passage (Detail)
	the passage (or author) indicates (Detail)
	the passage (or author) implies/suggests (Infer/Imply/Suggest)
	it can reasonably be inferred (Infer/Imply/Suggest)
	the author would most likely agree (Infer/Imply/Suggest)
	the author's perspective, the author's point of view (Infer/Imply/Suggest)
	as used in line…most nearly means (Vocabulary-in-Context)
	provides the best evidence (Best Evidence)
	best supports (Best Evidence)
	the main idea, the main theme (General)
	summarizes (General)
Why Questions	the purpose
	in order to
	most likely to
	serves to
	the primary purpose (General)
How Questions	weaken
	strengthen
	structure of the passage (General)
	the main focus shifts (General)

Chapter 6
Introduction to the Writing and Language Strategy

CAN YOU REALLY TEST WRITING ON A MULTIPLE-CHOICE TEST?

We'd say no, but the PSAT 8/9 (and a heck of a lot of other tests) seems to think the answer is yes. To that end, the PSAT 8/9 is giving you 30 minutes to answer 40 multiple-choice questions that ask about a variety of grammatical and stylistic topics. If you like to read and/or write, this test may frustrate you a bit because it may seem to boil writing down to a couple of dull rules. But as you will see, we will use the next few chapters to suggest a method that keeps things simple for pro- and anti-grammarians alike.

It is worth noting that the Writing and Language section of the PSAT 8/9 is very similar to that of both the PSAT and the SAT. It is a little shorter, but it tests almost all of the same topics. All of the rules and strategies you learn in this section can also be used on those tests if and when you take them in the future.

WHERE DID ALL THE QUESTIONS GO?

One thing that can seem a little strange about the Writing and Language section of the PSAT is that many of the questions don't have, well, questions. Instead, many of the questions look something like this:

When you think of a queen, or any member of a royal family, you probably don't imagine floppy **1** ears a tail and fur.

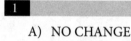

A) NO CHANGE
B) ears, a tail and,
C) ears, a tail, and
D) ears a tail, and

How are you supposed to pick an answer when there's no question?

Well, actually, what you'll find throughout this chapter and the next two is that the PSAT 8/9 gives you a *lot* of information in this list of answer choices. (The answer is (C), by the way, but stick with us for a second here.)

Look at these pairs, and you'll see just what we mean. As you read through these pairs of answer choices, think about what each question is probably testing.

1. A)   could of
   B)   could have

2. A)   tall, dark, and handsome
   B)   tall, dark and handsome

3. A)   let them in
   B)   let Sister Susie and Brother John in

4. A)   We arrived in Paris on a Sunday. Then we took the train to Nantes. Then we took the train to Bordeaux.
   B)   We arrived in Paris on a Sunday. Then we took the train to Bordeaux. Then we took the train to Nantes.

If you were able to see the differences in these answer choices, you're already more than halfway there. Now, notice how the differences in these answers can reveal the question that is lurking in the heart of each list of answer choices.

1. The difference between the word "of" and "have" means that this question is asking *Is the correct form "could of" or "could have"?*
2. The difference between having a comma after the word "dark" and not having one there means that this question is asking *How many commas does this sentence need, and where do they belong?*
3. The difference between "them" and "Sister Susie and Brother John" means that this question is asking *Is "them" adequately specific, or do you need to refer to people by name?*
4. The difference in the order of these sentences asks *What order should the sentences be in?*

Therefore, what we have noticed in these pairs of answer choices is something that may seem fairly simple but which is essential to success on the PSAT 8/9.

THE ANSWER CHOICES ASK THE QUESTIONS

At some point, you've almost certainly had to do the English-class exercise called "peer editing." In this exercise, you are tasked with "editing" the work of one of your fellow students. But this can be really tough, because what exactly does it mean to "edit" an entire essay or paper when you aren't given any directions? It's *especially* tough when you start getting into the subtleties between whether things are wrong or whether they could merely be improved.

Look, for example, at these two sentences:

> *It was a beautiful day outside birds were singing cheerful songs.*

> *It was a beautiful day outside; birds were singing cheerful songs.*

You'd have to pick the second one in this case because the first has a grammatical error: it's a run-on sentence. Or for the non-grammarians out there, you have to break that thing up.

Now, look at these next two sentences:

> *The weather was just right, so I decided to play soccer.*

> *Just right was how I would describe the weather, so a decision of soccer-playing was made by me.*

In this case, the first sentence is obviously better than the second, but the second technically doesn't have any grammatical errors in it. The first may be *better,* but the second isn't exactly *wrong.*

What made each of these pairs of sentences relatively easy to deal with, though, was the fact that you could compare the sentences to one another. In doing so, you noted the differences between those sentences, and so you picked the *better* answer accordingly.

Let's see how this looks in a real PSAT 8/9 situation.

Stormie's loyal subjects, the other dogs at the dog park, **2** starting to recognize her natural leadership abilities.

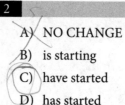

2
A) NO CHANGE
B) is starting
C) have started
D) has started

Here's How to Crack It

First, look at what's changing in the answer choices. The verb is underlined, and the answer choices have different verb forms. The question, then, seems to be asking, *Which verb makes the sentence complete and correct?*

Choice (A) makes the sentence incomplete, so it can be eliminated. Choices (B) and (D) are the wrong number: the subject of the sentence is *subjects*, which is plural, so the verb also needs to be plural. Both *is* and *has* are singular, so (B) and (D) can be eliminated. Only (C) produces a complete sentence and contains a verb that agrees with the subject of the sentence.

Notice how the entire process started with asking *What's changing in the answer choices?* With that question, we figured out what was being tested, and we used POE to do the rest.

When other dogs approach, Stormie's instinctive judgment, which categorizes each dog as friend or foe, tells **3** those how to respond.

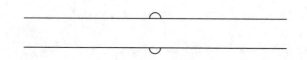

3
A) NO CHANGE
B) one
C) them
D) her

Here's How to Crack It

As always, start with what's changing in the answer choices. It looks like the change is among the words *those, one, them,* and *her,* which are all pronouns. As such, this question seems to be asking, *What is the appropriate pronoun to use in this context?*

Start by determining what the pronoun refers back to. A pronoun should clearly refer to a noun. The subject of the sentence is *Stormie's instinctive judgment.* Your judgment tells you what to do, so Stormie's judgment tells "her" how to respond. Eliminate (A), (B), and (C). Only (D) provides a pronoun that works in the context of this sentence.

LEARN FROM THE ANSWER CHOICES

Sometimes, a sentence on the Writing and Language section may sound perfectly fine to you, but it actually has an error. That's because the way we speak is often very different from the way we write. The PSAT 8/9 is more concerned on this test with how we write and with the stricter set of rules that go along with writing.

As such, not only can the answer choices tell us what a particular question is testing, they can also reveal mistakes that we might not have otherwise seen (in the original sentence) or heard (in our heads).

Let's see another.

At home, Stormie perches regally atop a pile of pillows and crosses her **4** two pause, surveying the living room that is her domain.

4
A) NO CHANGE
B) two paws,
C) to pause,
D) to paws,

Here's How to Crack It

First, as always, check what's changing in the answer choices. In this case, that step is especially important because you can't really hear the error. People often misuse words like *to* and *paws* in writing because these words sound similar to *two* and *pause*, respectively, but each spelling has its own meaning. The fact that similar-sounding words are not the same, that they *change*, tells us precisely what to pay attention to when we use POE.

Start the Process of Elimination. *Paws* refer to animal feet, and *pause* refers to a short break. A dog can cross its *paws*, but it can't cross "a short break," so eliminate (A) and (C). Next, consider the difference between (B) and (D). *Two* is a number, whereas *to* is a directional word (e.g., we went *to* the park). In this case, there are two *paws*, so eliminate (D). The correct answer is (B).

Notice, though, that looking at the answer choices revealed the problem that you might not have otherwise been able to see or hear. Then, POE got you the rest of the way.

ALL OF THE QUESTIONS CAN'T BE WRONG ALL OF THE TIME

Now that our strategy is basically set, let's look at one more tough one.

─────────────○─────────────

As the dog queen, she **5** collects a tax on all cheese and peanut butter consumed in the house.

5

A) NO CHANGE
B) assembles
C) profits
D) organizes

Here's How to Crack It

First, as always, check what's changing in the answer choices. Even if the original sentence sounds fine, it's important to check the answers in order to identify any possible errors that weren't obvious. In this case, the vocabulary is changing. Read the sentence and determine what meaning would best fit in the underlined portion. The part after the underlined portion is *a tax*, and the subject is *she*. The underlined portion should mean something like "takes." *Collects* matches with "takes," so keep (A). *Assembles* means "puts together," which doesn't match with "takes" in this context, so eliminate (B). *Profits* means "makes money from," which doesn't match with "takes," so eliminate (C). *Organizes* means "puts together," which doesn't match with "takes," and it also wouldn't be correct to suggest that a dog could *organize* something, so eliminate (D). The correct answer is (A).

Remember, NO CHANGE is right sometimes! However, do not automatically pick NO CHANGE simply because the sentence sounds fine. You may find that in some cases the correct answer does not "sound right." Alternatively, a wrong answer could "sound fine." Learn the rules in the following chapters, and use those rules along with Process of Elimination to maximize your correct answers.

─────────────○─────────────

HOW TO ACE THE WRITING AND LANGUAGE SECTION: A STRATEGY

- Check what's changing in the answer choices.
- Figure out what the question is testing and let the differences reveal potential errors.
- Use Process of Elimination.
- If you haven't eliminated three answers, pick the shortest one that is most consistent with the rest of the sentence.

In the next few chapters, we'll get into some of the more technical issues in Writing and Language, but we'll be using this strategy throughout. Try the drill on the next page to get some of the basics down.

Writing and Language Drill 1

The purpose of this drill is to get a basic idea of what each question is testing from only the answer choices. Check your answers in Part IV.

1

A) NO CHANGE
B) singers' preferred songwriters
C) singer's preferred songwriter's
D) singers' preferred songwriters'

What's changing in the answer choices?

apostrophe position

What is this question testing?

grammer skills

2

A) NO CHANGE
B) had
C) has
D) has had

What's changing in the answer choices?

What is this question testing?

3

A) NO CHANGE
B) Even though
C) If
D) Since

What's changing in the answer choices?

What is this question testing?

4

A) NO CHANGE
B) seem attractive for their
C) seems attractive for its
D) seems attractive for their

What's changing in the answer choices?

possessive

What is this question testing?

5

A) NO CHANGE
B) smooth, as in completely lumpless.
C) smooth, like talking not a single lump.
D) smooth.

What's changing in the answer choices?

What is this question testing?

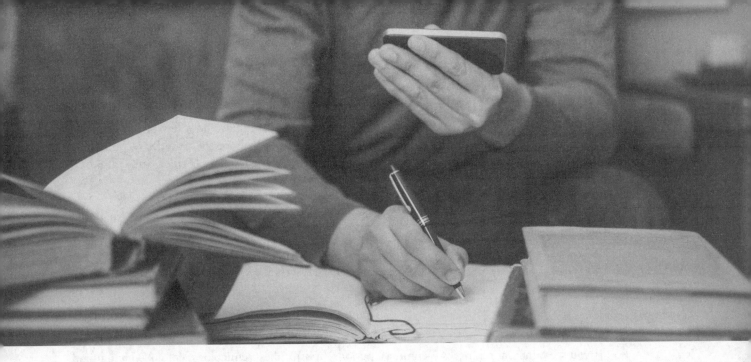

Chapter 7
Punctuation

WHAT, ARE, COMMAS, FOR, ANYWAY?

The writers of the PSAT 8/9 want you to know how to use commas and a few other types of weird punctuation as well. In this chapter, we're going to talk about the varieties of punctuation that the PSAT wants you to know how to use. Learn these few simple rules, and you'll be all set on the punctuation questions.

First and foremost, remember how you can spot a question that's asking about punctuation. Start by asking,

> What's changing in the answer choices?

If you see punctuation marks—commas, periods, apostrophes, semicolons, colons—changing, then the question is testing punctuation. Then, as you work the problem, make sure to ask the big question:

> Does this punctuation need to be here?

The particular punctuation mark you are using—no matter what it is—must have a specific role within the sentence. You wouldn't use a question mark without a question, would you? Nope! Well, all punctuation works that way, and in what follows, we'll give you some basic instances in which you would use some type of punctuation. Otherwise, let the words do their thing unobstructed!

COMPLETE AND INCOMPLETE IDEAS

In order to decide what type of punctuation is needed to connect ideas in a sentence, you must be able to identify whether the ideas being connected are complete or incomplete. A complete idea can stand on its own. It might be its own sentence, or it might be part of a longer sentence, but it's allowed to be by itself. Here are some examples.

> *The view is beautiful.*
> *Look at that sunset!*
> *How high is the summit?*
> *I gazed at the majestic mountains before me.*

As you can see, commands and questions can be complete ideas. However, they are rarely tested on the PSAT 8/9. Most complete ideas on the PSAT 8/9 will be statements. In general, a complete idea must have a subject and a verb. Sometimes it needs more than that. Consider the following idea:

> *The tour guide told us we will need*

This idea has a subject (*tour guide*) and a verb (*told*), but it's missing the rest of the idea—what *we will need*. Therefore, this idea is incomplete. An incomplete idea could also be missing the subject, verb, or both, as in the examples below, all of which are incomplete ideas.

> *Bought hiking boots*
>
> *To get to the top of the mountain*
>
> *The people in our group*

In addition, some transition words and conjunctions can make an idea incomplete even when it has a subject and a verb. Consider the following statement.

> *We began to descend into the canyon*

The idea above is complete. It has a subject (*we*) and a verb (*began*). However, look what happens when we add some transition words.

> *Because we began to descend into the canyon*
>
> *When we began to descend into the canyon*
>
> *Though we began to descend into the canyon*
>
> *As we began to descend into the canyon*

All of the ideas above are incomplete. Even though each has a subject and a verb, the transition word at the beginning makes each idea incomplete.

Now that we have established the difference between complete and incomplete ideas, let's take a look at the different types of punctuation that can connect two ideas.

STOP, GO, AND THE VERTICAL LINE TEST

Let's get the weird ones out of the way first. Everyone knows that a period ends a sentence, but even particularly nerdy grammarians can get lost when things get more complicated. Because of this confusion, we've come up with a basic chart that summarizes the different times you might use what the PSAT calls "end-of-sentence" and "middle-of-sentence" punctuation.

STOP
- Period (.)
- Semicolon (;)
- Comma + FANBOYS
- Question mark (?)
- Exclamation mark (!)

HALF-STOP
- Colon (:)
- Long dash (—)

GO
- Comma (,)
- No punctuation

> **FANBOYS** stands for **F**or, **A**nd, **N**or, **B**ut, **O**r, **Y**et, and **S**o.

> STOP punctuation can link only complete ideas.
>
> HALF-STOP punctuation must be preceded by a complete idea.
>
> GO punctuation can link anything except two complete ideas.

Let's see how these work. Here is a complete idea:

Samantha studied for the PSAT.

Notice that we've already used one form of STOP punctuation at the end of this sentence: a period.

Now, if we want to add a second complete idea, we'll keep the period.

Samantha studied for the PSAT. She ended up doing really well on the test.

In this case, the period is linking these two complete ideas. But the nice thing about STOP punctuation is that you can really use any of the punctuation in the list to do the same thing, so we could also say this:

Samantha studied for the PSAT; she ended up doing really well on the test.

What the list of STOP punctuation shows us is that essentially, a period and a semicolon are the same thing. We could say the same for the use of a comma plus one of the FANBOYS words.

Samantha studied for the PSAT, and she ended up doing really well on the test.

You can also use HALF-STOP punctuation to separate two complete ideas, so you could say

Samantha studied for the PSAT: she ended up doing really well on the test.

Or

Samantha studied for the PSAT—she ended up doing really well on the test.

There's a subtle difference, however, between STOP and HALF-STOP punctuation: for STOP, both ideas have to be complete, but for HALF-STOP, only the first one does.

Let's see what this looks like. If we want to link a complete idea and an incomplete idea, we can use HALF-STOP punctuation as long as the complete idea is first. For example,

Samantha studied for the PSAT: all three sections of it.

Or

Samantha studied for the PSAT: the silliest test in all the land.

When you use HALF-STOP, there has to be a complete idea before the punctuation, so these examples wouldn't be correct:

Samantha studied for: the PSAT, the SAT, and every AP test in between.

The PSAT—Samantha studied for it and was glad she did.

When you are not linking two complete ideas, you can use GO punctuation. So you could say, for instance,

Having studied for the PSAT, Samantha was confident going into the test.

Or

Samantha studied for the PSAT, all three sections of it.

These are the three types of mid-sentence or end-of-sentence punctuation: STOP, HALF-STOP, and GO. You'll notice that there is a bit of overlap between the concepts, but the writers of the PSAT couldn't possibly make you get into the minutiae of choosing between, say, a period and a semicolon. If you can figure out which of the big three (STOP, HALF-STOP, and GO) categories you'll need, that's generally all you need to be able to do.

In the following exercise, choose the type of punctuation that will correctly work in the blank.

Some questions have more than one answer! Check your answers on the next page.

> The PSAT 8/9 actually does not expect you to know when to use a semicolon. While you will see semicolons appear in the answer choices, most likely they won't be correct. However, we've included all the types of punctuation here because you'll need to know them later on for the more advanced versions of the PSAT and the SAT. When it comes to punctuation on the PSAT 8/9, you will be most commonly tested on commas in lists and sentences that don't need punctuation at all. The examples you see in this chapter will give you a good idea of what you can expect from punctuation questions on the PSAT 8/9.

	STOP	HALF-STOP	GO
The other day I went to the stadium _____ and bought a ticket.			✓
I had saved up all week _____ I couldn't think of anything better to spend the money on!	but	✗	
Some of my favorite sports include _____ hockey, baseball, and tennis.			✓
There's always something _____ for me to see at the stadium.			✗
When I arrived _____ I was thrilled to see that I had bought great seats.			✗
Some people from my school were sitting next to me _____ we're all in the same math class.	✗	✗	
The game was exciting _____ a goal in the first five minutes!		✗	✗
The crowd was extremely diverse _____ men, women, and children in the stands.		✗	
I didn't want to go home _____ even though I had school the next day.			✗
You can be sure of one thing _____ I'll be back as soon as I can.	✗	✗	

	STOP	HALF-STOP	GO
The other day I went to the stadium _____ and bought a ticket.			X
I had saved up all week _____ I couldn't think of anything better to spend the money on!	X	X	
Some of my favorite sports include _____ hockey, baseball, and tennis.			X
There's always something _____ for me to see at the stadium.			X
When I arrived _____ I was thrilled to see that I had bought great seats.			X
Some people from my school were sitting next to me _____ we're all in the same math class.	X	X	
The game was exciting _____ a goal in the first five minutes!		X	X
The crowd was extremely diverse _____ men, women, and children in the stands.		X	
I didn't want to go home _____ even though I had school the next day.			X
You can be sure of one thing _____ I'll be back as soon as I can.	X	X	

Let's see what this will look like on the PSAT 8/9.

One day Stormie decided she wanted to go on an **1** _____ adventure; while her human companion was at work.

1

A) NO CHANGE

B) adventure. While

C) adventure while

D) adventure, this was while

Here's How to Crack It

As always, check what's changing in the answer choices. In this case, most of the words stay the same. All that changes in three of the answers is the punctuation, and notice the types of punctuation that are changing: STOP and GO.

When you see STOP punctuation changing in the answer choices, you can use a technique that we like to call the Vertical Line Test.

Draw a line where you see the punctuation changing—in this case, between the words *adventure* and *while*. Then, read up to the vertical line and identify the idea as complete or incomplete: *One day Stormie decided she wanted to go on an adventure*. That's Complete. Now, read after the vertical line: *while her human companion was at work*. That's Incomplete.

By the time you're done, your page should look like this:

                                        Complete | Incomplete

One day Stormie decided she wanted to go on an **1** adventure; | while her human companion was at work.

So, let's think: we have a complete idea and an incomplete idea. What kind of punctuation do we need in order to connect these two ideas? According to the STOP/GO punctuation rules, we need either GO or HALF-STOP. While either of these will work to connect the two ideas in the question, notice that the answer choices contain only GO punctuation. Eliminate (A) and (B) because both choices contain STOP punctuation, which cannot connect a complete idea to an incomplete idea.

Both (C) and (D) have GO punctuation, but notice that the words change in (D). Read the second part of the sentence in (D): *this was while her human companion was at work*. That's a complete idea, so with (D) the sentence contains two complete ideas. A comma cannot be used to connect two complete ideas, since it is GO punctuation, so eliminate (D). The correct answer is (C). No punctuation is needed at all. Notice that we needed to repeat part of the Vertical Line Test test when new words were added to the sentence; the same would be true if words had been removed from the sentence.

Let's try another.

She wanted to search for her favorite
2 toy. | A bumpy blue bone made of nylon.

2

A) NO CHANGE

B) toy, and a

C) toy—a

D) toy a

Here's How to Crack It

Check the answer choices. What's changing? Punctuation is changing, and some of that punctuation is STOP or HALF-STOP. Let's use the Vertical Line Test. Draw a vertical line where you see the punctuation: between *toy* and *A* in the underlined portion.

What's before the vertical line? *She wanted to search for her favorite toy* is complete. Next, *a bumpy blue bone made of nylon* is incomplete. Therefore, because we have a complete idea followed by an incomplete idea, we can't use STOP punctuation, thus eliminating (A) and (B) because both a period and a comma + *and* are forms of STOP punctuation.

Now, what's different between the last two choices? Choice (C) contains HALF-STOP punctuation, and (D) contains GO punctuation. Both can work to connect a Complete idea to an Incomplete idea, so consider whether there is a reason to use either type of punctuation. A long dash (and HALF-STOP punctuation, in general) is used to create a small separation between or to slow down ideas. The second part of the sentence provides an explanation or definition of a concept in the first part; the two ideas should have separation between them so they don't sound like one continuous thought, so there is a reason to use a dash (a colon could also be used). Keep (C). Choice (D) doesn't include a punctuation mark that indicates a separation, or pause, so eliminate (D). The correct answer is (C). By the way, a comma could have worked here as well, but it wasn't an option (other than the comma + FANBOYS in (B)—which is STOP punctuation). Always use POE with the options that are provided, instead of trying to fix the sentence on your own.

Let's see one more.

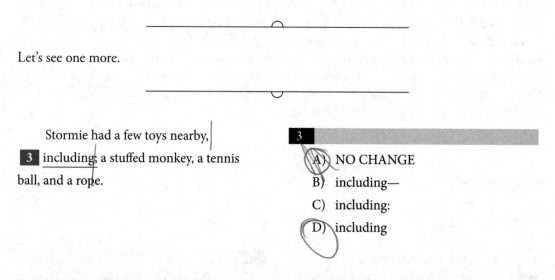

Here's How to Crack It

First, ask what's changing in the answer choices. Punctuation is changing, and some choices contain STOP and HALF-STOP punctuation, so let's use the Vertical Line Test. Put the line between *including* and *a*. The first idea, *Stormie had a few toys nearby, including,* is incomplete, and the second idea, *a stuffed monkey, a tennis ball, and a rope,* is also incomplete. Therefore, STOP and HALF-STOP can't be used—only GO punctuation can connect two incomplete ideas. Eliminate (A), (B), and (C) because they are all either STOP or HALF-STOP punctuation. The correct answer is (D).

A SLIGHT PAUSE FOR COMMAS

Commas can be a little tricky. You may recall that GO punctuation sometimes includes a comma and sometimes does not. You can think of that comma as signaling a pause or a shift in ideas. What are some other reasons to use a comma? Take a look at the list below.

If you can't cite a reason to use a comma, don't use one.

On the PSAT, there are only four reasons to use a comma:

- in STOP punctuation, with one of the FANBOYS
- in GO punctuation, to separate incomplete ideas from complete ideas
- in a list of three or more things
- in a sentence containing unnecessary information

We've already seen the first two concepts, so let's look at the third and fourth.

Try this one.

However, she wasn't satisfied with any of those toys. Unfortunately, she was trapped in a hallway by two closed **4** doors; a gate with wooden bars and a wall.

4

A) NO CHANGE

B) doors, a gate with wooden bars, and

C) doors, a gate with wooden bars, and,

D) doors, a gate with wooden bars; and

Here's How to Crack It

First, check what's changing in the answer choices. The original underlined portion has STOP punctuation, so use the Vertical Line Test and draw the line between *doors* and *a*. The first idea, *Unfortunately, she was trapped in a hallway by two closed doors* is a complete idea, but *a gate with wooden bars and a wall* is incomplete. Therefore, STOP punctuation can't be used. Eliminate (A). Choice (D) also has STOP punctuation, but in a different spot, so draw a line between *bars* and *and*. The second part of the sentence, *and a wall*, is incomplete, so the semicolon (STOP punctuation) can't work. Eliminate (D). Notice that (B) and (C) only have commas changing, and the items in the underlined portion are part of a list of three things: 1) doors, 2) a gate with wooden bars, and 3) a wall. There should be a comma after each item before the word *and*, but there shouldn't be a comma after *and*, so eliminate (C). The correct answer is (B).

On the PSAT, there should be a comma after every item in a series. Think of it this way. There's a potential misunderstanding in this sentence:

I went to the park with my parents, my cat Violet and my dog Stuart.

Without a comma after *Violet*, it sure sounds like this person has some interesting parents. If there's no comma, how do we know that this sentence isn't supposed to say that the parents are *my cat Violet and my dog Stuart*? The only way to remove the ambiguity is to add a comma, like this:

I went to the park with my parents, my cat Violet, and my dog Stuart.

Let's try another.

The gate, intended to block off doorways for [5] babies, made a scary rattling noise anytime Stormie touched it.

5

A) NO CHANGE
B) babies
C) babies;
D) babies—

Here's How to Crack It

First, check what's changing in the answer choices. Some of the choices contain STOP and HALF-STOP punctuation, so draw the vertical line between *babies* and *made*. The first part of the sentence, *The gate, intended to block off doorways for babies*, is incomplete. Neither STOP nor HALF-STOP can be used because both require the first part to be complete. Eliminate (C) and (D). Now consider whether a comma should be used.

The comma in (A) comes after the phrase *intended to block off doorways*. This phrase also has a comma before it, which indicates that the phrase is unnecessary. You can also try reading the sentence without the phrase: *The gate made a scary rattling noise anytime Stormie touched it.* This still makes sense and has the same meaning as the original sentence, so the phrase is unnecessary and needs commas both before and after it. (Note that these commas work similarly to two parentheses. Two dashes can also be used in the same way.)

Therefore, because the phrase does need a comma after it, eliminate (B). The correct answer is (A).

Let's try a few more. Try to figure out whether the word or idea in italics is necessary to the meaning of the sentence.

1. A student *who has prepared for the PSAT 8/9* will feel more confident.
2. Katie wants to go to Yale *which has a really good theater program.*
3. The team *that scored five touchdowns* won the game in a landslide.
4. The PSAT 8/9 *which is administered by the College Board* is not as common as the PSAT 11.
5. Rising senior *Liam* is hoping to ace the SAT.

Answers are on page 164.

Let's put this all together in this question.

This was the [6] barrier, that would determine whether Stormie would be able, to retrieve her blue bone.

6

A) NO CHANGE
B) barrier that would determine whether Stormie would be able,
C) barrier, that would determine whether Stormie would be able
D) barrier that would determine whether Stormie would be able

Here's How to Crack It

Check what's changing in the answer choices. There are varying numbers of commas in varying places. Remember, the rule of thumb with commas is that if you can't cite a reason to use a comma, *don't use one.*

It looks like the phrase *that would determine whether Stormie would be able* is being set off by commas. Let's see whether this phrase is necessary or unnecessary information. Read the original sentence, and then read the sentence again without the phrase: *This was the barrier to retrieve her blue bone.* This changes the meaning of the sentence and doesn't clearly indicate what the barrier's role is. Therefore, the phrase in question is necessary to the meaning of the sentence, so it shouldn't be surrounded by commas.

In the end, there aren't reasons to put commas anywhere in this sentence. The correct answer is (D). Sometimes the PSAT 8/9 will test unnecessary punctuation explicitly, so make sure you have a good reason to use commas when you use them!

YOUR GOING TO BE TESTED ON APOSTROPHE'S (AND INTERNET SPELLING IS A TERRIBLE GUIDE!)

As with commas, apostrophes have only a very limited set of applications. Apostrophes are a little trickier, though, because you can't really hear them in speech, so people misuse them all the time. Think about the header of this section. The apostrophes are wrong there. Here's the correct way of punctuating it: You're going to be tested on apostrophes. Can you hear the difference? Neither can we.

Therefore, as with commas:

> If you can't cite a reason to use an apostrophe, *don't use one.*
>
> On the PSAT 8/9, there are only two reasons to use an apostrophe:
>
> - possessive nouns (NOT pronouns)
>
> - contractions (shortened forms of two words, such as *it's* instead of *it is*)

Here are some examples.

Annoyed by **7** humans method's for keeping dogs from being free, Stormie vowed to somehow get past that fence.

7

A) NO CHANGE
B) humans methods'
C) human's methods
D) humans' methods

Here's How to Crack It

Check what's changing in the answer choices. In this case, the words are all the same, but apostrophes are changing. Remember, you must have a good reason to use an apostrophe.

Does anything belong to *humans*? Yes! The *methods* are used by *humans*, so the first word does need an apostrophe. Eliminate (A) and (B). No remaining answer has an apostrophe on *methods*—it doesn't need one because it is simply plural, not possessive. Next consider the difference between *human's* and *humans'*. The word *human's* means "belonging to one human," whereas *humans'* means "belonging to more than one human." In this case, a plural noun is needed, as *Annoyed at human's methods* would not be a correct usage—you could say *the human's methods* or *a human's methods*, but it's not correct to simply say *human's*. Eliminate (C). The correct answer is (D).

Let's have a look at another.

This was the day when all dogs would learn to revere **8** their queen, who would do the impossible.

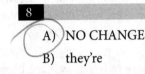

8

A) NO CHANGE
B) they're
C) they are
D) there

Here's How to Crack It

Check what's changing in the answer choices: different spellings of the pronoun *their* and the use of apostrophes. First, consider *their* versus *they're*: *they're* means "they are." This actually means that neither (B) nor (C) could be correct because they are exactly the same. However, to be sure, try reading the sentence that way: *This was the day when all dogs would learn to revere they are queen.* This doesn't work—the *queen* belongs to the *dogs*, so a possessive pronoun is needed, which doesn't use apostrophes. Eliminate (B) and (C).

Now consider the meaning of *there*. It is used to refer to a particular place. No place is being referenced in this sentence, so eliminate (D). The correct answer is (A).

Phew! These apostrophes can get a little tricky, so let's try a few more. On these (as on many parts of the PSAT 8/9), you'll find that using your ear, sounding things out, doesn't really help all that much.

Circle the option that works. The big question is this: apostrophes or no apostrophes?

1. *Salims/Salim's* teacher said *hes/he's* allowed to miss next *Tuesdays/Tuesday's* exam.

2. *Its/It's* really not going to hurt my feelings if you don't want to go to *they're/their* party with me.

3. Whatever the *justification's/justifications* for *your/you're* attitude, *there/they're* is no reason to be so obnoxious about it.

4. *Were/We're* going to get back to them as soon as their *application's/applications* are processed.

5. *They're/Their* *they're/their* nachos, but they *wont/won't* share any unless *its/it's* absolutely necessary or we share *ours/our's*.

Answers are on page 164.

CONCLUSION

In sum, we've looked at all the punctuation you'd ever need on the PSAT 8/9. It's really not so much, and you probably knew a lot of it already. In general, checking what's changing in the answer choices can help reveal mistakes that you may not have heard, and POE can help you narrow those answers down.

Punctuation rules are easy to learn, as is the biggest rule of all about punctuation.

> Know why you are using punctuation, whether that punctuation is STOP, HALF-STOP, GO, commas, or apostrophes. If you can't cite reasons to use these punctuation marks, don't use them!

In the last few pages of this chapter, try out these skills on a drill.

Answers to Questions on Page 161:

1. NECESSARY to the meaning of the sentence (no commas). If you remove the italicized part, the sentence is not adequately specific.

2. UNNECESSARY to the meaning of the sentence (commas). If you remove the italicized part, the sentence is still complete and does not change meaning.

3. NECESSARY to the meaning of the sentence (no commas). If you remove the italicized part, the sentence is not adequately specific.

4. UNNECESSARY to the meaning of the sentence (commas). If you remove the italicized part, the sentence is still complete and does not change meaning.

5. NECESSARY to the meaning of the sentence (no commas). If you remove the italicized part, the sentence is no longer complete.

Answers to Questions on Page 163:

1. Salim's, he's, Tuesday's
2. It's, their
3. justifications, your, there
4. We're, applications
5. They're, their, won't, it's, ours

Writing & Language Drill 2

Time: 5–6 minutes. Check your answers in Part IV.

Marie Van Brittan Brown: Staying Safe

In the 1960s, a woman named Marie Van Brittan Brown **1** lived in Queens, New York, where she worked as a nurse. Both she and her husband Albert, an electrician, often worked odd hours. Their neighborhood had a high crime rate, and since they often had to come and go during the night, the two were concerned about safety. They were not always both there during the night to protect each **2** other; their home, and their two children. Furthermore, Brown had noticed that local **3** residents calls' to the police did not always receive a quick response. With these concerns in mind, Brown wondered whether **4** there was a way to see who was at her door from any room in the house and quickly contact the authorities.

1

A) NO CHANGE
B) lived, in
C) lived, in,
D) lived: in

2

A) NO CHANGE
B) other,
C) other:
D) other

3

A) NO CHANGE
B) residents call's
C) resident's calls
D) residents' calls

4

A) NO CHANGE
B) they're
C) they are
D) their

At that time, if someone **5** knocked on your door you might have to look out a window (potentially allowing an intruder to see who you were) or a small peephole. A potential intruder could also be standing right outside the door, and if he or she did not make a noise, you would have no way to know that someone was there, preparing to break in. If the person did try to break in, you would have to run to the phone and call the **6** police this could use up precious time in the days when most homes had only one phone, with a cord.

5

A) NO CHANGE
B) knocked, on your door,
C) knocked on your door,
D) knocked, on your door

6

A) NO CHANGE
B) police, which
C) police, this
D) police. Which

In 1966, Brown, along with Albert; filed a patent for the first home security system. In Brown's invention, a door would have several peepholes with a camera looking outside. The video would be transmitted to a monitor that could be **8** placed, it was in any room in the house. This would allow residents to see who was outside their door without having to constantly look out. In addition, Brown's patent included a set of microphones to allow the resident to talk to the person outside. A remote control could lock or unlock the door from a distance, and the invention included an additional **9** feature, and a panic button that would call the police immediately.

Brown's patent application was approved in 1969, and she later won an award from the National Scientists Committee. Her idea formed the basis for many security systems in place today in **10** homes, offices, and outdoor spaces. In fact, it's estimated that over 100 million security cameras are now in place, utilizing Brown's innovative idea.

7

A) NO CHANGE
B) Albert
C) Albert—
D) Albert,

8

A) NO CHANGE
B) placed in
C) placed; in
D) placed. In

9

A) NO CHANGE
B) feature. A
C) feature—a
D) feature a

10

A) NO CHANGE
B) homes, offices and,
C) homes offices and
D) homes offices, and

Chapter 8
Words

THE WORDS CHANGE, BUT THE SONG REMAINS THE SAME

In the last chapter, we looked at what to do when the PSAT 8/9 is testing punctuation. In this chapter, we're going to look at what to do when the PSAT 8/9 is testing the parts of speech—mainly verbs, nouns, and pronouns.

Our basic strategy, however, has remained the same. As we saw in the previous two chapters, when faced with a PSAT 8/9 Writing and Language question, you should always

> Check out what's changing in the answer choices and use POE.

As you will notice, throughout this chapter, we talk a lot about certain parts of speech, but we don't really use a lot of grammar terms. That's because we find that on the PSAT 8/9, the best answers across a lot of different parts of speech can be summed up more succinctly with three basic terms: **consistency**, **precision**, and **concision**.

You don't need to know a ton of grammar if you can remember these three basic rules.

> **Consistency:** Correct answers are consistent with the rest of the sentence and the passage.
>
> **Precision:** Correct answers are as precise as possible.
>
> **Concision:** Barring other errors, correct answers are as concise as possible.

Let's look at some examples of each.

CONSISTENCY

Let's see how the PSAT 8/9 might test consistency.

Dogs **1** was knowing that they are not supposed to try to escape confinement.

A) NO CHANGE
B) has known
C) knows
D) know

Here's How to Crack It

First, as always, check what's changing in the answer choices. In this case, the forms of the verb *to know* change. Therefore, because the verbs change, we know that the question is testing verbs.

When you see verbs changing in the answer choices, the first thing to check is the subject of the sentence. Is the verb consistent with the subject? In this case, it's not. The subject of the sentence is *dogs*, which is plural. Therefore, (A), (B), and (C) can all be eliminated because they are singular verbs. Only (D), *know*, is a plural verb and can therefore work in this sentence.

Thus, when you see verbs changing in the answer choices, check the subject first. Even though the above answer choices provided verbs in different tenses, you didn't have to decide which tense is needed—only one choice has a verb that is the correct number (singular or plural) to match with the subject. Subjects and verbs need to be consistent with each other.

Let's have a look at another.

In preparation for her adventure, Stormie 2 plot about how to get past the fence and considered the potential risks involved.

2

A) NO CHANGE
B) is plotting
C) plotted
D) plots

Here's How to Crack It

Check what's changing in the answer choices: the verbs. Remember from the first question that whenever you see verbs changing, you want to make sure the verb is consistent with the subject. The subject of the sentence is *Stormie*, which is singular, so you can eliminate (A), *plot*, which is a plural verb (you can test this with the words *it* and *they*—you'd say "it plots" and "they plot," so *plot* is plural because it goes with *they*).

Then, because all of the remaining verbs are consistent with the subject, make sure they are consistent with the other verbs in the sentence. The sentence states that Stormie *considered* the risks, so the underlined verb must be consistent with *considered*, which is in past tense. Eliminate (B) and (D) because they are in present tense. Only (C) is consistent, and it's the correct answer.

As you can see, verbs are all about consistency.

> When you see verbs changing in the answer choices, make sure those verbs are:
>
> **Consistent** with their subjects
>
> **Consistent** with other verbs in the sentence and surrounding sentences

Let's see how Consistency can be tested with pronouns.

Stormie had a few ideas in her mind, since she couldn't write **3** herself down, for how to do so.

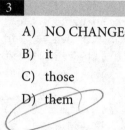

3

A) NO CHANGE

B) it

C) those

D) them

Here's How to Crack It

Check what's changing in the answer choices. Here, pronouns are changing. Pronouns must always be consistent with the nouns they are replacing. Identify the noun that the underlined pronoun needs to refer back to. In this sentence, the pronoun should refer to the *ideas*, which is plural. Eliminate (A) and (B) because they aren't plural, so those pronouns aren't consistent.

Next consider whether *those* or *them* is more consistent. The word *those* is used to refer to a specific group of something. The sentence refers to a particular group of ideas, but the use of *those* would imply that, while she can't write down the particular ideas mentioned in the sentence, there are other ideas she could write down. Dogs can't write anything down, so *those* doesn't work here. Eliminate (C). The correct answer is (D).

Consistency applies across the test. Let's see another question in which the idea of Consistency might help us.

She thought there might be a way to dig underneath the fence to tunnel her way out. She had **4** thus considered whether she could climb or leap over it.

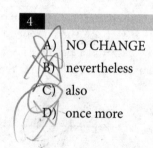

4

A) NO CHANGE

B) nevertheless

C) also

D) once more

Here's How to Crack It

First, what's changing in the answer choices? Transition words. Transition questions also test consistency. The transition must be consistent with the relationship between the sentence with the underlined portion and the sentence before it. Check the two sentences to determine their relationship.

The first sentence tells about one of the dog's ideas. The second sentence reveals a second idea. Thus, the two sentences agree. Eliminate any opposite-direction transitions. Choice (B), *nevertheless*, is a contrasting transition, so eliminate it. Now consider the remaining options. Choice (A), *thus*, is used to present a conclusion that follows a set of evidence. That isn't the relationship here, so eliminate (A). Choice (C), *also*, is used to add on to previous information, which is consistent with the relationship between these sentences, so keep (C). Choice (D), *once more*, indicates something that happened again, but there is no evidence that this idea had already occurred to her before, so eliminate (D). Only (C) is consistent with the relationship between these two sentences.

Consistency can show up in other ways as well. Let's have a look at the next question.

To see whether digging would be a possible strategy, [5] Stormie's paws were scratched on the ground below the gate and attempted to break through.

5
A) NO CHANGE
B) Stormie quickly scratched her paws on the ground below the gate
C) scratching on the ground below the gate
D) paws were scratched on the ground below the gate by Stormie

Here's How to Crack It

Look at what's changing in the answer choices. Here, it's not as obvious as in some questions. Notice that the order of the words changes, but the answers all provide roughly the same meaning. This is often a good indication that the question is testing modifiers. A modifier is a phrase that describes a noun. Here's an example:

> **Hoping to ace the test,** *I studied for an hour every day.*

The phrase *hoping to ace the test* describes, or modifies, the pronoun *I*, so this sentence is correct. Let's take a look at one with an error:

> **Hoping to ace the test,** *studying for an hour every day was necessary.*

This sentence might sound okay, because you can probably tell what it's supposed to mean, but it contains a grammar error called a misplaced modifier. In this sentence, *hoping to ace the test* describes *studying*, which doesn't make sense: the verb *studying* can't be *hoping* for something because it's not a person. Therefore, the rule for modifiers is that modifier (describing phrase) must come as close as possible to the person or thing it's describing.

Back to question 5. The first part of the sentence contains a modifier: *To see whether digging would be a possible strategy*. Ask yourself: who or what wanted to see whether digging would be possible? It's Stormie, so you can eliminate any answer that doesn't have *Stormie* right after the comma. This means that (A), (C), and (D) are all wrong: *Stormie's paws*, *scratching*, and *paws* are not the ones trying to see something. The correct answer is therefore (B).

If you identify that the order of words is changing and recognize the modifier, you can often answer these questions very quickly. As you can see, only the first word of the answer mattered here.

Let's have a look at some more of these modifiers. Rewrite each sentence below so the modifier makes the precise sense that it should.

1. Given all its logical twists and turns, many people struggle with philosophy.

2. Readers in different times tend to gravitate toward different philosophers and places.

3. Once cracked, you can find incredible guidance and solace in philosophy.

4. I first learned about Pragmatism from a professor in college at 20.

5. Boring and uninteresting, Jack didn't care much for the work of William James.

Answers are on page 179.

In addition to verbs, pronouns, transitions, and modifiers, the PSAT 8/9 will sometimes test consistency as its own topic. Here's an example.

6 Stormie made her best efforts to dig, but she wasn't able to break through the hard tiled floor.

6

A) NO CHANGE

B) I can't tell you how hard Stormie tried to dig,

C) I'm serious that Stormie dug so hard,

D) Stormie dug to the max,

Here's How to Crack It

Check what's changing in the answer choices. Again, it isn't quick and obvious, but you may notice that the answer choices use different levels of language. Choices (B) and (C) introduce personal pronouns: *I* and *you*, and (D) uses the slang-y phrase *to the max*. The question doesn't test specific grammar rules so much as consistency in general. All PSAT 8/9 passages will be written in a somewhat formal, academic tone. They won't use slang or casual language. Eliminate (D) because it's not consistent with the tone of the passage. So far, this passage hasn't used the pronoun *I* or *me*, and these personal pronouns are not likely to be used on the Writing and Language on the PSAT 8/9—most, if not all, passages will be written in the third person. Therefore, (B) and (C) are incorrect. You may also notice that the phrases *I can't tell you* and *so hard* are also overly casual. Only (A) is consistent with the tone of the passage. As always, consistency is key!

Consistency

- When the verbs are changing in the answer choices, make sure those verbs are consistent with their subjects and with other verbs.

- When the nouns are changing in the answer choices, make sure those nouns are consistent with the other nouns in the sentence and the paragraph.

- When transition words are changing in the answer choices, choose a transition that is consistent with the relationship between that sentence and the one before.

- When the order of the words changes in the answer choices, look for modifier errors.

- When some answers have more casual language or switch to first or second person (using *I* or *you*), eliminate options that aren't consistent with the style and tone of the rest of the passage.

PRECISION

Consistency is probably the most important thing on the Writing and Language section of the PSAT 8/9, but precision is a close second. Once you've made sure that the underlined portion is consistent with the rest of the sentence, make sure that the underlined portion is as precise as possible. Perfect grammar is one thing, but it won't matter much if no one knows what the writer is talking about!

Let's hear that one more time.

> Once you are sure that a word or phrase is consistent with the non-underlined portion of the sentence, make that word or phrase as precise as you can.

Frustrated, Stormie frowned and **7** thought why her first approach hadn't been successful.

7

A) NO CHANGE
B) admired
C) interrogated
D) wondered

Here's How to Crack It

Check what's changing in the answer choices. The choice of words or vocabulary changes, which is an indication that the question is testing precision. For these questions, you'll need to choose the word with the most precise meaning in the context of the sentence. The words you'll see in the answers may have related or similar definitions, but some may not work grammatically or may provide a meaning that is slightly different from what is needed in that particular context.

For these questions, try ignoring the underlined portion and filling in your own word. Here, you could say Stormie "considered" *why her first approach hadn't been successful.* Then use Process of Elimination. While *thought* is similar to "considered," the phrase "thought why" isn't correct—it would need to be "thought about." Eliminate (A). Choice (B), *admired*, means "viewed with respect," which doesn't match with "considered," so eliminate it. Choice (C), *interrogated*, means "asked questions to," which doesn't work in this context—there must be a person or animate object being interrogated, which isn't the case here. Eliminate (C). Choice (D), *wondered*, does match with "considered," and it fits in the context of the sentence, so it's the correct answer.

Most likely, you will be familiar with the words in the answer choices for these questions. As you can see, though, you'll have to consider slight differences in their definitions as well as how they should be used in a sentence. If you come across a word you don't know or can't tell the difference between two words, just take your best guess and move on.

———————◯———————

Precision can show up in some other ways as well. Have a look at this question.

———————◯———————

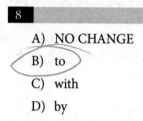

She turned her attention **8** on the wooden gate, which had scared her since she was a puppy.

8
A) NO CHANGE
B) to
C) with
D) by

Here's How to Crack It

Check what's changing in the answer choices. Here, it's again the individual words, but this time they're all prepositions (directional words such as *of, for, from, with, by,* and *in*). When you see prepositions changing in the answer choices, it's a good clue the question is testing idioms. Idioms are phrases that are just said a certain way: *depend on, afraid of, arrive at, talk about,* and so on. Why do we say *arrive at* instead of *arrive to*? No good reason—it's just an idiom. For these questions, you might be able to eliminate answers where the preposition doesn't make sense. Beyond that, however, if you don't know the idiom you'll just have to guess.

In this case. the idiom is "attention to," so the correct answer is (B). If you weren't sure about that, rest assured that you can expect to see only one or two questions like this on the test. Unfortunately, there isn't a good way to prepare for idiom questions because any number of words can be tested. As with vocabulary questions, do the best you can with what you know and don't waste too much time on these. Focus your study efforts on the more consistently rule-based questions, such as the ones we've already discussed.

CONCISION

When it comes to consistency and precision, you may find yourself sometimes choosing an answer that uses more words but makes the meaning more clear. This is fine—sometimes more words are needed. However, when the additional words don't make the meaning more precise, it's best to leave them out. For example, if you were to ask for directions, which answer would you rather receive?

> *Turn right at Main Street and walk four blocks.*

Or

> *Since this street, Elm Street, is facing in a northerly direction, and your destination is due northeast, go east when you arrive at the intersection of Elm and Main. Going east will entail making a right turn in quite that easterly direction. After having made this turn and arrived on the perpendicular street…*

The first one. Obviously.

And that's because concision (being concise) is key when you want to communicate meaning. Really, as long as everything else is in order—as long as the grammar and punctuation are good to go—the best answer will almost always be the shortest.

Let's see an example.

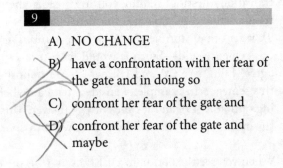

Perhaps she would have to
[9] possibly confront her fear of the gate and cast it aside in order to prevail in her adventure.

9

A) NO CHANGE

B) have a confrontation with her fear of the gate and in doing so

C) confront her fear of the gate and

D) confront her fear of the gate and maybe

Here's How to Crack It

Check what's changing in the answer choices. In this case, the answer choices all say roughly the same thing, but some use more words than others. Typically, if you see a list of answer choices in which one answer is short and the rest mean the same thing but are longer, the question is testing concision.

Start with the shortest answer, in this case (C), and read the sentence that way: *Perhaps she would have to confront her fear of the gate and cast it aside in order to prevail in her adventure.* This is grammatically sound and makes sense, so now look at the other options and consider whether the additional words make the sentence more precise or not. Choice (A) adds the word *possibly*, but the sentence already says *perhaps*, so this is redundant. Eliminate (A). Choice (B) changes *confront* to *have a confrontation with*. This isn't wrong, but it's a wordier way of saying the same thing. Likewise, it adds the words *in doing so* to the end of the phrase, which just aren't needed. Eliminate (B) because it's not as concise as (C). Choice (D) adds the word *maybe*, which, like (A), is redundant with *perhaps*. Eliminate (D). Choice (C) is concise and clear, so it's the correct answer.

Remember, however, that the shortest option is not always correct. Sometimes a sentence needs more words to be complete or to make the meaning clear. Always check all four answers using Process of Elimination.

Let's see one more.

10 Nevertheless, Stormie knew now that her struggle to retrieve her treasured blue bone rested not only on the structures of her confinement but also on her ability to overcome her own anxieties.

10

A) NO CHANGE

B) However,

C) For example,

D) DELETE the underlined portion, adjusting the capitalization as needed.

Here's How to Crack It

As always, check what's changing in the answer choices: transitions. As we discussed before, transition questions require you to consider the relationship between the sentence containing the underlined portion and the sentence before it. Look at the sentence before (from question 9): it says that Stormie might have to *confront her fear*. This sentence confirms what the previous sentence said—Stormie would have to *overcome her own anxieties*—so the two sentences agree. Eliminate (A) and (B), which are opposite-direction transitions. Now consider (C): is this sentence an example of an idea that came before? No, so (C) can't work. The only remaining option is (D), and it's the correct answer. This sentence doesn't need a transition at all, and the options provided definitely don't work to connect these two sentences.

When you see the option to DELETE in (D), the question could be testing concision. Consider the other three options along with the option to DELETE. If the three options provided do not make the sentence complete or precise, then choose (D). If the additional words are needed, however, don't pick it!

As we have seen in this chapter, when the PSAT is testing words (i.e., any time the words are changing in the answer choices), make sure that those words are

- **Consistent.** Verbs, nouns, and pronouns should agree within sentences and passages.
- **Precise.** The writing should communicate specific ideas and events.
- **Concise.** When everything else is correct, the shortest answer is the best.

Answers to Questions on Page 174:

1. Many people struggle with philosophy given all its logical twists and turns.

2. Readers in different times and places tend to gravitate toward different philosophers.

3. Once cracked, philosophy can provide incredible guidance and solace.

4. I first learned about Pragmatism from a college professor when I was 20 years old.

5. Jack didn't care much for the work of William James, which he found boring and uninteresting.

Note: These are just some ways to fix the original modifier errors. If you wrote something different, just make sure that if you keep the modifier, it comes as close as possible to the person or thing it's describing.

Writing and Language Drill 3

Time: 7–8 minutes. Check your answers in Part IV.

Landscape Mode

Today we are accustomed to seeing photographs of beautiful, natural places. The idea of painting a landscape may seem old-fashioned or lacking **1** when comparing the high-definition photos we're used to, but an artist's unique painting style can provide the viewer with much more than simply a visually pleasing scene. Acclaimed painter Chiura Obata embodies this idea: his landscapes comprise unique styles that have made his work highly influential over the past century.

Born in Japan, Obata **2** will immigrate to the United States as a teenager in 1903, hoping to find more contact with nature. A later trip to the Sierra Nevada mountain range in California **3** kindles his lifelong passion for landscapes. During Obata's trip, the mountains and trees, among other stunning natural features, led **4** him to create over 100 sketches. Reverent of the beautiful space surrounding him, Obata even used water from the nearby lakes and streams to incorporate into his watercolor paintings. *San Francisco Chronicle* art critic Charles Desmarais wrote that many of Obata's works "are nominally landscapes that are less descriptive than visionary reactions to the natural world."

1
A) NO CHANGE
B) in comparison to
C) as comparing to
D) as a comparison to

2
A) NO CHANGE
B) has immigrated
C) immigrates
D) immigrated

3
A) NO CHANGE
B) kindled
C) was kindling
D) will kindle

4
A) NO CHANGE
B) them
C) one
D) those

Not long after his trip, Obata returned to Japan and was able to have his sketches printed using **5** a traditional woodblock printing technique. This idea was fortunate because the colored prints were visually striking and different from landscapes that people had seen before. **6** Despite this, Obata won a prize in Japan and later showcased his work in many successful American art exhibits. The landscapes, including a famous print called *Lake Basin in the High Sierra*, **7** contrast the size and timelessness of the mountains with the relative insignificance of humans. Obata aimed to make the viewer feel the almost mystical experience he had had while in these natural spaces. The paintings are mysterious and **8** depict fine details even as they showcase immense features of the land.

5

A) NO CHANGE

B) an accustomed

C) a stable

D) a seasoned

6

A) NO CHANGE

B) Again,

C) In other words,

D) As a result,

7

A) NO CHANGE

B) contrasts

C) contrasting

D) is contrasting

8

A) NO CHANGE

B) draw

C) interpret

D) announce

As a professor at the University of California, **9** many students were introduced to his Japanese techniques and aesthetics, which then became defining attributes of the California Watercolor School art movement. Today, museum exhibits allow Obata's art to continue spreading and **10** influence to artists. His landscapes and their reflection on the relationship between impermanent human societies and enduring environmental features are as evocative today as ever.

9

A) NO CHANGE

B) there were many students who were introduced

C) Obata introduced many students

D) an introduction was made between students and Obata

10

A) NO CHANGE

B) artist influences.

C) to influence artists.

D) influencing artists.

Chapter 9
Questions

AND THEN THE PSAT 8/9 WAS LIKE, "HEY, CAN I ASK YOU A QUESTION?"

In the previous two chapters, we saw most of the concepts that the PSAT 8/9 will test on the Writing and Language portion of the exam. In this chapter, we're not going to learn a lot of new stuff in the way of grammar. Instead, we'll look at some of the questions that the PSAT 8/9 asks.

As we've seen, a lot of the questions on the Writing and Language Test aren't technically questions at all. They're just lists of answer choices, and you start the process of answering them by asking a question of your own: "What's changing in the answer choices?" Because you need to move quickly through this test, you may fall into the habit of not checking for questions. Even when you do read the questions, you may read them hastily or vaguely. Well, we are here to tell you that neither of these approaches will work.

> The most important thing about Writing and Language questions is that you notice those questions and then *answer* those questions.

This may seem like just about the most obvious advice you've ever been given, but you'd be surprised how much less precise your brain is when you're working quickly.

Here's an example. Do these next 10 questions as quickly as you can.

1. $2 + 1 =$ *3*
2. $1 + 2 =$ *3*
3. $3 + 1 =$ *4*
4. $3 + 2 \neq$ *6*
5. $1 + 2 =$ *3*
6. $2 - 1 <$ *5*
7. $2 \pm 2 =$ *+1*
8. $3 + 1 =$ *4*
9. $3 + 2 =$ *5*
10. $3 + 3 \neq$ *9*

Now check your answers.

1. 3
2. 3
3. 4
4. Anything but 5
5. 3
6. Any number greater than 1 (but not 1!)

7. 0 or 4

8. 4

9. 5

10. Anything but 6

Now, it's very possible that you got at least one of those questions wrong. What happened? It's not that the questions are hard. In fact, the questions are about as easy as can be. So why did you get some of them wrong? You were probably moving too quickly to notice that the signs changed a few times.

This is a lot like the Writing and Language section. You might miss some of the easiest points on the whole test by not reading carefully enough.

As you will see throughout this chapter, most of the questions will test concepts with which you are already familiar.

WORDS AND PUNCTUATION IN REVERSE

Many of the concepts we saw in the Punctuation and Words chapters show up explicitly with questions, but usually there's some kind of twist.

Here's an example.

The gate that kept Stormie confined to the hallway consisted of a wooden frame with thin vertical and horizontal rods. These horizontal and vertical rods making up the frame prevented her from slipping through the fence.

1

Which choice most effectively combines the sentences at the underlined portion?

A) rods, and these effectively prevent

B) rods; these, in contrast, prevent

C) rods, with the effect being the prevention of

D) rods, preventing

Here's How to Crack It

First and foremost, it's important to notice the question. This one is asking for the most effective way to combine the two sentences. Now that we have covered punctuation rules, consistency, precision, and concision, you have all the tools you need to answer this type of question. Questions on combining sentences require you to choose an option that uses correct punctuation and isn't overly wordy. A great strategy for these questions is to start with the shortest option. In this case, that's (D). Try reading the sentence with (D): *The gate that kept Stormie penned in to the hallway consisted of a wooden frame with thin vertical and horizontal rods, preventing her from slipping through the fence.* This doesn't seem to have any punctuation or grammar errors, so keep it, but check the other options to see whether the additional words help the meaning in some way.

Choice (A) adds a few more words but doesn't make the meaning more clear, so eliminate it because it's not as concise as (D). Choice (B) adds the phrase *in contrast*, which isn't the correct relationship between these sentences, so eliminate it. Like (A), (C) adds more words, but those words don't make the meaning more precise. Eliminate (C) because it's not as concise as (D). Therefore, (D) is the correct answer.

For these questions, the shortest answer is often the correct one—but not always. Start with the shortest option, but still consider the other choices. Remember that sometimes more words are necessary in order to make the meaning precise.

As you can see, questions that ask you to combine sentences are just another way to test the rules you already know.

The gate was only a few feet tall, but it posed a **2** toxic problem: if someone bumped it or knocked it over, the gate would make an extremely loud noise, frightening Stormie.

2

Which choice best maintains the style and tone of the passage?
A) NO CHANGE
B) significant
C) wicked
D) super rough

Here's How to Crack It

Notice what the question is asking for: a word that *maintains the style and tone of the passage.* Do the answer choices look familiar here? In the Words chapter, we saw that PSAT 8/9 questions can test you on appropriate language. Well, you'll see the same thing sometimes with an actual question. Sometimes the PSAT 8/9 will explicitly ask you to pick a word that is consistent with the passage's style and tone, as in the question above, and in other cases there won't be a question, as we saw in the Words chapter. Either way, the key is consistency!

Choices (C) and (D) are overly casual, so they aren't consistent with the passage's tone. Never pick an answer with slang words such as *cool, super, chill,* or *awesome*—unless the word is used in a non-slang context (for instance, weather could be described as *cool,* but describing an idea as *cool* is too casual for the PSAT).

Choice (A) is overly strong. The *problem* described in the sentence isn't *toxic* (poisonous), so eliminate (A). On these questions, you may also see answers that are too strong, too dramatic, or too flowery to be consistent with the passage's tone—for instance, stating that scientists "hoped with all their hearts" instead of just saying "hoped."

Only (B) is consistent with the passage's tone, so it's the correct answer.

───────────────○───────────────

Let's look at another that deals with one of the topics we saw earlier.

───────────────○───────────────

3 Today, however, Stormie recognized that the loud noise could not hurt her—she would find a way to get over the gate.

Stormie had two possible ideas for how to get over the gate: climbing and jumping. First, she tried climbing. Stormie reached her paws up and grabbed on to the horizontal wooden rods. Although she tried to use her upper body strength to pull herself up, Stormie quickly fell to the ground. It seemed that climbing wasn't a feasible strategy after all.

3

Which sentence provides the best transition to the next paragraph?

A) NO CHANGE

B) Stormie knew that she would not be able to overcome her fear of the gate.

C) Whenever Stormie had to go near the gate, she would move slowly to avoid causing the noise.

D) Stormie knew that she would have to find another way to escape, since getting over the gate wouldn't be an option.

Here's How to Crack It

The question is asking for a *transition to the next paragraph.* This is another great example of the importance of reading the question. When we discussed transitions in the previous chapter, we considered the relationship between sentences. Likewise, when a question asks about a transition between paragraphs, you'll think about the relationship between paragraphs.

Can we go ahead and answer this question as soon as we see the box with the number? No! We need to know what the next paragraph is about before we can figure out which option would be most consistent with that new idea. Read the paragraph after the underlined portion if you haven't already.

The paragraph leading up to the underlined portion (questions 1 and 2) provides details about the gate. The next paragraph introduces *two possible ideas for how to get over the gate* and then explains what happened when Stormie tried one of them. Use Process of Elimination, looking for an answer that refers back to the details about the gate and transitions into the new topic about how she could get over it.

Choice (A) does exactly that: it uses the word *however* to imply a contrast between the idea that the gate was scary and the idea that she would try to get past it anyway. In addition, the phrase *find a way to get over the gate* is consistent with the first sentence of the following paragraph. Keep (A). Choices (B) and (D) don't transition into the next paragraph because they both imply that Stormie won't try to get over the gate, but the first sentence of the next paragraph indicates that she will. Choice (C) tells us more about the gate, so it's consistent with the first paragraph, but again, it doesn't do what the question is asking—transition into the next paragraph. Therefore, (A) is the answer.

For transition questions, the answer should move smoothly from the topic of one paragraph into the topic of the next paragraph. Make sure you read enough to know what those topics are. Similarly, you may see questions asking you what sentence would best introduce or conclude a paragraph. In the same way, you'll need to read the entire paragraph and consider its main idea before tackling one of these questions.

> If a question asks for the best introduction or conclusion to a paragraph, you MUST read the whole paragraph first. If it asks for a transition, you MUST read that paragraph and the one after.

Questions like #3 are why…

> The most important thing about Writing and Language questions is that you notice that a question is being asked and answer that particular question.

PRECISION QUESTIONS

Not all questions will just be applications of punctuation and parts of speech. Some questions will ask you to do more specific things. Remember the three terms we kept repeating in the Words chapter: Consistency, Precision, and Concision. We'll start with the Precision-related questions. Even in those where Precision is not asked about directly, or when it is mixed with Consistency or Concision, remember this:

> Answer the question in the most precise way possible. Read literally!

Let's try one.

Next, she decided to try leaping over the gate. Stormie knew she was capable of jumping high, but she was worried that if her leap wasn't quite high enough, she would run into the gate **4** and hurt herself.

4

The writer is considering deleting the underlined portion, adjusting the punctuation as needed. Should the underlined portion be kept or deleted?

A) Kept, because it emphasizes Stormie's ability to jump high.

B) Kept, because it explains the reason Stormie was worried.

C) Deleted, because it blurs the paragraph's focus on the need for scaling the gate.

D) Deleted, because it does not explain exactly how tall the gate was.

Here's How to Crack It

The question asks whether we should keep or delete the phrase *and hurt herself*. Without the phrase, the sentence reads *Stormie knew she was capable of jumping high, but she was worried that if her leap wasn't quite high enough, she would run into the gate.* This isn't grammatically incorrect, but it's not quite as clear as the sentence with the phrase is: when the sentence includes the phrase *and hurt herself*, it identifies the risk associated with running into the gate. Therefore, the phrase should be kept. You want to be as precise as possible! Eliminate (C) and (D).

Choice (A) is not a good match because the phrase doesn't mention anything related to how high she could jump. Choice (B), however, is supported: getting *hurt* is a *reason Stormie was worried*. Therefore, (B) is the answer.

Let's try another.

The tiled floor was hard and could be painful if she fell on it from a height of several feet. **5** Stormie decided to be confident in her jumping skills—the blue bone would be worth all of the risk and effort. She readied herself and crouched into jumping position.

5

The writer is considering adding the following sentence.

> Some of the rooms in the house were carpeted, while other areas had wood floors.

Should the writer make this addition here?

A) Yes, because it supports the author's point in the previous sentence that Stormie could fall on the ground.

B) Yes, because it provides further details on the different types of flooring within the house.

C) No, because it fails to explain why the floors were made of different materials.

D) No, because it adds a detail that is irrelevant to the paragraph's focus on jumping over the gate.

Here's How to Crack It

The proposed sentence might seem interesting (let's be honest, though—probably not in this case!), but it isn't closely related to the focus of the paragraph. Therefore, it should not be added, eliminating (A) and (B). Remember, consistency is key!

While (C) is true, it doesn't provide a good reason not to add the sentence. The sentence doesn't need to *explain why the floors were made of different materials*—even if it did, this idea still wouldn't be relevant to the paragraph's focus. Choice (D) provides a good reason not to add the sentence.

In general, for questions asking whether a phrase or sentence should be added or kept, ask yourself whether there is a good reason to add or keep it (i.e., is it consistent with the text?). If not, it should be removed or not added. Process of Elimination, as always, is also huge on these questions—you'll be able to eliminate some options that simply aren't true. For instance, if an answer choice states that the information was provided earlier in the passage, but it wasn't, you can cross that option off right away.

CONSISTENCY QUESTIONS

Just as questions should be answered as precisely as possible, they should also be answered with information that is consistent with what's in the passage.

When answering consistency questions, keep this general rule in mind:

> Writing and Language passages should be judged on what they do say, not on what they could say. When dealing with Style, Tone, and Focus, make sure to work with the words and phrases the passage has already used.

Let's look at two questions that deal with the idea of consistency.

[1] As Stormie rose into the air, she reached a maximum height of between 2 and 3 feet and made contact with the top of the gate. [2] She reminded herself that the gate couldn't hurt her—it was only a noise that she was afraid of. [3] The force of her leap knocked the gate over with a thundering crash. [4] She looked around and realized that she was free. [5] **6** Once she was sure she hadn't been hurt, Stormie sat down and chewed the toy that she loved, reveling in the satisfaction of succeeding in her adventure. **7**

6

Which choice provides an important detail about what Stormie did that sets up the information given in the rest of the sentence?

A) NO CHANGE

B) After cleaning her fur and paws,

C) After locating her blue bone,

D) Sweating in the warm temperature,

7

The writer wants to add the following sentence to the paragraph.

> Stormie landed on the ground on top of the gate and quickly scampered, feeling timid from the loud noise.

To make the paragraph most logical, the sentence should be placed

A) after sentence 1.

B) after sentence 2.

C) after sentence 3.

D) after sentence 5.

Here's How to Crack Them

Let's look at question 6 first. In this case, the question tells us exactly what to look for: something that would *set up the information given in the rest of the sentence*. When the question asks you to fulfill a specific purpose, it's crucial that you understand what that purpose is. In fact, it's a good idea to underline the purpose stated in the question. Typically, for these questions you won't have to worry about grammar or punctuation—it's all about whether the meaning of the answer choice matches what the question is asking you to do.

Here, we need to see what information is in the rest of the sentence. It says that Stormie *sat down and chewed the toy that she loved*, so the correct answer needs to set this up. Choices (A), (B), and (D) could all be things that she did, but they don't have anything to do with the rest of the sentence. You might like them, but they can't be right. Only (C) mentions *the toy that she loved*: the *blue bone*. Therefore, (C) is the answer.

As for question 7, we need to find some very literal way to make the new sentence consistent with the rest of the paragraph. Look for words and phrases that will link this sentence to another sentence. Remember, it's not what the passage *could* say; it's what the passage *does* say. The new sentence mentions *the loud noise*, so it should be placed after some mention of a loud noise. Sentence 3 mentions *a thundering crash*. Therefore, this sentence should go after sentence 3, so (C) is correct.

As we have seen, these questions are not difficult, but they do require very specific actions on your part. Make sure you read the questions carefully and that you answer those questions as precisely and consistently as you can.

The same goes for charts and graphs on the Writing and Language Test. Don't let the strangeness of the charts throw you off! Just read the graphs with as much precision as you can and choose the most precise answers possible.

Let's have a look at one that we've added to the previous paragraph.

As Stormie rose into the air, she reached a maximum height of **8** between 2 and 3 feet and made contact with the top of the gate.

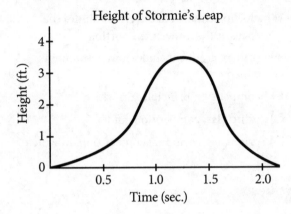

Height of Stormie's Leap

Which choice uses accurate information from the graph to complete the point being made in the sentence?

A) NO CHANGE

B) between 3 and 4

C) over 4

D) an unknown number of

Here's How to Crack It

This question is asking for the choice that agrees with the graph—again, consistency is key. From what we have seen, these questions are usually pretty straightforward. You don't have to do anything overly complex with the graphs, and that's certainly the case here.

The sentence mentions the *maximum height* of Stormie's leap, and the vertical axis of the graph describes height, so look for the peak. Then, draw a horizontal line from the peak to the axis on the left side. The line should cross the axis between 3 and 4 feet, so the correct answer is (B).

In general, graphs on the PSAT 8/9 Reading and Writing and Language Tests are very straightforward, and the fundamental question they ask is this: "Can you read a graph?" These are easy points as long as you read the graphs carefully and use POE.

CONCLUSION

As we have seen in this chapter, the PSAT 8/9 can ask a lot of different kinds of questions, but the test won't throw anything really crazy at you. The biggest things to remember, aside from the punctuation rules, are PRECISION and CONSISTENCY. If you pick answers that are precise and consistent with other information in the passage, you should be good to go. Just make sure to answer the question!

Take a Breather
You've made it through the entire Writing and Language section! Next up is Math, so feel free to take a break before diving in. Grab a snack, relax with a book, go for a walk—anything that will help you refresh before reviewing more content. Remember that study breaks can make you more productive, so don't deprive yourself of some needed relaxation time.

Writing and Language Drill 4

Time: 10 minutes. Check your answers in Part IV.

Gause's Law: It's a Competition

By the nineteenth and early twentieth centuries, scientists had observed many ecological **1** principles, including the principle of competition. In this principle, different organisms or species compete for a limited supply of a certain resource. Scientists posited that whenever two species are in competition, they will not coexist with constant population sizes. **2** To prevent going extinct, a species can either evolve or develop a new niche—the species's unique role in a certain environment. While this idea had been proposed earlier, biologist Georgy Gause was **3** born in Moscow, Russia, in 1910.

1

Which choice most effectively combines the sentences at the underlined portion?

A) principles, this includes competition, in which

B) competition principles, in which

C) principles, competition, and

D) principles, including competition, in which

2

At this point, the writer is considering adding the following sentence.

> That is, one species will benefit from a certain advantage it has and increase its population, and the other species could eventually go extinct.

Should the writer make this addition here?

A) Yes, because it elaborates on a concept and clarifies the connection between competition and extinction.

B) Yes, because it explains the significance of Gause's research.

C) No, because it provides information that is unrelated to the paragraph's main idea.

D) No, because it contradicts information given earlier in the paragraph.

3

Which choice best sets up the information that follows in the passage?

A) NO CHANGE

B) the first to prove the validity of the principle of competitive exclusion, in 1932.

C) later awarded a prize for his life-saving work on antibiotic medications.

D) an ecologist who published a number of influential books.

[1] In order to demonstrate this theory, Gause conducted a laboratory experiment. [2] He used two species of *Paramecium* (a type of microscopic organism) known as *P. aurelia* and *P. caudatum*. [3] To test the theory of competitive exclusion, Gause also combined the two species and observed what happened. [4] For the experiment, he created separate groups of each organism as control groups. [5] He provided the control and combined groups with the same amount of food and water and used a sample to determine the population of each species every day. [6] He wanted to see whether the two species would grow equally **4** well or whether, as the principle of competitive exclusion suggests, one group would become dominant and overtake the other. **5**

4

Which choice best maintains the style and tone of the passage?

A) NO CHANGE

B) nicely

C) amazingly

D) wonderfully

5

To make this paragraph most logical, sentence 4 should be placed

A) where it is now.

B) after sentence 1.

C) after sentence 2.

D) after sentence 5.

6 The experiment contradicted scientists' expectations. In the control groups, the two species had similar populations to each other. However, in the group that was combined, 7 Gause saw no clear pattern: as the two species competed for resources, *P. aurelia* emerged as the dominant organism. Initially, the two species grew at a similar rate, but *P. aurelia* soon surpassed *P. caudatum* and approached the population levels seen in the individual groups. *P. caudatum* decreased in population, 8 but it later increased and caused the *P. aurelia* to go extinct.

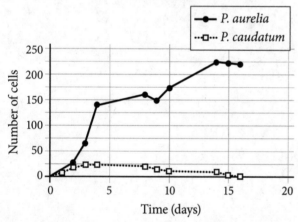

P. aurelia and *P. caudatum* populations when combined

6

Which choice, if added here, would most effectively introduce the main topic of the paragraph?

A) NO CHANGE

B) Gause's results confirmed the theory.

C) It is important for scientific experiments to contain control groups.

D) Gause eventually published his results in a book.

7

Which choice most effectively sets up the results that follow in the sentence?

A) NO CHANGE

B) both species continued to grow at the same rate:

C) Gause saw a difference in the populations emerge:

D) Gause decided to do more experiments:

8

Which choice uses information from the graph to accurately describe *P. caudatum* over the 16-day span?

A) NO CHANGE

B) never containing more than 5 cells.

C) going extinct in fewer than 10 days.

D) eventually being eliminated entirely from the sample.

Scientists continue to study competitive exclusion today, among plants, animals, and even humans, and Gause's experiments are credited for demonstrating this ecological idea experimentally. **9** Ecologists know that, at least under the controlled conditions of a laboratory, **10** when two species compete for the same resources, one will overtake the other one.

9

At this point, the writer is considering adding the following information:

> Gause had earned his first degree at Moscow University a few years before publishing his results.

Should the writer add the sentence here?

A) Yes, because it shows that Gause's scientific research was trustworthy.

B) Yes, because it helps the reader understand the passage's main points.

C) No, because it contradicts the author's claim about Gause in the previous sentence.

D) No, because it adds unnecessary information that is unrelated to the main topic of the paragraph.

10

The author wants a conclusion that summarizes the main finding of Gause's experiment. Which choice best accomplishes this goal?

A) NO CHANGE

B) two species can coexist without competing for resources.

C) competition for resources causes both organisms to go extinct.

D) when two species compete, one will adapt to find a new niche.

Chapter 10
Math Basics

Although we'll show you which mathematical concepts are most important to know for the PSAT 8/9, this book relies on your knowledge of basic math concepts. If you're a little rusty, this chapter is for you. Read on for a review of the math basics you'll need to know before you continue.

HOW TO CONQUER PSAT 8/9 MATH

So what do you need to do? There are three important steps:

1. Know the basic content. Obviously you do need to know the basics of arithmetic and algebra. We'll cover what you need to know in this chapter.

2. Learn some PSAT 8/9-specific problem-solving skills. Since these basic concepts appear in ways you're probably not used to from math class, you need to prepare yourself with a set of test-specific problem-solving skills designed to help you solve PSAT 8/9 Math problems. We'll cover the most important ones in the next chapter.

3. Have a sound overall testing strategy. This means knowing what to do with difficult questions or when calculator use is not allowed, and having a plan to pace yourself to get the maximum number of points in the time allotted. Be sure to read carefully the material in Chapter 2 to make sure you're using the strategy that will get you the greatest number of points in the time you have.

(PERSONAL) ORDER OF DIFFICULTY

The Math sections on the PSAT 8/9 are Sections 3 and 4. Section 3 contains 10 multiple-choice questions and 3 Grid-In questions. Section 4 contains 21 multiple-choice questions and 4 Grid-In questions. Within each question type, there is a loose order of difficulty, with most of the questions being of medium difficulty. (This means that the first few multiple-choice and first Grid-In questions are likely to be rated as easy, and the last few multiple-choice and last Grid-In questions are typically considered the most difficult.) More important than any order of difficulty is your own Personal Order of Difficulty. Though the last questions of each type in a section are likely to be the hardest, use your own personal strengths and weaknesses to decide which questions to do and which to skip.

Yes Calculator

1
2
3
4
5
6
7
8
9
10
11
12
13
14
15
16
17
18
19
20
21
Grid-In   22
23
24
25

No Calculator

1
2
3
4
5
6
7
8
9
10
Grid-In   11
12
13

13 Questions /
25 minutes

25 Questions /
40 minutes

USING YOUR CALCULATOR

You are allowed to use a calculator on Section 4 of the PSAT 8/9, and you should definitely do so. You can use any graphing, scientific, or plain old four-function calculator, provided that it doesn't have a keyboard.

There are a few simple rules to remember when dealing with your calculator:

1. Use the calculator you're most comfortable with. You definitely don't want to be trying to find the right button on test day. Ideally, you should be practicing with the same calculator you'll use on test day.

2. Change or charge your batteries the week before the test. If they run out during the test, there's nothing you can do about it.

Not sure whether your calculator is acceptable? Check College Board's website for a list of approved calculators.

3.   Be sure to hit the "clear" or "on/off" button after each calculation to reset the calculator after an operation. A common mistake to make when using your calculator is to forget to clear your last result.

4.   Your calculator is very good at calculating, but watch out for mis-keying information. (If you type the wrong numbers in, you'll get the wrong result.) Check each number on the display as you key it in.

5.   For the most part, you'll use your calculator for the basic operations of addition, subtraction, multiplication, and division; the ability to convert fractions to decimals and vice versa; and the ability to do square roots and exponents. Don't forget, though, that it likely has handy buttons for things like sine, cosine, and *i*, should you encounter those on the test.

6.   Then, there's one really big, important rule whenever you think about using your calculator:

A calculator can't think; it can only calculate.

What does this mean? It means that a calculator can't think through a problem for you. You have to do the work of understanding and setting up the problem correctly to make sure you know what the right calculation will be to get the answer. Only then can you use the calculator, when it is allowed, to calculate the answer.

So use your paper and pencil to practice your problem-solving skills on all Math questions. You should always be sure to set up the problem in your test booklet—writing it down is still the best method—which will help you catch any errors you might make and allow you to pick up where you left off if you lose focus. Then, for questions in Section 4, move quickly to your calculator to chug your way through the calculations, and be careful to enter each number and operator correctly. Remember, using your calculator is already saving you time on these questions—don't rush and lose the advantage that it gives you.

As you work through this book, look for calculator symbols next to questions on which calculator use would be allowed. If you don't see the symbol, don't use your calculator!

Math Basics Drill 1

DEFINITIONS

One of the reasons that good math students often don't get the credit they deserve on the PSAT 8/9 is that they've forgotten one or more of these definitions—or they read too fast and skip over these "little" words. Be sure you know them cold and watch out for them!

Match the words with their definitions, and then come up with some examples. Answers can be found in Part IV.

1. integers

2. positive numbers

3. negative numbers

4. even numbers

5. odd numbers

6. factors

7. multiples

8. prime numbers

9. distinct

10. digit

a. numbers that a certain number can be divided by, leaving no remainder
   Examples: _____

b. integers that cannot be divided evenly by 2
   Examples: _____

c. numbers that have no fractional or decimal parts
   Examples: _____

d. numbers that are greater than zero
   Examples: _____

e. having a different value
   Examples: _____

f. integers that can be divided by 2 evenly (with no remainder)
   Examples: _____

g. numbers that are less than zero
   Examples: _____

h. numbers that have exactly two distinct factors: themselves and 1
   Examples: _____

i. numbers that can be divided by a certain number with no remainder
   Examples: _____

j. a figure from 0 through 9 that is used as a placeholder
   Examples: _____

11. consecutive numbers

12. divisible

13. remainder

14. sum

15. product

16. difference

17. quotient

18. absolute value

k. the result of addition
   Examples: _____

l. a whole number left over after division
   Examples: _____

m. the result of subtraction
   Examples:_____

n. can be divided with no remainder
   Examples: _____

o. a number's distance from zero; always a
   positive value
   Examples: _____

p. numbers in a row
   Examples: _____

q. the result of division
   Examples: _____

r. the result of multiplication
   Examples: _____

EQUATIONS AND INEQUALITIES

An **equation** is a statement that contains an equals sign, such as $3x + 5 = 17$.

To solve an equation, you must get the variable x alone on one side of the equals sign and everything else on the other side.

The first step is to put all of the variables on one side of the equation and all of the numbers on the other side, using addition and subtraction. As long as you perform the same operation on both sides of the equals sign, you aren't changing the value of the variable.

Then you can divide both sides of the equation by the coefficient, which is the number in front of the variable. If that number is a fraction, you can multiply everything by its reciprocal.

For example,

$$
\begin{array}{lll}
3x + 5 = 17 & & \\
\underline{ -5 \quad -5} & & \text{Subtract 5 from each side.} \\
3x \quad\ = 12 & & \\
\underline{\div 3 \qquad \div 3} & & \text{Divide each side by 3.} \\
x \quad\ = 4 & &
\end{array}
$$

Always remember the rule of equations:

> Whatever you do to one side of the equation, you must also do to the other side.

The example above was fairly simple. The PSAT 8/9 may test this idea with more complex equations and formulas, though. Just keep trying to isolate the variable in question by undoing the operations that have been done to it. Here's an example.

7

In the equation $T = UVW$, all variables are positive. Which of the following expresses W in terms of the variables T, U, and V?

A) $W = \dfrac{T}{UV}$

B) $W = TUV$

C) $W = T - UV$

D) $W = UV - T$

Here's How to Crack It

The question asks for one variable in an equation in terms of the others. To isolate W, which is multiplied by U and V, divide both sides of the equation by U and V. The result is $\dfrac{T}{UV} = W$. Flip the two sides of this equation to get $W = \dfrac{T}{UV}$. The correct answer is (A).

An **inequality** is any statement with one of these signs:

<	(less than)
>	(greater than)
≤	(less than or equal to)
≥	(greater than or equal to)

You can solve inequalities in the same way you solve equations, with one exception: whenever you multiply or divide an inequality by a negative value, you must change the direction of the sign: < becomes >, and ≤ becomes ≥.

For example,

$$3x + 5 > 17$$

$$\underline{\quad -5 \quad -5 \quad}$$ Subtract 5 from each side.

$$3x \quad > 12$$

$$\underline{\div 3 \qquad \div 3 \quad}$$ Divide each side by 3.

$$x \quad > \ 4$$

In this case, we didn't multiply or divide by a negative value, so the direction of the sign didn't change. However, if we were to divide by a negative value, we would need to change the direction of the sign.

$$-3x + 5 > 15$$

$$\underline{\quad -3 \quad -3 \quad}$$ Subtract 3 from each side.

$$-4x \quad > 12$$

$$\underline{\div -4 \qquad \div -4 \quad}$$ Divide each side by 4.

$$x \quad > \ 4$$

Now let's look at how the PSAT 8/9 may make this more complicated with a question about a range of values.

4

$$8 \geq 2x - 6$$

The inequality above can be expressed as which of the following?

A) $x \leq 2$

B) $x \leq 4$

C) $x \leq 6$

D) $x \leq 7$

Here's How to Crack It

The question asks for an inequality to be solved for a variable. Treat inequalities as you would equations, isolating the variable and performing the same operations on both sides. Start by adding 6 to both sides of the inequality to get $14 \geq 2x$, then divide both sides by 2 to get $7 \geq x$. The answer choices have x on the left side if the inequality, so just flip this to get $x \leq 7$. If there were also an answer of $x \geq 7$ as an option, you'd have to make sure that you flipped the inequality sign properly, but that's not an issue here. The correct answer is (D).

SIMULTANEOUS EQUATIONS

Simultaneous equations occur when you have two equations at the same time. Occasionally, all you have to do is stack the equations, and then add or subtract them, so try that first. Sometimes, it won't get you exactly what you want, but it will get you close to it.

8

$$-c + d = 5$$
$$c + 2d = 13$$

What is the value of c if the solution to the system of equations above is (c, d) ?

A)   1

B)   6

C)   8

D)   18

Here's How to Crack It

The question asks for the value of c in the system of equations. Stacking and adding the equations will not give you the value of c, but it will make the c terms disappear, making it easy to solve for d.

$$\begin{array}{r} -c + d = 5 \\ c + 2d = 13 \\ \hline 3d = 18 \end{array}$$

Now divide both sides by 3 to get $d = 6$. Plug this into the first equation to get $-c + 6 = 5$, then subtract 6 from both sides to get $-c = -1$. Multiplying both sides by -1 gives you $c = 1$. The correct answer is (A).

That was pretty simple, but simultaneous equations on the PSAT 8/9 can be tougher. Let's look at a really challenging one.

22

A debate team takes part in 12 different debates over a season. A win is worth 3 points and a loss is worth 1 point for participation. There are no ties. If the debate team scores a total of 30 points over the season, what is the difference between their number of wins and number of losses for the season?

Here's How to Crack It

The question asks for the difference between wins and losses for a debate team. Read the information in the question carefully to translate it into equations that can be solved. Start with a straightforward piece of information, such as the fact that there were 12 debates. There were only wins and losses, no ties, so represent wins with w and losses with l. You can translate the first sentence as $w + l = 12$. Now you can move on to the points, of which the team scored 30 in total. The team got 3 points for every win, so those points can be represented as $3w$. The team got 1 point for every loss, so those points can be written as $1l$ or just l. This makes the second equation $3w + l = 30$. Since the l term in both equations has no coefficient, that will be the easiest term to eliminate. To do so, multiply the first equation by -1 to get $-w - l = -12$. Now stack and add the equations.

$$
\begin{array}{r}
-w - l = -12 \\
3w + l = 30 \\
\hline
2w = 18
\end{array}
$$

Now divide both sides of the resulting equation by 2 to get $w = 9$. Plug this into the original version of the first equation to get $9 + l = 12$, so $l = 3$. Finally, the question asks for the difference in numbers of wins and losses, so subtract to get $9 - 3 = 6$. The correct answer is 6.

WRITING YOUR OWN EQUATIONS

For the most part, we've been looking at solving equations given to you in questions. That last question, though, required you to create one of your own. The PSAT 8/9 Math sections are testing not only your math skills, but also, and possibly even more important to your score improvement, your reading skills. It is imperative that you read the questions carefully and translate the words in the problem into mathematical symbols.

English	Math Equivalents
is, are, were, did, does, costs	=
what (or any unknown value)	*any variable (x, y, k, b)*
more, sum	+
less, difference	−
of, times, product	× *(multiply)*
ratio, quotient, out of, per	÷ *(divide)*

Sometimes you'll be asked to take a word problem and create equations or inequalities from that information. Usually they will not ask you to solve these equations/inequalities, so if you are able to locate and translate the information in the problem, you have a good shot at getting the correct answer. Always start with the most straightforward piece of information. What is the most straightforward piece of information? Well, that's up to you to decide. Consider the following problem.

3

Drew is distributing water bottles during a marathon. She starts with 3,500 bottles of water and distributes an average of 70 bottles each hour. Which of the following best demonstrates the relationship between the remaining number of water bottles, w, and the amount of time h, in hours, Drew spends distributing water bottles?

A) $w = 3{,}500h - 70$

B) $w = 3{,}500 - 70h$

C) $h = 3{,}500 - 70w$

D) $h = 3{,}500w - 70$

Here's How to Crack It

The question asks for an equation to model a relationship between variables. Start with an easy piece of information—Drew starts with 3,500 bottles of water, and then she gives some away. This means that the correct equation must have 3,500 in it, then some value subtracted from it.

Unfortunately, all the equations have some piece like this, so translate another piece. The variable w is defined as the number of remaining water bottles, so the equation should be set equal to w. Eliminate (C) and (D), as those two are in terms of h. Now determine where the h should go, since that's the only difference between (A) and (B). Drew hands out 70 water bottles per hour, with h representing the number of hours. This means that the equation must include the term $70h$. Eliminate (A). The correct answer is (B).

Now let's look at harder one. The following question has a lot more words and more than one inequality in each answer choice. This makes it even more important to translate one piece at a time and eliminate after each step.

5

A sports memorabilia store sells a number of rare cards, r, for \$20 each. It also sells a number of common cards, c, for \$2 each. On a given day, a sports enthusiast purchases 40 cards for a total of \$296. Which of the following systems of equations illustrates the relationship between r and c ?

A) $\begin{cases} 20r + 2c = (40)(296) \\ r + c = 296 \end{cases}$

B) $\begin{cases} 20r + 2c = (40)(296) \\ r + c = 40 \end{cases}$

C) $\begin{cases} 40r + 40c = 296 \\ 20r = 2c \end{cases}$

D) $\begin{cases} 20r + 2c = 296 \\ r + c = 40 \end{cases}$

Here's How to Crack It

The question asks for the system of equations that represents the situation. Rather than taking the time to create your own system based on the information, then looking to match yours to one of the answer choices, use Bite-Sized Pieces and Process of Elimination. Just translate one small, straightforward piece, such as the fact that 40 cards were sold. Those cards were either rare, represented by r, or common, represented by c. Therefore, one equation must be $r + c = 40$. Eliminate any answers that don't include this equation, such as (A) and (C). Now, rather than translating the other equation needed, take a moment to compare the remaining answers. The difference between the two is that (B) has (40)(296) as the right side of the first equation, while (D) only has 296 there. The number 296 appears in the question as the total amount of money the sports enthusiast spent, so this value should not be multiplied by 40, the number of cards purchased (the enthusiast did NOT spend \$296 on of each of the cards). Thus, you can eliminate (B) and know that the correct answer is (D). Using POE in small pieces this way is very efficient!

Math Basics Drill 2

Answers can be found in Part IV.

3

Which of the following values is 6 less than 5 times itself?

A) 1

B) $\dfrac{3}{2}$

C) 5

D) 6

5

David is trying to take up to 31 unique photos, one for each day in January. He has already taken 4 nature photos and 7 architectural photos. Which of the following inequalities represents all possible values of p if p represents the remaining number of photos David could take over the month of January?

A) $0 \le 31 - (4 + 7) - p$

B) $31 \le p - 11$

C) $0 \ge 31 - (4 + 7) - p$

D) $31 \ge p - 11$

9

If $8(2 - x) = 10 - 5(x + 3)$, what is the value of x ?

A) 1

B) $\dfrac{31}{13}$

C) 7

D) $\dfrac{17}{2}$

7

What value of c is a solution to the equation $-3c - 2 + 9 = c - 2 - 3c$?

A) -9

B) -2

C) 2

D) 9

10

$$2a - b = 11$$
$$4a - b = 7$$

What is the value of a if the solution to the system of equations above is (a, b) ?

A) 4

B) 6

C) -2

D) -15

19

$$-(x^2 - 2) + x^4 + (2x^2 - 8)$$

Which of the following expressions is equivalent to the expression above?

A) $x^4 + x^2 - 6$

B) $x^4 + x^2 - 10$

C) $x^4 - x^2 - 10$

D) $2x^8 - 6$

20

Bill can purchase eight hockey pucks and two water bottles for $22 or twelve hockey pucks and ten water bottles for $54. For his team's hockey practice, Bill needs sixteen water bottles. How much will it cost for Bill to purchase the sixteen water bottles given the above costs?

A) $20

B) $22

C) $48

D) $54

THE COORDINATE PLANE

You will definitely see some questions on the coordinate plane, or *xy*-plane, on the PSAT 8/9. Let's start by covering the basics here. You'll see more advanced concepts in the Advanced Math chapter. So let's just review:

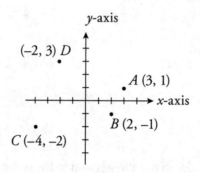

The *x*-axis is the horizontal axis, and the *y*-axis is the vertical axis. Points are given on the coordinate plane with the *x*-coordinate first. Positive *x*-values go to the right, and negative ones go to the left; positive *y*-values go up, and negative ones go down. So point *A* (3, 1) is 3 points to the right on the *x*-axis and 1 point up from the *y*-axis. Point *B* (2, –1) is 2 points to the right on the *x*-axis and 1 point down from the *y*-axis.

Slope is a measure of the steepness of a line on the coordinate plane. On most slope problems, you need to recognize only whether the slope is positive, negative, or zero. A line that goes up and to the right has positive slope; a line that goes down and to the right has negative slope, and a flat line has zero slope. In the figure below, ℓ_1 has positive slope, ℓ_2 has zero slope, and ℓ_3 has negative slope.

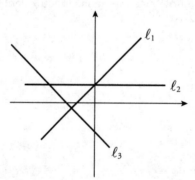

If you do need to calculate the slope, and the graph is drawn for you, here's how: slope $= \dfrac{y_2 - y_1}{x_2 - x_1}$.

The *slope* of a line is equal to $\dfrac{rise}{run}$. To find the slope, take any two points on the lines and count off the distance you need to get from one of these points to the other.

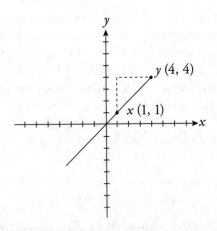

In the graph above, to get from point x to point y, we count up (rise) 3 units, and count over (run) 3 units. Therefore, the slope is $\frac{rise}{run} = \frac{3}{3} = 1$. Always remember to check whether the slope is positive or negative when you use $\frac{rise}{run}$.

If you're not given a figure and you can't draw one easily using the points given, you can find the slope by plugging the coordinates you know into the slope formula. Just remember to plug the numbers into the formula carefully!

Knowing how to find the slope is useful for solving questions about perpendicular and parallel lines. **Perpendicular lines** have slopes that are negative reciprocals of one another. **Parallel lines** have the same slope and no solutions. You may also be given two equations that have infinitely many solutions.

Take a look at an example.

19

$$15x - 12y = 63$$

$$ay + 5x = 21$$

The system of equations above has infinitely many solutions. If a is a constant, what is the value of a ?

A) −12

B) −4

C) −3

D) 3

> **To Infinity...**
> **and Beyond!**
> When given two equations with infinitely many solutions, find a way to make them equal. The equations represent the same line.

Here's How to Crack It

The question asks for the value of a in a system of equations with infinitely many solutions. The equations are in the standard form of a line, $Ax + By = C$, so they represent two lines in the xy-plane. The only way for a system of two lines to have infinitely many solutions is if the two equations represent the same line. The problem is that these two equations don't really look the same. Start by rearranging the terms in the second equation to be in the same order as the first equation. The second equation becomes $5x + ay = 21$. You may notice that $5x$ can be multiplied by 3 to get to $15x$. The same holds true for the right side of the second equation (if you multiply the 21 by 3, you get 63). Therefore, you should multiply the entire second equation by 3 to get it looking more like the first equation. The result is $15x + 3ay = 63$. Now each term can be compared easily, and the $-12y$ in the first equation is equal to the $3ay$ in the second equation. Therefore, $-12y = 3ay$, and you can divide both sides of that equation by $3y$ to get $-4 = a$. The correct answer is (B).

The equation of a line can take multiple forms. The most common of these is known as the **slope-intercept form**. If you know the slope and the y-intercept, you can create the equation of a given line. A slope-intercept equation takes the form $y = mx + b$, where m is the slope and b is the y-intercept.

Here's an example.

3

$$y = \frac{1}{3}x + 6$$

The graph of the equation above in the xy-plane crosses the y-axis at $(0, b)$. What is the value of b ?

A) $\dfrac{1}{6}$

B) $\dfrac{1}{3}$

C) 3

D) 6

Here's How to Crack It

The question asks for the value of b, the y-coordinate of the point where a line crosses the y-axis. This is also known as the y-intercept, and the equation is already in slope-intercept form. The b in $y = mx + b$ corresponds to 6 in the equation in the question, and this is also the b in the point $(0, b)$. Another approach to answer this question is to plug the given point into the equation. The 0 is the x and the b is the y, so the equation becomes $b = \frac{1}{3}(0) + 6 = 0 + 6 = 6$. Either way, the correct answer is (D).

As we saw in question 19 above, another form of the line equation that may show up on the PSAT 8/9 is the **standard form**. In this form, $Ax + By = C$, the slope is $-\dfrac{A}{B}$ and the y-intercept is $\dfrac{C}{B}$. Knowing these shortcuts can help you avoid having to convert a line in standard form to the slope-intercept form.

The **distance formula** looks quite complicated. The easiest way to solve the distance between two points is to connect them and form a triangle. Then use the Pythagorean Theorem. Many times, the triangle formed is one of the common Pythagorean triplets (3-4-5 or 5-12-13).

The **midpoint formula** gives the midpoint of a line segment on the coordinate plane. For example, the line ST has points $S(x_2, y_2)$ and $T(x_2, y_2)$. To find the midpoint of this line segment, simply find the average of the x-coordinates and the y-coordinates. In our example, the midpoint would be $\dfrac{x_1 + x_2}{2}, \dfrac{y_1 + y_2}{2}$.

To find the **point of intersection** of two lines, find a way to set them equal and solve for the variable. If the equations are already in $y = mx + b$ form, set the $mx + b$ part of the two equations equal and solve for x. If the question asks for the value of y, plug the value of x back into either equation to solve for y. It may also be possible to Plug In the Answers (see Chapter 11 for more on this) or graph the equations on your calculator. These skills will also help find the points of intersection between a line and a non-linear graph such as a parabola.

Sometimes, it's a little trickier. Let's look at a difficult question that combines several of the previous concepts.

Questions 10–12 refer to the following information.

Two construction workers are digging holes using shovels and measuring their dig rates to determine who is faster. Both construction workers start in holes below ground level at their assigned dig sites and dig vertically down through the dirt.

The depth below ground level d, in meters (m), that construction worker Elijah has reached in terms of time t, in minutes, after he started digging is described by the function $d(t) = 1.8t + 4.5$.

Construction worker Betty begins in a hole below ground level. Betty's depth below ground level, in m, for the first 5 minutes of digging is described in the table below. Betty's dig rate is constant throughout the competition.

Time (min)	Depth below ground level (m)
0	6.5
1	8.7
2	10.9
3	13.1
4	15.3
5	17.5

Where's question 10?

On the PSAT 8/9, you will often see a set of questions based on shared information. You'll see this content again with question 10 in the next chapter.

11

How long will it take Betty, in minutes, to reach a depth of approximately 19.7 meters below ground level?

A) 5

B) 6

C) 7

D) 8

Here's How to Crack It

The question asks for the time in minutes that it will take Betty to dig 19.7 meters below ground. When dealing with sets of questions, it is important to take the time to find the right information. The chart gives data about Betty. You might be tempted to find the slope and the equation of the line for Betty's progress, but start by ballparking. Based on the chart, Betty is only 17.5 meters below ground at 5 minutes, so the correct answer cannot be 5. The depth of 19.7 meters is not too far below a depth of 17.5 meters, so it is unlikely to take her 3 more minutes to get there, making (D) less probable. Use the numbers on the chart to determine how far Betty digs in one minute. From minute 4 to minute 5, she dug from 15.3 m to 17.5 m, which is 2.2 meters. From minute 5 to minute 6, she'll dig an additional 2.2 meters to reach a depth of 17.5 + 2.2 = 19.7 meters. This is the depth the question asked about, so the correct answer is (B).

Now let's look at one that does require finding the slope.

12

Zeb begins to dig in an additional hole at the same time as Elijah. Zeb's depth below ground level, in m, for the first 5 minutes of digging is described in the table below. If Zeb digs at a constant rate, how many minutes will it take Zeb and Elijah to be at the same depth below ground level?

Time (min)	Depth below ground level (m)
0	6.0
1	7.7
2	9.4
3	11.1
4	12.8
5	14.5

A)   1.7

B)   4.5

C)   10

D)   15

Here's How to Crack It

The question asks for the number of seconds it will take for two workers to dig to the same depth. For Elijah, there is an equation to model his depth: $d(t) = 1.8t + 4.5$. If you had an equation for Zeb's depth, you could set the two equations equal and solve for t. To create that equation, start by using two points on the chart to calculate the slope. Two such points for $(t, d(t))$ are $(1, 7.7)$ and $(2, 9.4)$. The slope can be found with the expression $\frac{y_2 - y_1}{x_2 - x_1}$, which becomes $\frac{9.4 - 7.7}{2 - 1} = \frac{1.7}{1} = 1.7$. The y-intercept is the point at which x (or in this case t) is 0, so that value of y (or in this case $d(t)$) is 6.0. Therefore, the equation for Zeb becomes $d(t) = 1.7t + 6.0$. Since we want to know when the depth of the holes are the same, set the equations equal to each other to get $1.8t + 4.5 = 1.7t + 6.0$. Subtract $1.7t$ from both sides of the equation to get $0.1t + 4.5 = 6.0$. Subtract 4.5 from both sides to get $0.1t = 1.5$, then divide both sides by 0.1 to get $t = 15$. The correct answer is (D).

Math Basics Drill 3

Answers can be found in Part IV.

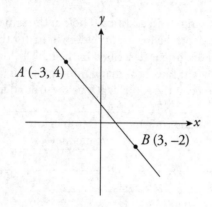

a. How many units do you count up (rise) to get from point *B* to point *A*? _____

b. How many units must you count over (run) to get from point *A* to point *B*? _____

c. What is the slope of the line above? _____
    (Remember, the line is going down to the right, so it must have a negative slope.)

d. What would be the slope of a line parallel to *AB*? _____

e. What would be the slope of a line perpendicular to *AB*? _____

f. What is the distance from point *A* to point *B*? _____

g. What is the midpoint of line segment *AB*? _____

4

$$y = x^2 + 8x + 23$$

What is the value of the *y*-intercept for the above equation when graphed in the *xy*-plane?

A) −8

B) 0

C) 8

D) 23

9

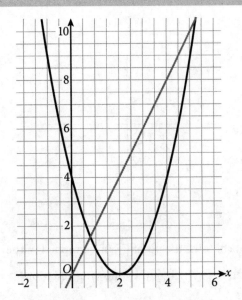

A system of equations is graphed in the *xy*-plane above. How many solutions does the system have?

A) None

B) One

C) Two

D) Three

6

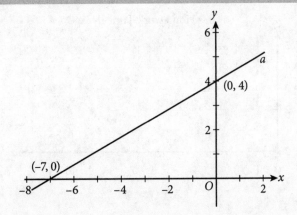

Line *a* is shown in the *xy*-plane above. Assuming line *b* lies parallel to line *a*, which of the following equations could represent line *b*?

A) $y = -\dfrac{7}{4}x - 2$

B) $y = -\dfrac{4}{7}x + 4$

C) $y = \dfrac{4}{7}x + 3$

D) $y = \dfrac{7}{4}x - 6$

9

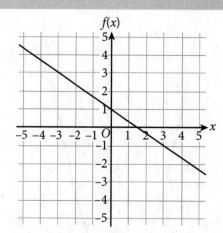

A line that contains the point $\left(\frac{3}{2}, 0\right)$ is graphed in the xy-plane above. Which of the following equations represents the line?

A) $f(x) = -3x + 2$

B) $f(x) = -\frac{3}{2}x - 2$

C) $f(x) = -2x + 3$

D) $f(x) = -\frac{2}{3}x + 1$

17

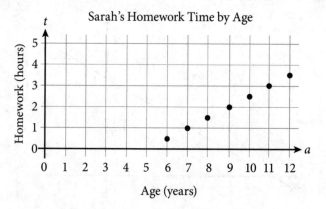

Sarah's parents tracked the amount of time she spent on homework as she grew up. The scatterplot above shows how the amount of time t, in hours, Sarah spent on homework in relation to her age a, in years. Which of the following equations best models this data, where $6 \le a \le 12$?

A) $t = -0.5a - 2.5$

B) $t = -2.5a - 0.5$

C) $t = 0.5a - 2.5$

D) $t = 2.5a - 0.5$

19

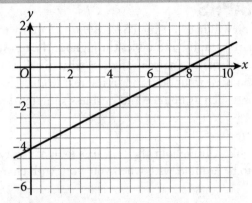

The *xy*-plane above shows a graph of the line $y = tx - r$, where *t* and *r* are constants. What is the value of *r*?

A)   −8

B)   −4

C)   4

D)   8

20

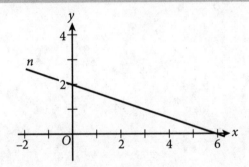

If the graph of line *n* in the *xy*-plane above is represented by the equation $y = mx + c$, where *m* and *c* are constants, which of the following set of inequalities is true about *m* and *c*?

A) $\begin{cases} m < 0 \\ c < -4 \end{cases}$

B) $\begin{cases} 0 < m < 1 \\ c > 0 \end{cases}$

C) $\begin{cases} m > 0 \\ c < 4 \end{cases}$

D) $\begin{cases} -1 < m < 0 \\ c > 0 \end{cases}$

CHARTS AND GRAPHS

Another basic math skill you will need for the PSAT 8/9 is the ability to read charts and graphs. The PSAT 8/9 includes charts, graphs, and tables throughout the test (not just in the Math sections) to present data for students to analyze. The test-writers believe this better reflects what students learn in school and need to understand in the real world. The situations will typically include real-life applications, such as finance and business situations, social science issues, and science.

Since you'll be seeing graphics throughout the test, let's look at the types you may encounter and the skills you'll need to be familiar with when you work with charts and graphs.

The Scatterplot

A scatterplot is a graph with distinct data points, each representing one piece of information. On the scatterplot below, each dot represents the number of televisions sold at a certain price point.

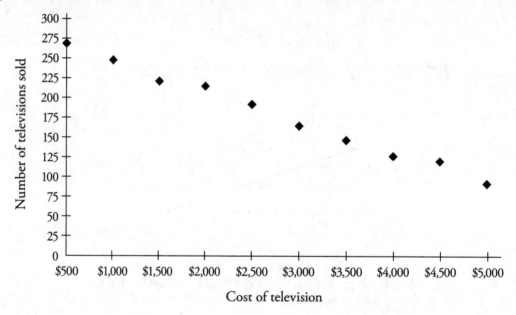

Here's How to Read It

To find the cost of a television when 225 televisions are sold, start at 225 on the vertical axis and draw a horizontal line to the right until you hit a data point. Use the edge of your answer sheet as a straightedge if you have trouble drawing your own straight lines. Once you hit a point, draw a straight line down from it to the horizontal axis and read the number the line hits, which should be $1,500. To determine the number of televisions sold when they cost a certain amount, reverse the steps—start at the bottom, draw up until you hit a point, and then move left until you intersect the vertical axis.

A question may ask you to draw a "line of best fit" on a scatterplot diagram. This is the line that best represents the data. You can use the edge of your answer sheet as a ruler to help you draw a line that goes through most of the data.

The Line Graph

A line graph is similar to a scatterplot in that it shows different data points that relate the two variables. The difference with a line graph, though, is that the points have been connected to create a continuous line.

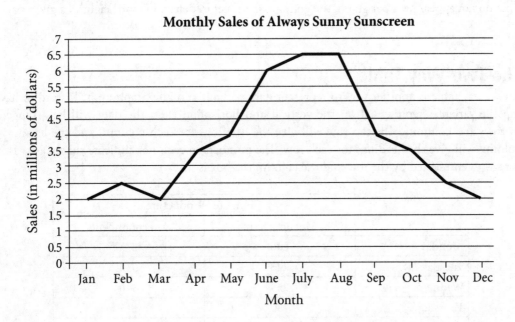

Monthly Sales of Always Sunny Sunscreen

Here's How to Read It

Reading a line graph is very similar to reading a scatterplot. Start at the axis that represents the data given, and draw a straight line up or to the right until you intersect the graph line. Then move left or down until you hit the other axis. For example, in February, indicated by an F on the horizontal axis, Always Sunny Sunscreen had 2.5 million in sales. Make sure to notice the units on each axis. If February sales were only $2.50, rather than $2.5 million, then this company wouldn't be doing very well!

The Bar Graph (or Histogram)

Instead of showing a variety of different data points, a bar graph will show how many items belong to a particular category. If the variable at the bottom is given in ranges, instead of distinct items, the graph is called a histogram, but you read it the same way.

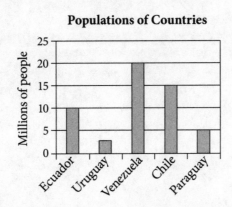

Populations of Countries

Here's How to Read It

The height of each bar corresponds to a value on the vertical axis. In this case, the bar above Chile hits the line that intersects with 15 on the vertical axis, so there are 15 million people in Chile. Again, watch the units to make sure you know what the numbers on the axes represent. On this graph, horizontal lines are drawn at 5-unit intervals, making the graph easier to read. If these lines do not appear on a bar graph, use your answer sheet to determine the height of a given bar.

The Two-Way Table

A two-way table is another way to represent data without actually graphing it. Instead of having the variables represented on the vertical and horizontal axes, the data will be arranged in rows and columns. The top row will give the headings for each column, and the left-most column will give the headings for each row. The numbers in each box indicate the data for the category represented by the row and the column the box is in.

	Computer Production	
	Morning Shift	Afternoon Shift
Monday	200	375
Tuesday	245	330
Wednesday	255	340
Thursday	250	315
Friday	225	360

Here's How to Read It

If you wanted to see the number of computers produced on Tuesday morning, you could start in the Morning Shift column and look down until you found the number in the row that says "Tuesday," or you could start in the row for Tuesday and look to the right until you found the Morning Shift column. Either way, the result is 245. Some tables will give you totals in the bottom row and/or the right-most column, but sometimes you will need to find the totals yourself by adding up all the numbers in each row or in each column. More complicated tables will have more categories listed in rows and/or columns, or the tables may even contain extraneous information.

THE BOX PLOT

A box plot shows data broken into quartiles, as follows:

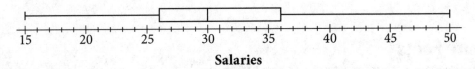

Salaries

Here's How to Read It

Here is what all the parts of the box plot represent.

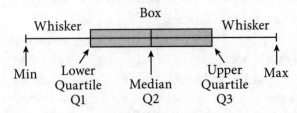

The line in the middle of the box shows the median value of the data, which is 30 in the example above. The "whiskers," which give this figure the alternate name "box-and-whisker plot," represent the highest value on the list with the end of the whisker on the right and the lowest value with the end of the whisker on the left. Thus, the minimum value of this data set is 15, and the maximum is 50. Then the data between the median and these minimum and maximum values is broken into two equal parts on each side, creating four "quartiles." The value halfway between the minimum and the median is the Q1 value on the left side of the box, at about 26, and the value halfway between the maximum and the median is the Q3 value on the right side of the box, at about 36.

The Stem-and-Leaf Plot

A stem-and-leaf plot shows data according to a common first digit.

```
2 | 0 1 7
3 | 2 2 4
4 | 0 1 5 7 7 8
5 | 1 1 4 5 5 7 9
6 | 2 5 8 8 9
7 | 0
```

A book club took a survey of the age, in years, of its members. The data is shown in the stem-and-leaf plot above.

Here's How to Read It

The numbers on the left of the vertical line are the initial digit of each age, and the numbers to the left of the vertical line are the following digits corresponding to the given first digit. This means that the ages of the members of the book club are 20, 21, 27, 32, 32, 34, etc. Questions using stem-and-leaf plots often ask for things like the range of the data, the median of the data, or the probability of selecting a certain number. We will look at all those statistical measures in the Math Techniques chapter.

From a stem-and-leaf plot or a box plot, you can determine the median and range of the set of data. It is also possible to calculate the mode and mean from a stem-and-leaf plot and the interquartile range from a box plot.

Figure Facts

Every time you encounter a figure or graphic on the PSAT 8/9, you should make sure you understand how to read it by checking the following things:

- What are the variables for each axis or the headings for the table?

- What units are used for each variable?

- Are there any key pieces of information (numbers, for example) in the legend of the chart that you should note?

- What type of relationship is shown by the data in the chart? For instance, if the chart includes curves that show an upward slope, then the graph shows a positive association, while curves that show a downward slope show a negative association.

- You can use the edge of your answer sheet as a ruler to help you make sure you are locating the correct data in the graph or to draw a line of best fit if necessary.

GRIDS-INS: THE BASICS

Keep Left

No matter how many digits in your answers, always start gridding in the leftmost column. That way, you'll avoid omitting digits and losing points.

You will see 7 questions on the PSAT 8/9 that ask you to bubble in a numerical answer on a grid, rather than answer a multiple-choice question. These Grid-In questions are arranged in a loose order of difficulty, meaning they start easier and get progressively harder, and can be solved according to the methods outlined for the multiple-choice problems on the test. Don't worry that there are no answer choices—your approach is the same.

The only difficulty with Grid-In questions is getting used to the way in which you are asked to answer the question. For each question, you'll have a grid like the following:

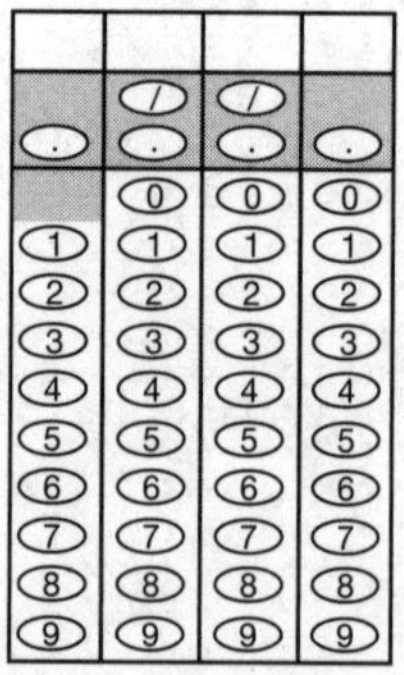

We recommend that you write the answer on top of the grid to help you bubble, but it's important to know that the scoring machine reads only the bubbles. If you bubble incorrectly, the computer will consider the answer to be incorrect.

Here are the basic rules of gridding:

1. If your answer uses fewer than four boxes, you can grid it anywhere you like. To avoid confusion, we suggest that you start at the leftmost box. For example,

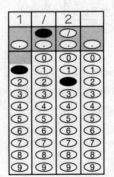

2. You can grid your answer as either a fraction or a decimal, *if* the fraction will fit. You can grid and answer of .5 as either .5 or $\frac{1}{2}$.

or

Relax

If your answer is a fraction and it fits in the grid (fraction bar included), don't reduce it. Why bother? You won't get an extra point for doing so. However, if your fraction doesn't fit, reduce it or turn it into a decimal on your calculator.

3. You do not need to reduce your fractions, *if* the fraction will fit. If your answer is $\frac{2}{4}$, you can grid it as $\frac{2}{4}$, $\frac{1}{2}$, or 0.5.

or   or

4. If you have a decimal that will not fit in the spaces provided, you *must grid as many places as will fit.*

If your answer is $\frac{2}{3}$, you can grid it as $\frac{2}{3}$, .666, or .667, but .66 or 0.66 are *not* acceptable.

You do not need to round your numbers, so we suggest that you don't. There's no reason to give yourself a chance to make a mistake if you don't have to.

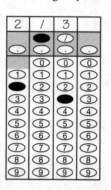 or 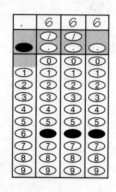 or

5. You cannot grid mixed numbers. Convert all mixed numbers to ordinary fractions.

If your answer is $2\frac{1}{2}$, you must convert it to $\frac{5}{2}$ or 2.5; otherwise the computer will read your 2 1/2 as 21/2.

Don't Mix

Never grid in a mixed number. Change it into an improper fraction or decimal. To convert mixed fraction into improper fractions, all you have to do is multiply the denominator with the whole number in from of the fraction, then add that product to the numerator, and finally put that number over the denominator you started with.

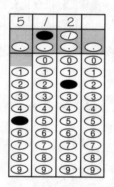 or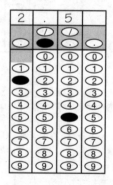

6. You can't grid π, square roots, variables, or negative numbers, so if you get an answer with one of those terms, you've made a mistake. Reread the final question and check your work.

Math Basics Drill 4

Answers can be found in Part IV.

11

The function $f(x) = -3x - 2$ is graphed in the *xy*-plane. Line *b* is perpendicular to function *f*. What is the slope of line *b* ?

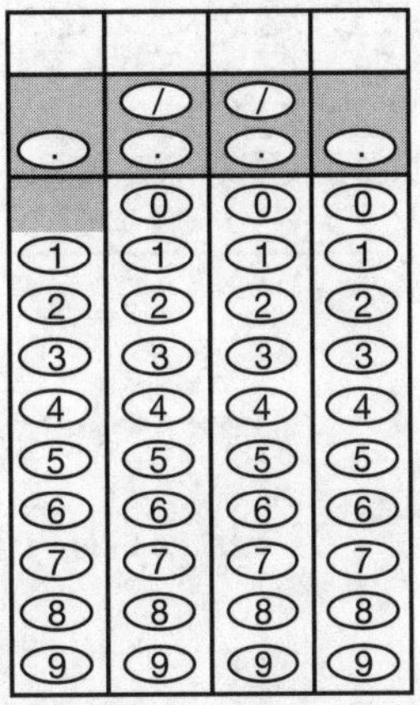

12

What value of *g* satisfies the equation $-8(g - 3) = -2g + 6$?

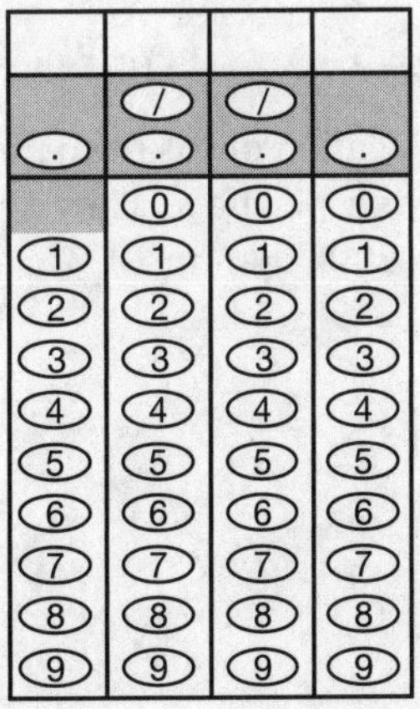

13

If $5x^2 = 125$, what could be the value of $5x$?

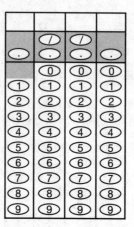

3

Average Gas Prices

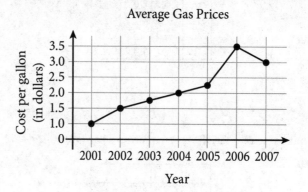

The average cost of a gallon of gas from 2000 to 2007 is displayed in the line graph above. How much more did a gallon of gas cost in 2007 than in 2003, according to the line graph?

A) $1.00

B) $1.25

C) $1.75

D) $3.00

Questions 14 and 15 refer to the following information.

John was interested in the effect caffeine had on his reading speed and graphed the relationship between caffeine intake, in milligrams per hour, and his reading speed, in pages per hour, in the scatterplot below.

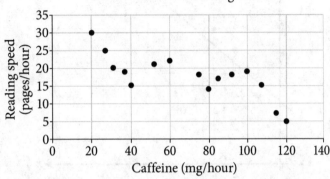

Caffeine Intake versus Pages Read

14

Based on the data John collected, over which of the following intervals is there a positive relationship between his caffeine intake, in milligrams per hour, and his reading speed, in pages per hour?

A) 40–60 and 60–75

B) 40–60 and 80–100

C) 25–40 and 40–60

D) 25–40, 60–80, and 100–120

15

John wants to estimate what his reading speed would be, in pages per hour, if he were to consume 45 mg of caffeine in an hour. Using the trend that he observed between 40 and 60 milligrams per hour, which of the following is closest to the reading speed, in pages per hour, that John can expect?

A) 13

B) 15

C) 17

D) 20

16

A data set showing the relationship between two variables is graphed in the xy-plane to produce the scatterplot below. A line of best fit is generated and is shown on the graph.

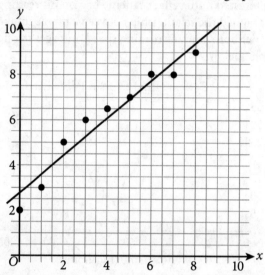

How much greater is the y-value of the data point at $x = 4$ than the y-value of the best fit line at the same x-value?

A) 12.5

B) 6.5

C) 6.0

D) 0.5

23

Charlie uses apple juice and cherry juice to make a punch for his birthday party. The expression $1.9a + 2.2c = 13.9$ models the recipe Charlie uses to make the punch, where a and c are the volumes, in liters, of apple juice and cherry juice, respectively. How many liters of cherry juice does Charlie need for the recipe if he uses 5 liters of apple juice?

Summary

o The Math sections are arranged in a loose Order of Difficulty, which can make it easier to spot the less difficult problems. However, remember that the test-writers' idea of "easier" problems is not necessarily the same as your idea. Let your Personal Order of Difficulty be your guide.

o Write in your test booklet to set up problems, and then use your calculator (when allowed) to figure out solutions. And remember to type carefully—your calculator won't check for mistakes.

o Review basic definitions again before the test to make sure you don't get stuck on the "little words."

o To solve equations for a variable, isolate the variable. Make sure you perform the same operations on both sides of the equation.

o Inequalities can be worked just like equations, until you have to multiply or divide by a negative number. Then you need to flip the inequality sign.

o To solve simultaneous equations, simply add or subtract the equations. If you don't have the answer, look for multiples of your solutions. When the simultaneous equation question asks for a single variable and addition and subtraction don't work, try to make something disappear. Multiply the equations by a constant to make the coefficient(s) of the variable(s) you want go to zero when the equations are added or subtracted.

o When writing a system of equations, start with the most straightforward piece of information.

o You can also use the equations in the answer choices to help you narrow down the possibilities for your equations. Eliminate any answers in which an equation doesn't match your equation.

o Parallel lines have the same slope and no solutions. If two lines have the same slope and infinitely many solutions, they are actually the same line. Perpendicular lines have slopes that are negative reciprocals of one another.

o Rather than worrying about the distance formula, connect the two points and make the resulting line the hypotenuse of a right triangle. Then you can use the Pythagorean Theorem to find the distance.

- The coordinates of the midpoint of a line segment with endpoints (x_1, y_1) and (x_2, y_2) will be $\dfrac{x_1 + x_2}{2}, \dfrac{y_1 + y_2}{2}$.

- When you encounter charts, carefully check the chart for information you should note, and remember that you can use your answer sheet as a ruler to help you locate information or to draw a line of best fit.

- When doing Grid-In questions, be sure to keep to the left, and don't bother reducing fractions if they fit in the allotted spaces.

Chapter 11
Math Techniques

In the previous chapter, we mentioned that one of the keys to doing well on the PSAT 8/9 is to have a set of test-specific problem-solving skills. This chapter discusses some powerful strategies, which—though you may not use them in school—are specifically designed to get you points on the PSAT 8/9. Learn them well!

PLUGGING IN

One of the most powerful problem-solving skills on the PSAT 8/9 is a technique we call Plugging In. Plugging In will turn nasty algebra problems into simple arithmetic and help you through the particularly twisted problems that you'll often see on the PSAT 8/9. There are several varieties of Plugging In, each suited to a different kind of question.

Plugging In Your Own Numbers

The problem with doing algebra is that it's just too easy to make a mistake.

> Whenever you see a problem with variables in the answer choices, use Plugging In.

Start by picking a number for the variable in the problem (or for more than one variable, if necessary), solve the problem using your number, and then see which answer choice gives you the correct answer.

Take a look at the following problem.

20

If a quantity c is decreased by 35%, which of the following is equivalent to the resulting value?

A) 65c

B) 35c

C) 0.65c

D) 0.35c

When to Plug In
- phrases like "in terms of" or "equivalent form" in the question
- variables in the question and/or answers choices

Here's How to Crack It

The question asks for the result of decreasing an unknown value by 35%. There is a variable in the answer choices, so Plugging In can help you make more sense of the calculations here. A great number to plug in for percent questions is 100, as any percent taken of 100 will just be the number of the percent. This means that 35% of 100 is 35. If 100 *is decreased* by 35, the result is 100 − 35 = 65. This is the target number, so circle it. Next plug in 100 for c in the answer choices to see which one matches the target. Choice (A) becomes 65(100) = 6,500, which doesn't match the target. Eliminate (A). Choice (B) becomes 35(100) = 3,500, which also can be eliminated. Choice (C) becomes 0.65(100) = 65. This matches the target, so keep it, but check (D) just in case. Choice (D) becomes 0.35(100) = 35, which is the amount of the decrease, not the resulting value after the decrease. Using Plugging In helped you avoid all the traps in (A), (B), and (D). Now you know that the correct answer is (C).

As you can see, Plugging In can turn messy algebra questions into more straightforward arithmetic questions. This technique is especially powerful when the PSAT 8/9 asks you to find the equivalent form of an expression.

5

Which of the following is an equivalent form of the expression $x^2 + 15x - 54$?

A) $(x + 3)(x - 18)$

B) $(x - 3)(x + 18)$

C) $(x - 9)(x + 6)$

D) $(x + 9)(x - 6)$

Here's How to Crack It

The question asks for an equivalent form of an expression. We looked at factoring in a previous question, but looking at the answer choices shows that there is room for mistakes with the signs on this one. Another approach to try is Plugging In. Pick a small and simple value to work with, such as $x = 2$. The original expression becomes $2^2 + 15(2) - 54 = 4 + 30 - 54 = 34 - 54 = -20$. Circle this target value, then you are ready to move on to the answer choices. Replace all those x's with 2's to determine which answer equals the target of -20. Choice (A) becomes $(2 + 3)(2 - 18) = 5(-16) = -80$. This doesn't match your target, so eliminate (A). Choice (B) becomes $(2 - 3)(2 + 18) = (-1)(20) = -20$. This works, but don't stop there! Remember to check all four answer choices when plugging in, in case more than one of them works. Choice (C) becomes $(2 - 9)(2 + 6) = (-7)(8) = -56$, and (D) becomes $(2 + 9)(2 - 6) = (11)(-4) = -44$. Neither matches the target, so you know that the correct answer is (B).

> **Plugging In: Quick Reference**
> - When you see *in terms of* or *equivalent form* and there are variables in the answer choices, you can use Plugging In.
> - Pick your own number for an unknown in the problem.
> - Do the necessary math to find the answer you're shooting for, which is the target number. Circle the target number.
> - Use POE to eliminate every answer that doesn't match the target number.

Plugging In is such a great technique because it turns hard algebra problems into medium and sometimes even easy arithmetic questions. Remember this when you're thinking of your POOD and looking for questions to do among the hard ones; if you see variables in the answers, there's a good chance it's one to try.

Don't worry too much about what numbers you choose to plug in; just plug in easy numbers (small numbers like 2, 5, or 10 or numbers that make the arithmetic easy, like 100 if you're looking for a percent). Also, be sure your numbers fit the conditions of the questions (for example, if they say $x \leq 11$, don't plug in 12).

What If There's No Variable?

Sometimes you'll see a problem that doesn't contain an *x*, *y*, or *z*, but which contains a hidden variable. If your answers are percents or fractional parts of some unknown quantity (total number of marbles in a jar, total miles to travel in a trip), try Plugging In.

Take a look at this problem.

9

Sam is making conical party hats for her daughter's birthday party. She makes one size for adults and one size for children, both of which have the same height. If the radius of the child-sized hats is one-third that of the adult-sized hats, then the volume of an adult-sized hat is how many times the volume of a child-sized hat?

A) 16

B) 9

C) 2

D) $\frac{1}{3}$

Here's How to Crack It

The question asks for a relationship between the volumes of the two hats. There is not much geometry on the PSAT 8/9, but there is a handy reference box at the start of each Math section. The formula for the volume of a cone is listed there as $V = \pi\frac{1}{3}r^2h$. There are no variables in the question, but there is some missing information. If you knew the height and radius of the adult-sized hat, you could determine the height and radius of the child-sized hat and easily compare the volumes. Whenever you need some missing information to solve a problem, see if you can plug it in! Both hats have the same height, so plug in $h = 6$ (using a value divisible by 3 will help with the fraction later). The radius of the child-sized hat is one-third that of the adult-sized hat, so make the adult $r = 9$ and the child $r = 3$. Plug these numbers into the formula to find that the volume of an adult-sized hat is $V = \frac{1}{3}\pi(9)^26 = \frac{6}{3}\pi(81) = 162\pi$. The volume of the child-sized hat is $V = \frac{1}{3}\pi(3)^26 = \frac{6}{3}\pi(9) = 18\pi$. To find *how many times* the adult hat is compared to the child-sized one, divide the volume of the adult one by the volume of the child one to get $\frac{162\pi}{18\pi} = 9$. The correct answer is (B).

MEANING IN CONTEXT

Some questions, instead of asking you to come up with an equation, just want you to recognize what a part of the equation stands for. It sounds like a simple enough task, but when you look at the equation, they have made it really hard to see what is going on. For this reason, Meaning in Context questions are a great opportunity to plug in real numbers and start to see how the equation really works!

First things first, though, you want to think about your POOD. Does this question fit into your pacing goals? It might take a bit of legwork to get an answer, and you may need that time to go collect points on easier, quicker questions.

If this question does fit into your pacing plan, you should read carefully, label everything you can in the equation, and POE to get rid of any answer choices that are clearly on the wrong track. Then, it's time to plug some of your own numbers in to see what is going on in there.

Here's one that is part of a set with a question we already worked on.

Two construction workers are digging holes using shovels and measuring their dig rates to determine who is faster. Both construction workers start in holes below ground level at their assigned dig sites and dig vertically down through the dirt.

The depth below ground level d, in meters (m), that construction worker Elijah has reached in terms of time t, in minutes, after he started digging is described by the function $d(t) = 1.8t + 4.5$.

Construction worker Betty begins in a hole below ground level. Betty's depth below ground level, in m, for the first 5 minutes of digging is described in the table below. Betty's dig rate is constant throughout the competition.

Time (min)	Depth below ground level (m)
0	6.5
1	8.7
2	10.9
3	13.1
4	15.3
5	17.5

> **Déjà vu?**
> You may remember Elijah, Betty, and Zeb from the previous chapter. This is the final question that belongs to this set.

10

Which of the following is the best description of the number 4.5 in the function $d(t) = 1.8t + 4.5$?

A) The depth below ground level, in meters, of Elijah's hole at the beginning of the competition

B) The depth below ground level, in meters, of Elijah's hole 4.5 minutes after digging begins

C) Elijah's dig rate, in meters per minute, at the beginning of the competition

D) Elijah's dig rate, in meters per minute, 4.5 minutes after digging begins

Here's How to Crack It

The question asks for the meaning of a number in a function. As with all sets, the first place to start is to determine where to find the information that you need. The function is in the introductory text, and it refers to Elijah's digging speed. Start by underlining the number in the equation that the question refers to, which is 4.5. Then label as much of the equation as possible to determine what everything represents. The depth is represented by d, so label the left side of the equation "depth." Time is represented by t, so label the t as "time." The number 4.5 is neither of these, so plugging in some numbers may help to determine what is happening here. Choice (A) refers to the depth *at the beginning of the competition*, or when $t = 0$. Plug this value into the equation to get $d(0) = 1.8(0) + 4.5 = 0 + 4.5 = 4.5$. This matches the value you underlined in the equations, so (A) is true. If you are not sure about this, you can always check the other answers to see if you can eliminate them. Choice (B) refers to the depth after 4.5 minutes, which cannot also be 4.5, since that's the depth at 0 minutes. Eliminate (B). Choices (C) and (D) both refer to *rate, in meters per second*. Slope relates to rate of change. Looking at the equation, you may have noticed that it is in slope-intercept form, $y = mx + b$. In this form, the slope is m, so the slope (and the rate of change) is 1.8, not 4.5. Therefore, you can eliminate (C) and (D). The correct answer is (A).

Here are the steps for using Plugging In to solve Meaning in Context questions:

Meaning In Context

1. Read the question carefully. Make sure you know which part of the equation you are being asked to identify.

2. Use your pencil to label the parts of the equation you can identify.

3. Eliminate any answer choices that clearly describe the wrong part of the equation, or go against what you have labeled.

4. Plug in! Use your own numbers to start seeing what is happening in the equation.

5. Use POE again, using the information you learned from plugging in real numbers, until you can get it down to one answer choice. Or, get it down to as few choices as you can, and guess.

Math Techniques Drill 1

Answers can be found in Part IV.

8

$$V = \pi r^2 h$$

The formula for the volume, V, of a cylinder is given above, where r is the radius of the cylinder and h is the height of the cylinder. Which of the following gives the height of the cylinder in terms of its volume and radius?

A) $h = \pi V r^2$

B) $h = \dfrac{\pi r^2}{V}$

C) $h = \dfrac{\pi V}{r^2}$

D) $h = \dfrac{V}{\pi r^2}$

9

Jean calculates how much money she spends on her dog Patches, and the results are shown below.

Expenses for Patches

Expense	Average Cost
dog food	$20 per week
dog walker	$30 per week

On top of these costs, Jean also pays an annual municipal licensing fee of $55. The cost, P, of caring for Patches for a given number of weeks, w, in the year can be calculated using the equation $P = 55 + (20 + 30)w$. When this function is graphed in the xy-plane, what does the slope represent?

A) The cost of food and dog-walking per week

B) The cost of licensing and food for a year

C) The total cost of care per week

D) The cost of licensing for a year

4

James joins a local billiards club. The club charges a monthly membership fee of $15 and each hour of play costs $1.50. Which of the expressions below shows James's monthly cost at the billiards club when he plays for h hours?

A) $(15 + h)1.50$

B) $(15 + h)0.50$

C) $0.50h + 15$

D) $1.50h + 15$

10

$$\text{Albert: } t = 9h$$

$$\text{Buster: } t = 3h$$

The equations above show the number of trees, t, chopped per hour, h, by two lumberjacks, Albert and Buster. Based on these equations, which of the following statements is true?

A) The rate at which Buster chopped trees per hour decreased at a slower rate than the rate at which Albert chopped trees per hour.

B) The rate at which Albert chopped trees per hour decreased at a slower rate than the rate at which Buster chopped trees per hour.

C) For every hour of chopping, the number of trees Albert chopped was one-third as many as the number of trees Buster chopped.

D) For every hour of chopping, the number of trees Buster chopped was one-third as many as the number of trees Albert chopped.

17

The power P, in watts, of an electrical circuit can be calculated using the formula $P = \dfrac{V^2}{R}$, where V is the voltage of the circuit, in volts, and R is the resistance of the circuit, in ohms. Assuming that the voltage does not change, what is the effect on the power when the resistance is multiplied by a factor of 2 ?

A) It is divided by 2.

B) It is divided by 4.

C) It is multiplied by 2.

D) It is multiplied by 4.

19

Research scientists are testing the effect of a new antibiotic on bacterial growth. They start with a colony of 1,500 bacteria and take counts every 10 minutes for an hour, as shown in the table below.

Bacterial Count Over Time
Following Antibiotic Treatment

Minutes (m)	Number of bacteria (b)
10	1,390
20	1,280
30	1,170
40	1,060
50	950
60	840

Which of the following represents the best interpretation of the y-intercept of the line created when these data points are plotted in the xy-plane if minutes, m, are plotted on the x-axis and number of bacteria, b, are plotted on the y-axis?

A) The number of bacteria at the start of the experiment

B) The rate at which bacteria is decreasing every 10 minutes

C) The number of intervals for which the number of bacteria is decreasing

D) The number of bacteria 60 minutes after the experiment begins

20

In the equation $F = 5(g + 2) - 3$, which of the following gives the value of g in terms of F?

A) $\dfrac{F-2}{5}$

B) $\dfrac{F+3}{5}$

C) $\dfrac{F-2}{5} + 3$

D) $\dfrac{F+3}{5} - 2$

PLUGGING IN THE ANSWERS (PITA)

You can also plug in when the answer provided to a problem is an actual value, such as 2, 4, 10, or 20. Why would you want to do a lot of complicated algebra to solve a problem, when the answer is right there on the page? All you have to do is figure out which choice it is.

How can you tell which is the correct answer? Try every choice until you find the one that works. Even if this means you have to try all four choices, PITA is still a fast and reliable means of getting the right answer.

If you work strategically, however, you almost never need to try all four answers. If the question asks for either the greatest or the least answer, start there. Otherwise, start with one of the middle answer choices. If that answer works, you're done. If the answer you started with was too big, try a smaller answer. If the answer you started with was too small, try a bigger answer. You can almost always find the answer in two or three tries this way. Let's try PITA on the following problem.

> **PITA = Plugging In the Answers**
>
> Don't try to solve problems like this by writing equations and solving for variables. Plugging In the Answers lets you use arithmetic instead of algebra, so you're less likely to make errors.

3

Lauren and Jolean are gardeners building plant containers in their local community garden. For every plant container, there are at most 110 seeds but no less than 70 seeds. If they build 3 plant containers, which of the following could be the total number of seeds in the 3 containers?

A) 465

B) 345

C) 225

D) 105

Here's How to Crack It

The question asks for the number of seeds that could be in the 3 containers. Label the answers as "seeds," and start somewhere in the middle. Try (B), 345 seeds. Divided among 3 containers, this would be 345 ÷ 3 = 115 seeds per container. This is outside the range of 70 to 110 seeds per container, so eliminate (B). The value was too large, so try (C) next. Divided among 3 containers, there would be 225 ÷ 3 = 75 seeds per container. Since this is within the range of seeds per container, you can stop here. The correct answer is (C), and you didn't even need to set up an inequality to solve!

Neat, huh? Let's try one more.

9

Given the equations $-a + 4b = 8$ and $2a + 4b = 20$, what is the value of a if (a, b) is the solution to the system of equations?

A) -12

B) 3

C) 4

D) 12

Here's How to Crack It

The question asks for the value of a in the system of equations. We already looked at how to solve systems, but let's try this one using PITA. Label the answers as a, and start in the middle with (C), 4. Plug this value of a into both equations and solve for b.

$$
\begin{array}{cc}
-4 + 4b = 8 & 2(4) + 4b = 20 \\
4b = 12 & 4b = 12 \\
b = 3 & b = 3
\end{array}
$$

Both equations yield the same value for b, so we've found the correct value of a. Always be on the look-out for opportunities to plug in or plug in the answers as you do your PSAT 8/9 practice. Once you get good at it, you can decide on any test question which way is faster—solving or Plugging In.

Math Techniques Drill 2

Answers can be found in Part IV.

3

What is the value of z given the equation $4(z + 3) - 6 = 5(z - 1)$?

A) 11

B) 7

C) 2

D) –2

6

If $\dfrac{7 - x}{x + 2} = \dfrac{5}{4}$, and $x \neq -2$, what is the value of x ?

A) 2

B) 3

C) 9

D) 27

9

Which of the following is a solution to the equation $p^2 + 20p + 75 = 0$?

A) –75

B) –15

C) 0

D) 20

12

Gail's homemade iced tea is a combination of green tea and raspberry purée. If the green tea and raspberry purée are in a ratio of 23 : 7, and a pitcher of iced tea can hold 900 mL, what is the amount of green tea, in mL, that Gail needs to make a pitcher of iced tea?

A) 63

B) 207

C) 210

D) 690

15

Which if the following is a solution to the equation
$\frac{7}{4}(x + 8) = 56$?

A) The equation has no solution.

B) 24

C) 32

D) 40

17

Strawberry	Chocolate Coating (g)
1	17.8
2	22.5
3	19.1
4	20.6
5	16.3
6	18.9
7	?

For more information on dealing with range and mean, see the next section of this chapter.

Chris is coating strawberries in chocolate for dessert. The table above displays 6 strawberries and their corresponding amounts of chocolate coating in grams (g). If Chris adds a 7th strawberry coated in chocolate, what is one possible value for the amount of chocolate coating that would decrease the mean of the data but increase the range?

A) 15.8 g

B) 17.1 g

C) 19.2 g

D) 23.1 g

18

In the expression $x^2 + cx - 8$, c is an integer. If the expression can be rewritten as the equivalent expression $(x - c)(x + 4)$, which of the following is the value of c ?

A) 4

B) 2

C) –2

D) –4

DATA ANALYSIS

In the calculator-allowed Math section (Section 4), there will be questions that will ask you to work with concepts such as averages, percentages, and unit conversions. Luckily, The Princeton Review has you covered! The rest of this chapter will give you techniques and strategies to help you tackle these questions.

Averages and $T = AN$

You probably remember the **average** formula from math class, which says Average (arithmetic mean) = $\dfrac{\text{total}}{\text{number of things}}$. However, the PSAT 8/9 will not always ask you to take a simple average. Of the three parts of an average problem—the average, the total, and the number of things—you're often given the average and the number of things, and finding the total will be the key to solving the question.

> **Total**
>
> When calculating averages, always find the total. It's the one piece of information that PSAT 8/9 loves to withhold.

If you multiply both sides of the above equation by # of things, you get (Average)(# of things) = total. It's easier to remember this as

$$T = AN$$

or, Total = Average × Number of Things. Once you know the total, you'll have the key information needed to finish solving the question.

Let's try this example.

8

12.0, 12.5, 13.0, 13.5, 14.0

The volumes, in milliliters, of five water bottles are shown above. What is the average volume, in milliliters, of the five bottles?

A) 14.0

B) 13.0

C) 12.0

D) 2.0

Here's How to Crack It

The question asks for the average volume of the five listed water bottle volumes. Use $T = AN$ to calculate the average. The *number of things* is 5, and the *total* of the 5 volumes is $T = 12.0 + 12.5 + 13.0 + 13.5 + 14 = 65$. Plug these values into the formula to get $65 = A(5)$, then divide both sides by 5 to get $13 = A$. You may also have noticed that since the 5 numbers are equally spread out by 0.5, the middle value will also be the average. Either way, the correct answer is (B).

Median

Another concept that is often tested along with average is median.

The **median** of a group of numbers is the number in the middle, just as the "median" is the large divider in the middle of a road. To find the median, here's what you do:

- First, put the elements in the group in numerical order from lowest to highest.
- If the number of elements in your group is odd, find the number in the middle. That's the median.
- If you have an even number of elements in the group, find the two numbers in the middle and calculate their average (arithmetic mean).

Try this on the following problem.

> **Finding a Median**
> To find the median of a set containing an even number of items, take the average of the two middle numbers after putting the numbers in order.

19

A baseball statistician analyzed 21 different games for the total number of runs scored by a baseball team. The distribution of the runs scored in each game is displayed in the frequency table below.

Runs scored	Frequency
0	3
1	4
2	2
3	4
4	2
5	1
6	3
7	0
8	1
9	0
10	1

What is the median number of runs scored of these games?

A) 2

B) 3

C) 4

D) 5

Here's How to Crack It

The question asks for the median number of runs based on the chart. The PSAT 8/9 will often make medians more difficult to calculate by putting the data in a chart or graph rather than in a list. On a frequency chart such as this one, there were three games that the team scored 0 runs, then 4 that the team scored 1 run, and on and on. Rather than listing out all 21 numbers, figure out which number would be in the middle if you did list them out. It would be the 11th number, as there would be 10 numbers before it and 10 after it. The first 7 numbers on the list are 0 or 1, then the 8th and 9th are 2. This means that the 10th through 13th numbers are 3, making the 11th number, and the median, 3. The correct answer is (B).

Mode and Range

Two more statistical concepts you may see on the PSAT 8/9 are mode and range, and they can often appear in the same question.

The **mode** of a group of numbers is the number that appears the most. (Remember: mode sounds like most.) To find the mode of a group of numbers, simply see which element appears the greatest number of times.

The **range** of a list of numbers is the difference between the greatest number on the list and the least number on the list. For the list 4, 5, 5, 6, 7, 8, 9, 10, 20, the greatest number is 20 and the least is 4, so the range is 20 − 4 = 16.

Let's look at a problem:

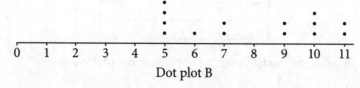
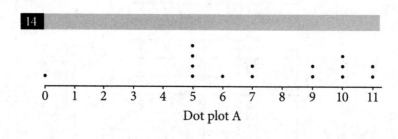

Dot plot A has 15 data points, and one of the data points is considered an outlier. Dot plot B has the 14 data points representing the same data as plot A without the outlier. Which of the following statements accurately describes the two dot plots?

A) The range of dot plot A is equal to the range of dot plot B.

B) The median of dot plot A is equal to the median of dot plot B.

C) The mode of dot plot A is equal to the mode of dot plot B.

D) The mean of dot plot A is equal to the mean of dot plot B.

Here's How to Crack It

The question asks for a description of the two dot plots, and all the answers contain statistics about the data. When given many options for data analysis, start with the easier ones and use POE. On a dot plot, the easiest thing to see is mode, as that will be the number with the most dots above it. On both dot plots, there are 4 dots at the value of 5, and no other values has 4 or more dots. This means that the mode of both dot plots is equal, making (C) the answer. If you aren't sure, you can check out the other measures. Range is the next easiest one to calculate. The range of dot plot A is 11 − 0 = 11, but the range of dot plot B is 11 − 5 = 6. Therefore, the ranges are not equal and (A) can be eliminated. The median of dot plot A will be the middle, or 8th, number. This is 7. The median of dot plot B will be the average of the 7th and 8th numbers, since there are an even number of numbers. The 7th number is 7, and the 8th number is 9, so the median of dot plot B is 8. This eliminates (B). The mean or average is the total divided by the number of things. Both lists will have the same total, as only the value of 0 is different. However, the total in A will be divided by 15 to get the average, while the total in B will only be divided by 14. This makes the average of A less than that of B, so eliminate (D). The correct answer is (C).

Rates

Rate is a concept related to averages. Cars travel at an average speed. Work gets done at an average rate. Because the ideas are similar, you can use Distance = Rate × Time ($D = RT$) or Work = Rate × Time ($W = RT$) to find the total distance traveled or work done.

Here's a simple example:

Problem: If a mover can load boxes onto a truck at a rate of 2 every 7 minutes, how long will it take him, in minutes, to load 37 boxes onto the truck?

Solution: Use the formula $W = RT$ to calculate the mover's time. The W, or work, is 37 boxes, and the rate is $\dfrac{2 \text{ boxes}}{7 \text{ minutes}}$, so the formula becomes $37 = \dfrac{2}{7}T$. Multiply both sides by $\dfrac{7}{2}$ to get $\dfrac{7}{2}(37) = T$, or $T = 129.5$ minutes.

Now let's look at a rate question.

23

Gabriel and David are assigned to clean a certain number of whiteboards during weekend detention. If Gabriel works alone, he can clean 7 boards per half-hour session. If David works alone, he can clean 5 boards per half-hour session. If the supervising teacher assigns them to work together in half–hour sessions, how many white boards will they clean in 2 hours?

Here's How to Crack It

The question asks for the number of whiteboard Gabriel and David will clean in two hours. Use the formula $W = RT$ to find the answer. They are working together, so their combined rate is $5 + 7 = 12$ boards in one half-hour session. Multiply this by two to get the combined rate: 24 whiteboards per hour. Now that the units of time match, plug the values of $R = 24$ and $T = 2$ into the formula to get $W = (24)(2) = 48$. The correct answer is 48.

PROBABILITY

One topic that is often tested with two-way tables is probability. Probability refers to the chance that an event will happen, and it is given as a percent or a fractional value between 0 and 1, inclusive. A probability of 0 means that the event will never happen; a probability of 1 means that it is certain to happen.

$$\text{Probability} = \frac{\text{number of outcomes you want}}{\text{number of possible outcomes}}$$

For instance, if you have a die with faces numbered 1 to 6, what is the chance of rolling a 2?

There is one face with the number 2 on it, out of 6 total faces. Therefore, the probability of rolling a 2 is $\frac{1}{6}$.

What is the chance of rolling an even number on one roll of this die? There are 3 faces of the die with an even number (the sides numbered 2, 4, and 6) out of a total of 6 faces. Therefore, the probability of rolling an even number is $\frac{3}{6}$, or $\frac{1}{2}$.

Let's look at how this concept will be test on the PSAT 8/9.

7

Number of cars owned in lifetime	Number of employees
0	25
1–2	110
3–4	120
More than 4	45

The data table above shows the results of a survey of 300 employees of a car dealership who were asked how many cars they had owned in their lifetimes. What is the probability that a randomly-selected employee had owned 3–4 cars?

A)   0.40

B)   0.20

C)   0.15

D)   0.08

Here's How to Crack It

The question asks for a probability based on a chart. The definition of probability is

$\dfrac{\text{number of outcomes you want}}{\text{number of possible outcomes}}$, and the question states that there were 300 total employees

surveyed. To determine the *want*, check the chart to see how many of those surveyed owned

3–4 cars. This number on the chart is 120, so the probability is $\dfrac{120}{300}$. The answers are in deci-

mal form, so divide 120 by 300 on your calculator to find that the probability is 0.40. The

correct answer is (A).

PERCENTS

Percent just means "divided by 100." So 20 percent $= \dfrac{20}{100} = \dfrac{1}{5}$, or .2.

Likewise, 400 percent $= \dfrac{400}{100} = \dfrac{4}{1} = 4$.

Any percent question can be translated into algebra—just use the following rules:

Percent	÷ 100
Of	×
What	x (or any variable)
Is, Are, Equals	=

Take a look at some examples of phrases you might have to translate on the PSAT 8/9:

8 percent of 10		$0.08 \times 10 = 0.8$
10 percent of 80		$0.1 \times 80 = 8$
5 is what percent of 80?	becomes	$5 = \dfrac{x}{100} \times 80$
5 is 80 percent of what number?		$5 = \dfrac{80}{100} x$
What percent of 5 is 80?		$\dfrac{x}{100} \times 5 = 80$

Try a question.

17

Joanna is a florist, and she estimates that of the 23 bouquets she sells in a day, 8.7% of them will not be gift-wrapped. At this rate, which of the following is the approximate total number of bouquets sold after 14 days that will not be gift-wrapped?

A) 2,800

B)   200

C)   28

D)   2

Looking for More Practice?

If you want some more difficult practice (or want a jump start on the PSAT), check out *Princeton Review PSAT/NMSQT Prep.*

Here's How to Crack It

The question asks for an approximation of the number of bouquets sold in 14 days that will not be gift-wrapped. Use the given percentage to determine how many are not gift-wrapped each day. Joanna sells 23 bouquets in a day, and 8.7% are not gift-wrapped. "Percent" means to divide by 100, so 8.7% can be written as $\dfrac{8.7}{100}$. This percent is *of the bouquets*, and "of" means to multiply, so this becomes $\dfrac{8.7}{100}(23) \approx 2$ bouquets each day that are not gift-wrapped. It is okay to round this, as the question asks for an approximate number and the answers are spread apart. Before you jump in and choose (D), make sure to pay attention to what the question actually asks for—the number of bouquets that are not gift-wrapped over the course of 14 days. If there are 2 per day, the result is (2)(14) = 28. The correct answer is (C).

RATIOS AND PROPORTIONS

Some questions in the calculator-allowed Math section (Section 4) will ask about ratios and proportions. With the strategies that you'll learn on the next few pages, you'll be well prepared to tackle these concepts on the PSAT 8/9.

Ratios

Ratios are about relationships between numbers. Whereas a fraction is a relationship between a part and a whole, a ratio is about the relationship between parts. So, for example, if there were 3 boys and 7 girls in a room, the fraction of boys in the room would be $\dfrac{3}{10}$. But the ratio of boys to girls would be 3:7. Notice that if you add up the parts, you get the whole: 7 + 3 = 10. That's important for PSAT 8/9 ratio problems, and you'll see why in a moment.

Ratio problems usually aren't difficult to identify. The problem will tell you that there is a "ratio" of one thing to another, such as a 2:3 ratio of boys to girls in a club. On the PSAT 8/9, you'll often be asked to compare different ratios. Use the definition that looks like a fraction (or, in other words, divide), and be sure to have the correct order (first term in the numerator, second term in the denominator).

Try this one.

> $$\text{Fraction} = \frac{\text{part}}{\text{whole}}$$
>
> $$\text{Ratio} = \frac{\text{part}}{\text{part}}$$

> **Gridding In**
>
> A ratio is usually expressed as 2:3 or 2 to 3, but if you need to grid a ratio, grid it as $\dfrac{2}{3}$.

5

The preferred pets of a random selection of high school students are shown in the table below. Students were asked to select their preferred pet from the following list: Dog, Cat, Fish, or Lizard.

Preferred Pet Based on High School Year

	Dog	Cat	Fish	Lizard
Freshmen	246	67	95	45
Seniors	89	113	62	75

Based on the results in the table above, the ratio for the least- to most-preferred pet of the senior class is about how many times greater than the ratio for the least- to most-preferred pet of the freshman class?

A) 1.2

B) 1.7

C) 3.0

D) 3.4

Here's How to Crack It

The question asks for a comparison of the ratios of least- to most-preferred pets for two different classes. It is important to read the question carefully and find the correct numbers for the ratios. Start with the freshman class. The freshmen's least preferred pet is the one with the smallest number of votes—lizard, with only 45. The freshmen's most preferred pet is a dog, with 246 votes. Strictly speaking, the ratio is 45:246, but the question says *about how many times*, indicating that you can estimate. Let's just call this 50:250, or 1:5. Ratios can be written as fractions, so that's $\frac{1}{5}$, or decimals, making it 0.20. This last version will be most useful for comparing the ratios. Now move on to the seniors, whose least-preferred pet was a fish with 62 votes and most-preferred pet was a cat with 113 votes. Again, round this to about 60:120 or 1:2, making the ratio 0.5. The question asks how many times greater the 0.5 ratio is than the 0.2 ratio, so take 0.5 and divide it by 0.2. The result is 2.5, which is closest to (C).

If you are nervous about rounding on one like this, given that the answers are somewhat close together, you can always do the exact calculations on your calculator, as calculator use is allowed on statistics questions. Just make sure to only do one bite-sized piece at a time and to write things down on your paper. That way, you won't get confused or miscalculate. Either way, the correct answer is (C).

Direct Variation

Direct variation or proportion problems generally ask you to make a conversion (such as from ounces to pounds) or to compare two sets of information and find a missing piece. For example, a proportion problem may ask you to figure out the amount of time it will take to travel 300 miles at a rate of 50 miles per hour.

To solve proportion problems, just set up two equal fractions. One will have all the information you know, and the other will have a missing piece that you're trying to figure out.

$$\frac{50 \text{ miles}}{1 \text{ hour}} = \frac{300 \text{ miles}}{x \text{ hours}}$$

Be sure to label the parts of your proportion so you'll know you have the right information in the right place; the same units should be in the numerator on both sides of the equals sign and the same units should be in the denominator on both sides of the equals sign. Notice how using a setup like this helps us keep track of the information we have and to find the information we're looking for, so we can use Bite-Sized Pieces to work through the question.

Now we can cross-multiply and then solve for x: $50x = 300$, so $x = 6$ hours.

$$\frac{x_1}{y_1} = \frac{x_2}{y_2}$$

Let's try the following problem.

3

A full water jug in an office contains 3,785 mL of water. What is the water jug's volume, in <u>liters</u>? (1 liter = 1,000 milliliters)

A)   3.785

B)   378.5

C)   378,500

D) 3,785,000

Here's How to Crack It

The question asks for the measure of a volume of 3,785 mL in liters. On these, try to ballpark if you can. A liter is a bigger unit of measurement than a milliliter, so the volume *in liters* must be a smaller number than the volume *in milliliters*. This enables you to eliminate (C) and (D). Sometimes this is not obvious, though, so only eliminate this way if you are sure you will not make a mistake, especially given that all of the answers are 3875 times a different power of

10. To make sure you always get proportions right and to decide between (A) and (B), set up two equal proportions with the known information and matching units in the numerators and denominators. For this question, that becomes $\dfrac{1\,\text{L}}{1{,}000\,\text{mL}} = \dfrac{x}{3{,}785}$. Cross-multiply to get $1{,}000x = 3{,}875$, then divide both sides by 1,000 to get $x = 3.875$. The correct answer is (A).

Inverse Variation

Inverse variation is simply the opposite of a direct, or ordinary, proportion. In a direct proportion when one variable increases, the other variable also increases; however, with inverse variation, when one variable increases, the other variable decreases, or vice versa. These types of problems are generally clearly labeled and all you have to do is apply the inverse variation formula:

$$x_1 y_1 = x_2 y_2$$

Once you memorize the formula, applying it will become second nature to you.

17

Vidhi is studying Boyle's Law, where the pressure of a gas varies inversely to its volume. If the pressure of a certain gas is 45 kilopascals for a volume of 5 liters, then what is the pressure of the gas in kilopascals when the gas is transferred to a container with a volume of 9 liters?

A) 16

B) 20

C) 25

D) 81

Here's How to Crack It

The question asks for the pressure of a gas in a container of a certain volume. According to the question, the pressure and the volume *vary inversely*, so use the inverse variation formula $x_1 y_1 = x_2 y_2$. Plug in the given values and P for the missing pressure to get $(45)(5) = (P)(9)$, which simplifies to $225 = 9P$. Divide both sides of the equation by 9 to get $25 = P$. The correct answer is (C).

Math Techniques Drill 3

Remember, answers to these drill questions can be found in Part IV!

a. If a student scores 70, 90, 95, and 105, what is the average (arithmetic mean) for these tests? _____

b. If a student has an average (arithmetic mean) score of 80 on 4 tests, what is the total of the scores received on those tests? _____

c. If a student has an average of 60 on tests, with a total of 360, how many tests has the student taken? _____

d. If the average of 2, 8, and x is 6, what is the value of x? _____

2, 3, 3, 4, 6, 8, 10, 12

e. What is the median of the group of numbers above? _____

f. What is the mode of the group of numbers above? _____

g. What is the range of the group of numbers above? _____

h. What percent of 5 is 6? _____

i. 60 percent of 90 is the same as 50 percent of what number? _____

j. Jenny's salary increased from $30,000 to $33,000. By what percent did her salary increase? _____

k. In 1980, factory X produced 18,600 pieces. In 1981, factory X produced only 16,000 pieces. By approximately what percent did production decrease from 1980 to 1981? _____

l. In a certain bag of marbles, the ratio of red marbles to green marbles is 7:5. If the bag contains 96 marbles, how many green marbles are in the bag? _____

m. One hogshead is equal to 64 gallons. How many hogsheads are equal to 96 gallons? _____

n. The pressure and volume of a gas are inversely related. If the gas is at 10 kPa at 2 liters, then what is the pressure when the gas is at 4 liters? _____

4

Kendall is baking a cake that requires 0.8 quarts of cream, but her measuring cup only measures liters. There are 1.06 quarts in 1 liter. Which of the following is the approximate number of liters of cream Kendall needs for the recipe?

A) 1.55

B) 0.85

C) 0.75

D) 0.26

5

Jeshua is making flashcards. He can make 18% of the flashcards he needs per hour, on average. If Jeshua continues at this rate, which of the following is the approximate number of flashcards he can make in one hour if he needs 398 flashcards?

A) 68

B) 72

C) 76

D) 80

8

Number of Times Jolly Retrieved the Toy
Throughout the Day

	9 a.m.	12 p.m.	3 p.m.	6 p.m.
Stuffed Animal	10	8	13	14
Ball	9	15	11	7

The two-way table above shows the number of times Jolly the puppy will retrieve a ball or a stuffed animal at different times of the day. What was the average number of times Jolly retrieved the stuffed animal throughout the day?

A) 10.50

B) 10.88

C) 11.25

D) 11.50

11

Fibi has a fish tank that can hold a given number of cubic centimeters of water. She measures her fish tank and finds that it has a length of 1,219 millimeters, a width of 0.305 meters, and a depth of 406 millimeters. What are the measurements (length, width, and depth, respectively) of her fish tank in centimeters? (Note: 1 centimeter = 10 millimeters, and 1 meter = 100 centimeters)

A) 121.9 cm × 30.5 cm × 4.06 cm

B) 121.9 cm × 30.5 cm × 40.6 cm

C) 12,190 cm × 305 cm × 4,060 cm

D) 12,190 cm × 305 cm × 406,000 cm

15

Brent, an accounting firm owner, donates a specific percentage of his firm's annual profit to charity. If Brent's firm made $654,000 last year and donated $52,320, how much money will his firm donate if its annual profit is $575,000 this year?

A) $46,000

B) $59,508

C) $79,000

D) $131,320

Questions 24–25 refer to the following information.

0.5 milliliters	essential oil
0.16 liters	rubbing alcohol
0.06 liters	aloe vera gel

One batch of hand sanitizer can be created using the materials and amounts listed in the table above. A single dose of hand sanitizer is 0.5 ounces and one batch of this recipe makes 4 doses.

24

Jack used d% of one batch of the hand sanitizer. If this amount contained 0.25 milliliters of essential oil, what is the value of d?

25

How many liters of rubbing alcohol are in one dose of this hand sanitizer?

Summary

o The test is full of opportunities to use arithmetic instead of algebra—just look for your chances to use Plugging In and Plugging In the Answers (PITA).

o If a question has in terms of or variables in the answer choices, it's a Plugging In problem. Plug in your own number, do the math, find the target number, and use POE to get down to one correct answer.

o If a question doesn't have variables but asks for a fraction or a percent of an unknown number, you can also plug in there. Just substitute your own number for the unknown and take the rest of the problem step by step.

o For Meaning in Context questions, start with RTFQ, labeling the equation, and using POE. If you still have more than one answer choice remaining, plug in to the equation to help you narrow down the answers.

o If a question has an unknown and asks for a specific amount, making you feel like you have to write an equation, try PITA instead.

o Average is defined as Average (arithmetic mean) $= \dfrac{\text{total}}{\text{\# of things}}$. Often on the PSAT 8/9, you'll be given the average and the number of things. Use $T = AN$ on those problems to determine the total.

o The median is the middle value in a list of consecutive numbers. If there are an odd number of elements, the median is the average of the two middle values.

o The mode is the most commonly occurring value in a list of numbers.

o The range is the difference between the greatest and least values in a list of numbers.

o Rates are closely related to averages. Use $D = RT$ or $W = RT$ just like you use $T = AN$. Remember that the PSAT 8/9 likes to make you find the totals (distance or work in rate questions).

- Probability is a fractional value between 0 and 1 (inclusive), and it is equal to the number of outcomes the question is asking for divided by the total number of possible outcomes. It can also be expressed as a percent.

- Percent simply means "per 100." Many percent questions can be tackled by translating English to math.

- Set up ratios like fractions. Take care to put the first term of the ratio in the numerator and the second term in the denominator.

- Sometimes you'll need to treat ratios like fractions or decimals. Use your calculator to turn the numbers into the easiest form to work the problem.

- Direct variation or proportion means as one value goes up, the other goes up. The formula is $\frac{x_1}{y_1} = \frac{x_2}{y_2}$.

- Inverse variation means as one value goes up, the other goes down. The formula is $x_1 y_1 = x_2 y_2$.

Chapter 12
Advanced Math

There will be 6 questions on the PSAT 8/9 that test what College Board calls "Passport to Advanced Math." This category includes topics such as functions, quadratics, and growth and decay. If you've learned these topics already in school, great! You'll have a step up on the PSAT 8/9. If not, fear not—this chapter will give you the foundation needed for tackling these questions on the PSAT 8/9.

FUNCTIONS

In the Math Basics chapter, we looked at some concepts related to the xy-plane. Here, we will look at some more complicated topics involving functions and graphs. The functions on the PSAT 8/9 mostly look like this:

$$f(x) = x^2 + 6x + 24$$

Just Follow the Instructions

Functions are like recipes. Each one is just a set of directions for you to follow. The College Board provides the ingredients and you work your magic.

Most questions of this type will give you a specific value to plug in for x and then ask you to find the value of the function for that x. Each function is just a set of instructions that tells you what to do to x—or the number you plug in for x—in order to find the corresponding value for $f(x)$ (a fancy name for y). Just plug your information into that equation and follow the instructions.

Let's try an easy one.

──────────○──────────

4

What is the value of $g(9)$ for the function g defined by $g(x) = x + 4$?

A)   4

B)   5

C)   9

D)   13

Here's How to Crack It

The questions asks for the value of $g(9)$ for the given function g. The value in the parentheses is the x value of the function, and $g(x)$ is the resulting y value. Plug in 9 for x in the function to get $g(9) = 9 + 4 = 13$. The correct answer is (D).

──────────○──────────

One way the PSAT 8/9 can make functions more complicated is to give you two functions to deal with together. If you approach these problems one piece at a time, they will be easier to handle.

Here's an example.

12

$$h(x) = 3x^2 + \frac{2}{3}$$

$$k(x) = \frac{1}{6}x + 8$$

Given the functions above, what is the value of $h(2) + k(2)$?

Here's How to Crack It

The question asks for the value of $h(2) + k(2)$, given the definitions of the two functions.

This is really no more complicated than a question dealing with a single function. Just

plug in the value for x and work the question in bite-sized pieces. Start with $h(2)$. Plug in

$x = 2$ to get $h(2) = 3(2)^2 + \frac{2}{3} = 3(4) + \frac{2}{3} = 12\frac{2}{3}$. Now plug $x = 2$ into the k function to

get $k(2) = \frac{1}{6}(2) + 8 = \frac{2}{6} + 8 = \frac{1}{3} + 8 = 8\frac{1}{3}$. Finally, add the values of $h(2)$ and $k(2)$ to get

$12\frac{2}{3} + 8\frac{1}{3} = 12 + 8 + \frac{2}{3} + \frac{1}{3} = 20 + \frac{3}{3} = 20 + 1 = 21$. The correct answer is 21.

Sometimes the PSAT 8/9 will use a word problem to describe a function, and then ask you to "build a function" that describes that real-world situation.

> **3**
>
> Vacay Homes Co. rents out vacation homes for periods
> ranging from 7 to 21 days for $115 per day plus a summer
> discount of $245. When $7 \le d \le 21$, which of the following
> functions B shows the amount of money a customer pays to
> Vacay Homes Co.?
>
> A) $B(d) = 21d - 245$
>
> B) $B(d) = 115d - 245$
>
> C) $B(d) = 115d + 2{,}170$
>
> D) $B(d) = 245d - 115$

Here's How to Crack It

The question asks for the function that represents the amount a customer must pay. Translate
the information in the question in bite-sized pieces and use Process of Elimination. The cost
per day is $115, and *d* represents day. Therefore, the correct function must include the term
115*d*. You can eliminate (A) and (D), as those have other coefficients for the *d* term. The question also mentions a *discount*, which will reduce the cost of the rental for the summer. The correct function must feature subtraction to show this reduction of cost. Now you can eliminate
(C), which adds an additional fee. The correct answer is (B).

QUADRATIC EQUATIONS

Ah, quadratics. You're likely to see several questions on the PSAT 8/9 that require you to
expand, factor, or solve quadratics. You may even need to find the vertex of a parabola or the
points of intersection of a quadratic and a line. So let's review, starting with the basics.

Expanding

Most often you'll be asked to expand an expression simply by multiplying it out. When working with an expression of the form (x + 3)(x + 4), multiply it out using the following rule:

> FOIL = **F**irst **O**uter **I**nner **L**ast

Start with the first figure in each set of parentheses: $x \times x = x^2$.

Now do the two outer figures: $x \times 4 = 4x$.

Next, the two inner figures: $3 \times x = 3x$.

Finally, the last figure in each set of parentheses: $3 \times 4 = 12$.

Add them all together, and we get $x^2 + 4x + 3x + 12$, or $x^2 + 7x + 12$.

Factoring

If you ever see an expression of the form $x^2 + 7x + 12$ on the PSAT 8/9, there is a good chance that factoring it will be the key to cracking it.

The key to factoring is figuring out what pair of numbers will multiply to give you the constant term (12, in this case) and add up to the coefficient of the x term (7, in this question).

Let's try an example:

$$x^2 + 7x + 12$$

Step 1: Draw two sets of parentheses next to each other and fill an x into the left side of each. That's what gives us our x^2 term.

$$(x \quad)(x \quad)$$

Step 2: 12 can be factored a number of ways: 1×12, 2×6, or 3×4. Which of these adds up to 7? 3 and 4, so place a 3 on the right side of one parenthesis and a 4 in the other.

$$(x \quad 3)(x \quad 4)$$

Step 3: Now we need to figure out what the correct signs should be. They should both be positive in this case, because that will sum to 7 and multiply to 12, so fill plus signs into each parenthesis.

$$(x + 3)(x + 4)$$

If you want to double-check your work, try expanding out $(x + 3)(x + 4)$ using FOIL and you'll get the original expression.

Now try the following problem.

11

When the expression $x^2 - 4x - 32$ is factored to $(x - 8)(x + h)$, where h is a constant, what is the value of h ?

Here's How to Crack It

The question asks for the value of h in the factored form of a quadratic. When the PSAT 8/9 gives you a factored quadratic, you almost always need to use FOIL to multiply it out in order to answer the question. Doing so on the factors $(x - 8)(x + h)$ results in $x^2 + hx - 8x - 8h$. Set this equal to the expression given in standard form to get $x^2 - 4x - 32 = x^2 + hx - 8x - 8h$. The constants on either side of the equation (the numbers with no x terms) must be equal, so $-32 = -8h$. Divide both sides by -8 to get $4 = h$.

Don't forget that you can plug in on a question like this instead. If you let $x = 2$, the given expression becomes $(2)^2 - 4(2) - 32 = 4 - 8 - 32 = -36$. The factored expression becomes $(2 - 8)(2 + h) = (-6)(2 + h)$, and this is equal to the -36 from the original expression. Therefore, $(-6)(2 + h) = -36$, and dividing both sides by -6 results in $2 + h = 6$. Subtracting 2 from both sides shows once again that $h = 4$. No matter how you approach this one, the correct answer is 4.

Solving Quadratic Equations

Sometimes you'll want to factor to solve an equation. In this case, there will be two possible values for x, called the roots of the equation. To solve for x, use the following steps:

Step 1: Make sure that the equation is set equal to zero.

Step 2: Factor the equation.

Step 3: Set each parenthetical expression equal to zero. So if you have $(x + 2)(x - 7) = 0$, you get $(x + 2) = 0$ and $(x - 7) = 0$. When you solve for each, you get $x = -2$ and $x = 7$. Therefore, -2 and 7 are the solutions or roots of the equation.

Try the following problem.

9

Which of the following is a solution to the equation $v^2 - 11v + 28 = 0$?

A) -11

B) $\quad 0$

C) $\quad 4$

D) $\quad 28$

Here's How to Crack It

The question asks for the solution to a quadratic, which is the value of v that will make the equation true. Now follow the steps:

1. Set the equation to zero. (This has already been done.)
2. Factor the left side to get $(v - 7)(v - 4) = 0$.
3. Set each factor equal to zero to get $v = 4$ and $v = 7$. Since only one of these is an option, the correct answer is (C).

An alternative approach to this question is to plug in the answers. Starting with (B), plug $v = 0$ into the equation to get $0^2 - 11(0) + 28 = 0$, or $28 = 0$. Since this is not true, eliminate (B). It is difficult to know which direction to go after this, so just pick a direction and try it out. Try (C). Plug $v = 4$ into the equation to $(4)^2 - 11(4) + 28 = 0$, or $16 - 44 + 28 = 0$. This simplifies to $0 = 0$, so you find that the correct answer is (C) using this method as well.

Sometimes, quadratic equations will be tested with word problems. Let's look at this type of question.

5

A biologist studying a population of birds on an island finds that the equation $P = -0.2w^2 + 10w + 120$ can be used to model the number of birds in the population, P, for each number of weeks, w, since she began her study. Which of the following values of w is most useful in determining the number of birds in the population when she began her study?

A) $w = 0$

B) $w = 10$

C) $w = 20$

D) $w = 120$

Here's How to Crack It

The question asks about the population when the biologist *began her study*. The time of her study is measured in weeks, represented by w. When she began the study, she hadn't put in any time yet, so the value for w would be 0. This matches the value in (A). Another option, given that calculator use is allowed, would be graphing the equation as $y = -0.2x^2 + 10x + 120$ to see what the graph looks like. If you are a visual learner, this may help you to better see what is going on with the population at the different times listed in the answer choices. Either way, the correct answer is (A).

SOLVING RATIONAL EQUATIONS

Since you are not always allowed to use your calculator on the PSAT 8/9, there will be some instances in which you will need to solve an equation algebraically. Even on the sections in which calculator use is permitted, you may find it faster and more effective to use your mathematical skills to efficiently answer a question.

Here is an example.

2

Given the proportion $\dfrac{120}{s} = \dfrac{10}{3}$, which of the following is the value of s ?

A) 20

B) 36

C) 60

D) 70

Here's How to Crack It

The question asks for the value of s in the given proportion. You are asked for a specific value and given numbers in the answer choices, so Plugging In the Answers is an option. However, if the answer you start with doesn't work, it may not be clear which direction to go next, and you may end up doing a bunch of unnecessary work. Instead, ones like this are faster to solve through cross-multiplication. Doing so results in $(s)(10) = (120)(3)$, which simplifies to $10s = 360$. Divide both sides of the equation by 10 to get $s = 36$. The correct answer is (B).

ABSOLUTE VALUES

Absolute value is just a measure of the distance between a number and 0. Since distances are always positive, the absolute value of a number is also always positive. The absolute value of a number is written as $|x|$.

When solving for the value of a variable inside the absolute value bars, it is important to remember that variable could be either positive or negative. For example, if $|x| = 2$, then $x = 2$ or $x = -2$ since both 2 and –2 are a distance of 2 from 0.

Here's an example.

> **PSAT 8/9 Smoke and Mirrors**
>
> When you're asked to solve an equation involving an absolute value, it is very likely that the correct answer will be the negative result. Why? Because the test-writers know that you are less likely to think about the negative result! Another way to avoid mistakes is to do all the math inside the absolute value symbols first, and then make the result positive.

4

For $|2x - 3| = 5$, which of the following is a possible value of x ?

A) −4

B) −1

C)   0

D)   1

Here's How to Crack It

The question asks for the value of x that is a solution to the absolute value. You could solve this by taking the part inside the absolute value symbol and setting it equal to 5 and −5, then solving both equations, but there is a lot of room for sign errors on that path. Instead, try PITA. Label the answers as "x" and start with (B), −1. The equation becomes $|2(-1) - 3| = 5$, which simplifies to $|-2 - 3| = 5$. This further simplifies to $|-5| = 5$, which is true. You can stop there—the correct answer is (B).

GROWTH AND DECAY

Another aspect of percent questions may relate to things that increase or decrease by a certain percent over time. This is known as "growth and decay." Real-world examples include population growth, radioactive decay, and credit payments, to name a few. While Plugging In can help on these, it is also useful to know the growth and decay formula.

> When the growth or decay rate is a percent of the total population:
>
> *final amount* = *original amount* $(1 \pm rate)^{number\ of\ changes}$

Let's see how this formula can make quick work of an otherwise tedious question.

6

$$y = 300(1.06)^x$$

The equation above describes the total money in an interest-generating savings account x months after it was opened. Which of the following best describes the meaning of the value of y for $x = 0$?

A) The account had a value of $0 when it was initially opened.

B) The account will have a value of $300 when it has been open for 300 months.

C) The account had a value of $300 when it was initially opened.

D) The account will have a value of $0 when it has been open for 300 months.

Here's How to Crack It

The question asks for the meaning of the value of y when $x = 0$. The x in the equation corresponds to the *number of changes* in the growth and decay formula. If that value is 0, there have been no changes, and the account only contains the *original amount*. In this case, the original amount was $300, as that is the value in front of the parentheses. This corresponds to the statement in (C). If you forget the formula for growth and decay, never fear! It is unlikely to come up in anything more complicated than this question, and these can be solved with POE and Plugging In, too. The value of x indicates the number of months, so if $x = 0$, you can eliminate (B) and (D), as those refer to *300 months*. The difference between (A) and (C) is the initial value of the account. Plugging $x = 0$ into the equation results in $y = 300(1.06)^0$. Any number raised to the power of 0 becomes 1, so this becomes $y = 300(1) = 300$. Thus, the value of the account when $x = 0$ is $300, not $0. Either way, the correct answer is (C).

ANALYSIS IN SCIENCE

If some of the questions you've seen so far are reminding you of science class, you're not crazy. One of the cross-test scores the PSAT 8/9 aims to measure is called Analysis in Science. This means that questions on science-based ideas will show up in Reading and Writing passages and also in Math questions.

One way this concept will be tested is through word problems. Many of the strategies we've already discussed, such as translating or Plugging In, will help you to answer these questions, regardless of the scientific context.

Here's an example.

23

A chemist uses different amounts of organic polymer and silica to produce certain thicknesses of a gel. The equation $3.9P - 0.89S = 40.15$ represents one such combination, where P and S represent the amounts of organic polymer and silica, respectively, in milligrams. If the chemist uses 16 milligrams of organic polymer, how many milligrams of silica are used?

Here's How to Crack It

The question asks how many milligrams of silica are used. Don't let the scientific context of the question throw you off. There is an equation and a given value, so focus on those. The value of 16 milligrams refers to the polymer, and the question states that the amount of polymer is represent by P. Plug $P = 16$ into the equation to get $3.9(16) - 0.89S = 40.15$. This simplifies to $62.4 - 0.89S = 40.15$, then you can subtract 62.4 from both sides to get $-0.89S = -22.25$. Divide both sides of the equation by -0.89 to get $S = 25$. This is the amount of silica, so the correct answer is 25.

Sometimes, you will be asked science questions based on a chart or graph. In those cases, carefully look up the numbers in question, do the required calculations, and eliminate answers that aren't true.

Let's look at one.

16

The scatterplot below shows how India's annual rainfall, in centimeters (cm), changed over time after the year 2000.

India's Annual Rainfall

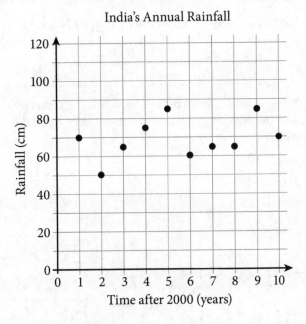

How many years after 2000 was the year in which India had the greatest annual rainfall?

A) 5

B) 10

C) 70

D) 85

Here's How to Crack It

The question asks about the year that India had the greatest rainfall. Start with Process of Elimination. The values for *years* on the horizontal axis only go from 0 to 10, so the correct answer must be in this range. Eliminate (C) and (D), which are answers you might get if you read the wrong axis. The amount of rainfall is measured on the vertical axis, so the greatest rainfall will be the dot closest to the top of the graph. This occurs right on the gridline for year 5, but make sure this represents 5 years after 2000. The question and the axis label both say *after 2000,* so there is no trick there. The correct answer is (A).

You may also be asked to graph the data presented in a table. Your knowledge of graphing in the *xy*-plane should help you with most of those. If anything gets too tricky, consider skipping it and spending your time on something else.

Advanced Math Drill

Answers can be found in Part IV.

3

The table below displays coordinate pairs of a function.

x	−2	−1	0	1	2
$f(x)$	10	6	2	−2	−6

Of the equations listed, which of the following correctly displays the relationship between the values of x and $f(x)$ in the table?

A) $f(x) = -5x$

B) $f(x) = -4x + 2$

C) $f(x) = -2x - 4$

D) $f(x) = 2x + 2$

7

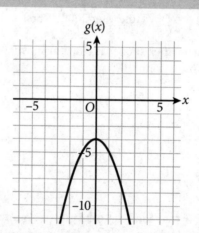

Which of the following functions represents the parabola graphed in the xy-plane above?

A) $g(x) = -(x - 4)^2$

B) $g(x) = -x^2 - 4$

C) $g(x) = (x - 4)^2$

D) $g(x) = x^2 - 4$

12

$$q(x) = -\frac{1}{3}x + 12$$

Given the function above, what value of c will make $q(c)$ equal to 6 ?

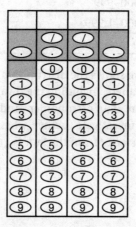

5

There are 210 members of a fitness center. A poll answered by a random sample of 30 members found that 7 of those members own exercise equipment at home. Approximately how many of the total members of the fitness center can be expected to own exercise equipment at home?

A) 187

B) 49

C) 37

D) 30

10

Distance from Sun (in millions of miles)	Number of planets
0–499	5
500–999	1
1,000–1,999	1
More than 2,000	2

The data table above shows the distribution of distance from the Sun for nine planets, including the dwarf planet Pluto, in Earth's solar system. If an astronomer randomly selects one of these planets to investigate further, what is the probability that the planet's distance from the Sun is greater than 999 million miles?

A) $\dfrac{1}{9}$

B) $\dfrac{1}{3}$

C) $\dfrac{4}{9}$

D) $\dfrac{1}{2}$

13

A group of students observed that there was a relationship between the hours a petri dish was left to incubate and the resulting number of cells in the petri dish. The graph below displays their findings as well as a best-fit line drawn by one of the students.

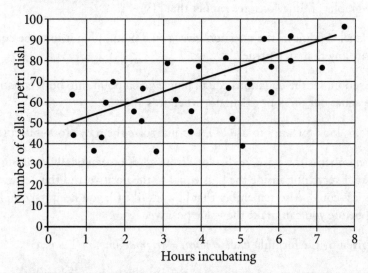

Which of the following is the correct approximate average hourly increase in the number of cells, based on the best-fit line in the graph?

A)   0.06

B)   0.43

C)   6.00

D)   92.00

Summary

o   Given a function, you put an x value in and get an $f(x)$ or y-value out.

o   Look for ways to use Plugging In and PITA on function questions.

o   For questions about the graphs of functions, remember that $f(x) = y$.

o   If the graph contains a labeled point or the question gives you a point, plug it into the equations in the answers and eliminate any that aren't true.

o   To find a point of intersection, set the equations equal, plug a given point into both equations to see if it works, or graph the equations on your calculator when it is allowed.

o   To solve rational equations, look for ways to use PITA or just solve them by cross-multiplying.

o   The absolute value of a number is the positive distance from zero, or practically, making the thing inside the || sign positive. Everything inside the || is equal to the positive and the negative value of the expression to which it is equal. Also remember that || work like ( ); you need to complete all the operations inside the || before you can make the value positive.

o   Growth and decay are given by the formula *final amount = original amount*$(1 \pm rate)^{number\ of\ changes}$.

o   Analysis in Science questions may seem weird, but they can usually be handled with the same strategies as those used for other math questions. Plug in or translate, read the chart or text carefully, and always use Process of Elimination to get rid of answers that don't match the data or don't make sense.

Part IV
Drill Answers
and Explanations

CHAPTER 5

"Why Does Music Feel So Good?" Drill (page 127)

34. **C** See Chapter 5 for explanation.

35. **D** The question asks what the word *moves* most nearly means in line 1. Go back to the text, find the word *moves*, and cross it out. Then read the window carefully, using context clues to determine another word that would fit in the text. The text says that music *moves people of all cultures*, but scientists don't understand *why listening to music can trigger such profoundly rewarding experiences*. Therefore, *moves* must mean something like "has an impact on." *Carries* does not match "has an impact on," so eliminate (A). *Persuades* means "convinces," which does not match "has an impact on," so eliminate (B). *Transports* does not match "has an impact on," so eliminate (C). *Affects* matches "has an impact on," so keep (D). Note that (A), (B), and (C) are Could Be True trap answers based on other meanings of *moves* that are not supported by the text. The correct answer is (D).

36. **D** The question asks for something *that research has not yet determined*, as indicated by the passage. Since there is no line reference, use the order of the questions to find the window. Q35 asks about line 1, so continue reading the first paragraph, looking for information about what has not yet been determined by research. Lines 3–7 state, *Nobody really understands why listening to music can trigger such profoundly rewarding experiences. Valorie Salimpoor and other neuroscientists are trying to figure it out with the help of brain scanners.* In other words, research has not yet determined why people get so much pleasure from listening to music. Eliminate answers that don't match this prediction. Choices (A), (B), and (C) do not match the prediction. These answers may be tempting because they mention topics that are discussed later in the passage, but none of these choices includes something that has not been determined by research. Eliminate (A), (B), and (C). Keep (D) because it matches the prediction. The correct answer is (D).

37. **A** The question is the best evidence question in a paired set. Because Q36 was easy to find, simply look at the lines used to answer Q36. Lines 3–5 gave the prediction for Q36. The correct answer is (A).

38. **B** See Chapter 5 for explanation.

39. **A** See Chapter 5 for explanation.

40. **C** The question asks for the reason *Salimpoor visited local music stores after collecting surveys of volunteers' music preferences*. Since there is no line reference, use lead words and the order of the questions to find the window for the question. The answer for Q39 was based on lines 35–41, so the window for Q40 most likely begins after these lines. Beginning with line 42, scan the passage, looking for the lead words *Salimpoor* and *music store*. Lines 49–57 discuss the process by which *Salimpoor* created a *list of unfamiliar songs*, and the end of the paragraph says that she *asked people who worked at local music stores* for song recommendations to help compile this list. Look for an answer choice that matches

this prediction. Choice (A) is a Mostly Right, Slightly Wrong trap answer. While *Salimpoor* did *seek information* from *music stores,* this information was not related to the cause of music preferences. Eliminate (A). Eliminate (B) because although *Salimpoor* looked for music *online* and *in stores*, she did not *compare* the two. This is a Right Words, Wrong Meaning trap answer. Keep (C) because it matches the prediction. Eliminate (D) because it is a Right Words, Wrong Meaning trap answer: the text says that *Salimpoor* asked the staff for recommendations, not for songs that the staff *had recommended to the study participants*. The correct answer is (C).

41. **A**   The question asks for the best support for the idea that *human responses to music can be tracked by measuring specific types of brain activity*. Use the line references given in the answer choices to find a statement that supports this idea. The lines for (A) say that certain *connections* among *brain areas could predict how much a participant was willing to spend on a given song*. Since the amount that a participant was willing to spend on a song was an indication of how much that participant liked the song, this choice supports the idea that *human responses to music can be tracked* by measuring *brain activity*. Keep (A). The lines for (B) say that a person's musical preference *depends* on the person's *past musical experiences*. This choice does not discuss *brain activity*, so eliminate (B). The lines for (C) say that different musical genres follow different sets of rules, and these genre-rule connections are *all implicitly recorded in your brain*. Likewise, (D) says that a listener is *constantly activating* memorized genre-rule connections by *listening to music*. While both choices either mention or refer to the *brain*, neither discusses how brain activity leads to musical preference. Eliminate (C) and (D). The correct answer is (A).

42. **B**   See Chapter 5 for explanation.

Dual Passage Drill (page 137)

26. **B**   The question asks what the speaker in Passage 1 implies about a *reason that the military draft is harmful to American society*. Since there is no line reference, use lead words and the order of the questions to find the window. Q26 is the first specific question, so the window is likely near the beginning of the passage. Scan the first paragraph of Passage 1, looking for the lead words *military draft*. Lines 3–6 indicate that the *military draft* mentioned in line 7 causes a *weakening of our social fiber* and *the undermining of the individual's faith in his Government and his hope for his future*. Eliminate answers that don't match this prediction. Eliminate (A), which is a Right Words, Wrong Meaning trap answer: the passage says that the military draft *undermines* (weakens) a person's *hope for his future*; it does not say that the draft gives a person a *false sense of hope*. Keep (B) because the phrase *reduce the public's trust in the government* matches *undermining of the individual's faith in his Government*. Eliminate (C) because the passage does not discuss the *nation's allies*. Eliminate (D), which is a Could Be True trap answer: you may know that some people left the United States because of the draft, but this fact is not included in the passage. The correct answer must be supported by the text. The correct answer is (B).

27. **D**   The question asks for a description of the *main shift in focus within lines 8–35 of Passage 1*. Use the given line reference to find the window. Lines 8–15 state that *voluntary recruitment* for the armed forces is *more acceptable and more consistent with historic American practice and tradition* than involuntary recruitment. Lines 24–35 state, *It is time to end the draft,* and then present a series of arguments for ending the draft. The main shift in these paragraphs is from arguments in favor of a volunteer military to arguments against the involuntary draft. Eliminate answers that don't match this prediction. Eliminate (A) because although the passage discusses *salary scales* for members of the military, it does not provide an *overview of careers in the military*. Eliminate (B) because there is no discussion about *equipment* in the passage. Eliminate (C) because, although the first paragraph mentions *Senate action*, this is not included in the lines that the question asks about. The passage also does not *outline all of the Senate's past actions* regarding a volunteer military, nor does it discuss Senate action on *other legislation*. Keep (D) because it matches the prediction. The correct answer is (D).

28. **D**   The question asks for an effect that would be caused by *raising wages for some members of the armed forces*, based on Passage 1. Notice that this is the first question in a paired set, so it can be done in tandem with Q29. Look at the answers for Q29 first. The lines for (29A) indicate that an all-volunteer military is *more acceptable and more consistent with historic American practice* than an involuntary military. These lines do not discuss the effects of *raising wages*, so they do not address Q28. Eliminate (29A). The lines for (29B) state that *a modest increase in pay for men in the lower ranks would sufficiently increase voluntary recruitment and reenlistments to supply manpower*. In other words, raising wages for some members of the armed forces would encourage enough people to volunteer for and reenlist in the military. Check the answers for Q28 to see whether any of the answers are supported by these lines. This information matches (28D). Draw a line connecting (29B) and (28D). The lines for (29C) indicate that increased wages for servicemen are *deserved and overdue* because people in the military are paid less than civilians (non-military members) who hold similar jobs. These lines discuss higher wages, but they don't describe an effect of raising wages, so they don't address Q28. Eliminate (29C). The lines for (29D) argue for ending the draft because it is *time to bring the American system into line with our professed ideals of individual freedom and personal choice*. These lines do not discuss the effects of *raising wages*, so they do not address Q28. Eliminate (29D). Without any support in the answers from Q29, (28A), (28B), and (28C) can be eliminated. The correct answers are (28D) and (29B).

29. **B**   (See explanation above.)

30. **A**   The question asks what the word *rigorous* most nearly means in line 30. Go back to the text, find the word *rigorous*, and cross it out. Then read the window carefully, using context clues to determine another word that would fit in the text. The text states that it is *time to stop sending to prison* people who are *deeply opposed to an unnecessary draft. Only a handful can meet the rigorous definition of the conscientious objector, the objector to all war. But other men are entitled to have their principled objections and scruples respected.* Therefore, *rigorous* must mean something like "exact" or "precise." *Strict* matches "precise," so keep (A). *Harsh* does not mean "precise," so eliminate (B). Note that (B) is a Could Be True trap answer based on another meaning of *rigorous* that is not supported by the passage. *Excessive* does not match "precise," so eliminate (C). *Unlikely* does not match "precise," so eliminate (D). The correct answer is (A).

31. **D**   The question asks what the word *extension* most nearly means in line 52. Go back to the text, find the word *extension*, and cross it out. Then read the window carefully, using context clues to determine another word that would fit in the text. Beginning with line 42, the text says, *there has been debate in this body for some weeks now on the need for the military draft…There have been arguments advanced in favor of its extension. Basically, the argument is that without the draft, our commitments as a nation and as a world leader cannot be fulfilled.* Therefore, *extension* must mean something like "being kept." Eliminate answers that do not match this prediction. *Reaching* does not mean "being kept," so eliminate (A). *Addition* does not mean "being kept," so eliminate (B). *Being enlarged* does not mean "being kept," so eliminate (C). Choices (A), (B), and (C) are Could Be True trap answers based on other meanings of *extension* that are not supported by the passage. *Being continued* matches "being kept," so keep (D). The correct answer is (D).

32. **C**   The question asks for a statement about *the military draft in the United States* that *both speakers* would agree with. Because this is a question about both passages, it should be done after the questions that ask about each passage individually. In Passage 1, line 41 states, *We must end the draft now!* The speaker in Passage 1 is opposed to the draft and would like to end it immediately. Eliminate answers that do not match the prediction for Passage 1. Eliminate (A) because Passage 1 does not discuss whether the *President* has *too much power* under the draft. Eliminate (B) because the speaker in Passage 1 is in favor of ending the draft immediately. Keep (C) because it matches the prediction. Eliminate (D), which is a Right Words, Wrong Meaning trap answer: the speaker of Passage 1 discusses replacing the draft with volunteer recruitment, but he doesn't discuss whether the draft could *replace a volunteer army*. The only answer remaining is (C). For this question, all but one answer can be eliminated based solely on Passage 1. However, Passage 2 must also support (C). There was only one individual question about Passage 2, so a large part of the passage is still unread. Continue reading Passage 2, looking for information about the speaker's view of the *draft*. Lines 58–65 state, *I favor a volunteer army…Because I do believe the volunteer army is a goal we can reach, I believe that the termination of the draft…within the next year, would be folly and do great damage to the ultimate adoption of a sound volunteer army concept.* In other words, although the speaker in Passage 2 does not want to end the draft immediately, he also favors voluntary recruitment rather than a draft. The correct answer is (C).

33. **A**   The question asks for the view expressed in Passage 2 about *Passage 1's central claim*. Because this is a question about both passages, it should be done after the questions that ask about each passage individually. First, consider the central claim of Passage 1. The speaker in Passage 1 states that volunteer recruitment for the military is *within practical reach* and says, *We must end the draft now!* Next, consider the point of view expressed in Passage 2 about replacing the draft with voluntary recruitment. Notice that Q33 is the first question in a paired set, so it can be done in tandem with Q34. Look at the answer choices for Q34. The lines for (34A) describe arguments that agree with the central claim in Passage 1. However, these lines do not express the point of view of the speaker in Passage 2, so they do not answer Q33. Eliminate (34A). The lines for (34B) state, *If I believed for one moment that the military could meet their manpower needs fully solely through volunteer enlistments, I would be in the forefront leading the charge for a volunteer army.* In other words, the speaker in

Passage 2 does not want to end the draft immediately because he believes that the military would not be able to recruit enough volunteers quickly. Check the answers for Q33 to see whether any of the answers are supported by these lines. This information matches (33A), so draw a line connecting (34B) and (33A). The lines for (34C) state that ending the draft *would be disastrous to the* Army's *planning* for *the volunteer army. The military must have the time to test various ideas, to work toward the volunteer army.* These lines do not support any of the answers for Q33, so eliminate (34C). The lines for (34D) state, *The argument that an immediate* end to the draft *would force the immediate adoption of the volunteer Army has been rejected at every point of its consideration of this legislation.* These lines do not support any of the answers for Q33, so eliminate (34D). Without any support in the answers from Q34, (33B), (33C), and (33D) can be eliminated. The correct answers are (33A) and (34B).

34. **B** (See explanation above.)

CHAPTER 6

Writing and Language Drill 1 (page 149)

1. Apostrophes; apostrophes and where they go

2. Verbs; verb tense

3. Words; transition words (direction)

4. Seem/Seems and their/its; verb number and pronoun number

5. Number of words; concision

CHAPTER 7

Writing and Language Drill 2 (page 165)

1. **A** Punctuation is changing in the answer choices, so this question is testing STOP, HALF-STOP, and GO punctuation. Use the Vertical Line Test and identify the ideas as complete or incomplete. Draw the vertical line between the words *lived* and *in*. The first part of the sentence, *In the 1960s, a woman named Marie Van Brittan Brown lived,* is a complete idea. The second part, *in Queens, New York, where she worked as a nurse,* is an incomplete idea. To connect a complete idea to an incomplete idea, HALF-STOP or GO punctuation is needed. Notice that each answer choice either uses HALF-STOP or GO punctuation, so consider the relationship between ideas and whether the point of punctuation interrupts a thought. The phrase *lived in Queens* is a continuous thought, so it does not need to be interrupted with a punctuation mark. Keep (A) because it does not use a punctuation mark. Eliminate (B), (C), and (D) because each uses a punctuation mark between *lived* and *in*. The correct answer is (A).

2. **B** Commas are changing in the answer choices, so this question is testing the four ways to use a comma. The sentence contains a list of three things: 1) *each other*, 2) *their home*, and 3) *their two children*. There should be a comma after each item in the list. Eliminate (A) because it has a semicolon, not a comma, after *other*. Keep (B) because it has a comma after each item in the list. Eliminate (C) and (D) because neither uses a comma after the word *other*. The correct answer is (B).

3. **D** Apostrophes are changing in the answer choices, so the question is testing apostrophe usage. When used with a noun, on the PSAT 8/9, an apostrophe indicates possession. In this sentence, the *calls* belong to *residents*, so an apostrophe is needed after *residents* but not after *calls*. In addition, because *residents* is plural, the apostrophe should be placed after the *s*. Eliminate (A) and (B) because neither contains the apostrophe on *residents*. Eliminate (C) because the apostrophe is before the *s*, which indicates a singular noun. This would imply only one resident, which is not correct. Choice (D) correctly places the apostrophe after the *s*. The correct answer is (D).

4. **A** Apostrophes are changing in the answer choices, so the question is testing apostrophe usage. When used with a pronoun, an apostrophe indicates a contraction. The sentence says that *Brown* wanted to find *a way to see who was at her door from any room in the house*. Keep (A) because the phrase *there was* indicates the introduction of a topic, and this sentence introduces the idea of seeing *who was at the door*. Choices (B) and (C) both mean the same thing—*they're* is a contraction of *they are*—so neither could be correct, since each question can have only one correct answer. Furthermore, with either one, the sentence would say *they are was*, which incorrectly uses two verbs; eliminate (B) and (C). Eliminate (D) because the sentence does not imply that two or more people own something; the possessive pronoun *their* is not appropriate. Choice (A) makes the meaning of the sentence most precise. No apostrophe is needed. The correct answer is (A).

5. **C** Commas are changing in the answer choices, so this question is testing the four ways to use a comma. Check to see whether any of the four ways can be cited as a reason to use commas: comma + FANBOYS, GO punctuation, list, or unnecessary information. There is no list in the question, and all of the information in the sentence is necessary (eliminating any information would change the meaning of the sentence), so check the other two reasons. There is no comma + FANBOYS, but there may be a reason to use GO punctuation. Consider the ideas before and after each comma to see how they are related and whether a comma is needed to show a shift in ideas. Commas change after *knocked*, but the phrase *knocked on your door* is a continuous thought, so there is no need to interrupt it with a comma. Eliminate (B) and (D). Commas also change after *door*. The idea before the comma gives a hypothetical situation, *someone knocked on your door*, and the idea after the comma explains what might happen *if someone knocked on your door*. These two ideas are two separate thoughts, not one continuous thought, so a comma should be used to separate them. Eliminate (A). The correct answer is (C).

6. **B** Punctuation is changing in the answer choices, so this question is testing STOP, HALF-STOP, and GO punctuation. Use the Vertical Line Test and identify the ideas as complete or incomplete. Draw the vertical line between the words *police* and *this*. The first part of the sentence, *If the person did try to break in, you would have to run to the phone and call the police*, is a complete idea. The second part, *this could use up precious time in the days when most homes had only one phone, with a cord*, is a complete idea. To connect a complete idea to a complete idea, STOP or HALF-STOP punctuation is needed. A lack of punctuation is GO punctuation, so eliminate (A). A comma without FANBOYS is GO punctuation, so eliminate (C). Choice (B) and (D) use different words, so consider the second part of the sentence, replacing *this* with *which*. The second part of the sentence, *which could use… with a cord* is an incomplete idea. To connect a complete idea to an incomplete idea, HALF-STOP or GO punctuation is needed. Keep (B) because a comma is GO punctuation. Eliminate (D) because a period is STOP punctuation. The correct answer is (B).

7. **D** Commas are changing in the answer choices, so this question is testing the four ways to use a comma. The phrase *along with Albert* is unnecessary information, so it should have commas both before and after it. Eliminate (A) because it has a semicolon, not a comma, after the phrase. Eliminate (B) because it does not place a comma after the phrase. Eliminate (C) because it has a long dash, not a comma, after the phrase. Choice (D) appropriately places commas both before and after the unnecessary phrase. The correct answer is (D).

8. **B** Punctuation is changing in the answer choices, so this question is testing STOP, HALF-STOP, and GO punctuation. Notice that (A) has extra words when compared to the other choices, so consider the meaning of this choice. The phrase *in any room of the house* refers to the *monitor*, which is already mentioned in the sentence, so there is no need to refer to it again with the pronoun *it*. Eliminate (A) because it is redundant and uses a comma to connect two complete ideas, which is not correct. Use the Vertical Line Test for the remaining choices and identify the ideas as complete or incomplete. Draw the vertical line between the words *placed* and *in*. The first part of the sentence, *The video would be transmitted to a monitor that could be placed*, is a complete idea. The second part, *in any room in the house*, is an incomplete idea. To connect a complete idea to an incomplete idea, HALF-STOP or GO punctuation is needed. Keep (B) because a lack of punctuation is GO punctuation. Eliminate (C) and (D) because both the semicolon and the period are STOP punctuation. The correct answer is (B).

9. **C** Punctuation is changing in the answer choices, so this question is testing STOP, HALF-STOP, and GO punctuation. Use the Vertical Line Test and identify the ideas as complete or incomplete. Draw the vertical line through the word *and*, between the words *feature* and *a*, because the FANBOYS word *and* is part of the STOP punctuation. The first part of the sentence, *A remote control could lock or unlock the door from a distance, and the invention included an additional feature*, is a complete idea. The second part, *a panic button that would call the police immediately*, is an incomplete idea. To connect a complete idea to an incomplete idea, HALF-STOP or GO punctuation is needed. Eliminate (A) because a comma + *and* is STOP punctuation. Eliminate (B) because a period is STOP punctuation. Keep (C) because a long dash is HALF-STOP punctuation and supports the idea that the phrase after the dash explains the idea before the dash. Eliminate (D) because, though a lack of

punctuation is GO punctuation, the phrase *additional feature a panic button* is not a continuous idea, so it needs to be interrupted. The correct answer is (C).

10. **A** Commas are changing in the answer choices, so this question is testing the four ways to use a comma. The sentence contains a list of three things: 1) *homes*, 2) *offices*, and 3) *outdoor spaces*. There should be a comma after each item in the list. Keep (A) because it has a comma after each item in the list. Eliminate (B) because there should not be a comma after the word *and*. Eliminate (C) and (D) because neither has a comma after every item in the list. The correct answer is (A).

CHAPTER 8

Writing and Language Drill 3 (page 180)

1. **B** Prepositions are changing in the answer choices, so this question is testing idioms. Look at the phrase before the preposition to determine the correct idiom. Use POE, and guess if there is more than one answer left. The sentence draws a comparison between two things: a *landscape painting* and *high-definition photos*. The correct idiom when comparing two items is *in comparison to* (*compared to* could work as well, but it's not an option here). Eliminate (A), (C), and (D). The correct answer is (B).

2. **D** Verbs are changing in the answer choices, so this question is testing consistency of verbs. A verb must be consistent with its subject and with the other verbs in the sentence. The subject of the verb is *Obata*, which is singular, and the sentence discusses an action done by *Obata* in the past. To be consistent, the underlined verb must also be singular and must be in past tense. Eliminate (A) because *will immigrate* is future, not past tense. Eliminate (B) because *has immigrated* is not in past tense. Eliminate (C) because *immigrates* is present, not past tense. Keep (D) because *immigrated* is past tense. The correct answer is (D).

3. **B** Verbs are changing in the answer choices, so this question is testing consistency of verbs. A verb must be consistent with its subject and with the other verbs in the sentence. The subject of the verb is *A trip*, which is singular, and this *trip* happened in the past. To be consistent, the underlined verb must also be singular and must be in past tense. Eliminate (A) because *kindles* is present, not past tense. Keep (B) because *kindled* is past tense. Eliminate (C) because *was kindling* is not the right type of past tense. The verb *was kindling* indicates an ongoing action, whereas the sentence describes something that happened one time. Eliminate (D) because *will kindle* is future, not past tense. The correct answer is (B).

4. **A**   Pronouns are changing in the answer choices, so this question is testing consistency of pronouns. A pronoun must be consistent in number with the noun it refers to. The underlined pronoun refers to the noun *Obata*, which is singular. To be consistent, the underlined pronoun must also be singular. Eliminate (B) and (D) because they contain the plural pronouns *them* and *those*, respectively. The pronoun *him* refers to a specific person, *Obata*, so it is appropriate in context. Keep (A). *One* refers generally to a person, which is not consistent with the specific mention of *Obata*, so eliminate (C). The correct answer is (A).

5. **A**   Vocabulary is changing in the answer choices, so this question is testing precision of word choice. Look for a word with a definition that is consistent with the other ideas in the sentence. The sentence says that *Obata returned to Japan* so that he could print his *sketches* with a specific *printing technique*. Since Obata traveled to Japan to access this printing technique, the correct word could mean something like "specific to Japan." *Traditional* can mean "specific to Japan" in the context of the sentence, so keep (A). *Accustomed* means "used to." A person could be *accustomed* to using a technique, but the technique itself can't be *accustomed*. Eliminate (B). *Stable* means "unlikely to change," which doesn't match "specific to Japan." Eliminate (C). *Seasoned* means "experienced." As with *accustomed*, a person can be *seasoned* with regard to a technique, but the technique itself cannot be described as *seasoned*. Eliminate (D). Choice (A) makes the meaning of the sentence most precise. The correct answer is (A).

6. **D**   Transitions are changing in the answer choices, so this question is testing consistency of ideas. A transition must be consistent with the relationship between the ideas it connects. The sentence before the transition states that Obata's *idea was fortunate* because the *colored prints* were unique, and the sentence that starts with the transition discusses accolades that *Obata won* for his works. These are both positive ideas, so eliminate (A) because it contains an opposite-direction transition. *Again* indicates that the idea that follows is a repeated idea, but Obata's accolades were not mentioned in the previous sentence, so eliminate (B). *In other words* indicates that the idea that follows is a restatement of the idea before it, but this is not what happens in the passage, so eliminate (C). *As a result* indicates that Obata's accolades were a result of the unique nature of his work. This relationship is supported by the passage, so keep (D). The correct answer is (D).

7. **A**   Verbs are changing in the answer choices, so this question is testing consistency of verbs. A verb must be consistent with its subject and with the other verbs in the sentence. The subject of the verb is *landscapes*, which is plural. To be consistent, the underlined verb must also be plural. Eliminate (B) and (D) because both are singular. Keep (A) because *contrast* is plural. Eliminate (C) because *contrasting* makes the sentence incomplete. The correct answer is (A).

8. **A** Vocabulary is changing in the answer choices, so this question is testing precision of word choice. Look for a word with a definition that is consistent with the other ideas in the sentence. The sentence mentions *fine details* shown in the *paintings*, so the correct word should mean "show" or "portray." *Depict* means "show," so keep (A). While *draw* means "illustrate," which is close to "show," it is not appropriate to say that the *paintings* draw. Eliminate (B). *Interpret* means "understand," which doesn't match "show." A painting cannot *interpret* something—only a person can. Eliminate (C). *Announce* means "make known," which doesn't match "show" in this context. Eliminate (D). Choice (A) makes the meaning of the sentence most precise. The correct answer is (A).

9. **C** The order of words is changing in the answer choices, so the question is testing precision. The underlined phrase follows a modifying phrase, so it must begin with the noun that the modifying phrase describes, or the subject of the sentence. The modifying phrase says *As a professor at the University of California*, so the phrase after the comma must begin with the person whom this phrase describes. Obata is the person being described, so eliminate answer choices that don't begin with Obata. Eliminate (A) and (B) because neither begins with Obata: *many students* weren't *a professor at the University of California*. Keep (C) because it correctly states that *Obata* was *a professor at the University of California*. Eliminate (D) because it does not begin with Obata: *an introduction* wasn't *a professor at the University of California*. The correct answer is (C).

10. **D** Words are changing in the answer choices, so the question is testing precision. Notice that the underlined portion contains a verb and is part of a list of two things that describe *Obata's art*. All items in a list must be consistent in structure, and all verbs in a list must be consistent. The first item in the list is *spreading*, so the underlined verb must have an *-ing* form to be consistent. Eliminate (A), (B), and (C) because none of these includes an *-ing* form. Keep (D) because it is consistent with the other item in the list: *museum exhibits allow Obata's art to continue spreading and influencing artists*. The correct answer is (D).

CHAPTER 9

Writing and Language Drill 4 (page 194)

1. **D** Note the question! The question asks how to effectively combine the underlined sentences, so it's testing precision and concision. Start with the shortest answer, which is (C). Choice (C) implies that the act of observing *many ecological principles* is *competition*, which is not consistent with the original sentence. It could also be read as a list of three things, which it shouldn't be. Eliminate (C). Consider the shortest of the remaining choices, which is (B). Choice (B) implies that scientists only observed *ecological principles* related to *competition*, not that competition is one of the ecological principles they studied. This is not consistent with the original sentences, so eliminate (B). Consider the shorter of the remaining choices, which is (D). Choice (D) preserves the meaning of the original sentence, so keep it. Choice (A) uses a comma to separate two complete ideas, which is not allowed. Eliminate (A). The correct answer is (D).

2. **A**   Note the question! The question asks whether a sentence should be added, so it's testing consistency. If the content of the new sentence is consistent with the ideas surrounding it, then it should be added. The paragraph discusses the definition of the *principle of competition*. The new sentence clarifies part of this definition, so it is consistent with the ideas in the text; the sentence should be added. Eliminate (C) and (D). Keep (A) because it is consistent with the purpose of the new sentence. The sentence after the new sentence mentions *extinction*, and this sentence introduces it as a possibility. Eliminate (B) because the new sentence does not explain the *significance of Gause's research*, as Gause is not mentioned here at all. The correct answer is (A).

3. **B**   Note the question! The question asks which choice *sets up the information that follows in the passage*, so it's testing consistency of ideas. Determine the main point of the information that follows, and find the answer that is consistent with this idea. The paragraph that follows the underlined portion discusses a laboratory experiment conducted by *Gause* to test the theory of competitive exclusion. Eliminate (A) because information about Gause's birth is not consistent with his experiment in the next paragraph. Keep (B) because Gause's proving the *validity of the principle of competitive exclusion* is consistent with the experiment in the next paragraph. Eliminate (C) and (D) because neither the *prize* that Gause later received nor the *influential books* he later published is consistent with the experiment discussed in the next paragraph. The correct answer is (B).

4. **A**   Note the question! The question asks for the choice that *best maintains the style and tone of the passage*, so it's testing consistency. The tone of the passage is formal and academic, so eliminate answer choices that are too informal or contain slang words. In addition, the underlined word should reflect the idea that Gause wanted to measure how the populations grew, so it should mean something like "successfully." Keep (A) because *well* matches the tone of the passage and matches the meaning of "successfully" in context. Although "nicely" can match "successfully," it more closely means "agreeably," which is not quite appropriate in context. Eliminate (B). Eliminate (C) because it is too informal to match the tone of the passage. Eliminate (D) because it is too strong. The passage has a mild tone, whereas *wonderfully* has a more excited connotation, which is not consistent. The correct answer is (A).

5. **C**   Note the question! The question asks where sentence 4 should be placed, so it's testing consistency of ideas. The sentence must be consistent with the ideas that come both before and after it. Sentence 4 says that Gause *created separate groups of each organism as control groups*, so it must come after some mention of the specific *organisms* studied by Gause. Sentence 2 discusses *P. aurelia* and *P. caudatum*, which are both *organisms*. Furthermore, sentence 3 uses the word *also* in describing the *combined* group, which implies that sentence 3 needs to come after some mention of other groups. Therefore, sentence 4 should follow sentence 2. The correct answer is (C).

6. **B**   Note the question! The question asks which choice *introduces the main topic of the paragraph*, so it's testing consistency of ideas. Determine the subject of the paragraph and find the answer that is consistent with that idea. The paragraph discusses the results of Gause's experiment, which proved the validity of the theory of competitive exclusion. Eliminate (A) because Gause's experiment

confirmed, not *contradicted*, the validity of the theory, which had been hypothesized previously by scientists. Keep (B) because it is consistent with the subject of the paragraph. Eliminate (C) because the importance of *control groups* to *scientific experiments* is not consistent with the results of Gause's experiment. Eliminate (D) because Gause's publication of his results does not convey the significance of his experiment. The correct answer is (B).

7. **C** Note the question! The question asks which choice *sets up the results that follow in the sentence*, so it's testing consistency of ideas. Determine the main point of the information that follows, and find the answer that is consistent with this idea. The phrase after the underlined portion says that, under competition, *P. aurelia emerged as the dominant organism*. Eliminate (A) because it contradicts the information that follows: the emergence of *P. aurelia* as a dominant organism is *a clear pattern*. Eliminate (B) because it is not consistent with the information that follows: the two species did not *grow at the same rate*. Keep (C) because it is consistent with the information that follows: Gause observed a *difference in the populations*. Eliminate (D) because it is not consistent with the information that follows: the sentence does not indicate that Gause did *more experiments*. The correct answer is (C).

8. **D** Note the question! The question asks which choice describes *P. caudatum over the 16-day span*, so it's testing consistency. Read the labels on the graph carefully, and look for an answer that is consistent with the information given in the graph. Choice (A) is not consistent with the graph because the population of *P. caudatum* did not increase to overtake that of *P. aurelia*. Eliminate (A). Eliminate (B) because it is not consistent with the graph: *P. caudatum* contained more than 5 cells for at least some time during the 16-day span. Eliminate (C) because it is not consistent with the graph: *P. caudatum* went extinct after 15 days. Keep (D) because it is consistent with the graph. The correct answer is (D).

9. **D** Note the question! The question asks whether a sentence should be added, so it's testing consistency. If the content of the new sentence is consistent with the ideas surrounding it, then it should be added. The paragraph discusses how Gause's work has influenced modern science. The new sentence identifies where *Gause* earned his *degree*, so it is not consistent with the ideas in the text; the sentence should not be added. Eliminate (A) and (B). Eliminate (C) because the new sentence does not *contradict* an earlier *claim about Gause*. Keep (D) because it states that the new sentence is not relevant to the main point of the paragraph. The correct answer is (D).

10. **A** Note the question! The question asks which choice *summarizes the main finding of Gause's experiment*, so it's testing consistency of ideas. Determine the main finding of Gause's experiment, and find the answer that is consistent with that idea. According to the text, in Gause's experiment, one organism *became dominant* and had a high population, while the other decreased in population until becoming wiped out. Keep (A) because it is consistent with the text. Eliminate (B) because the passage indicates that *competitive exclusion* means that one species becomes dominant—the two don't *coexist without competing*. Gause's findings matched with *competitive exclusion*, so this answer isn't supported. Eliminate (C) because only one species in the experiment went *extinct*, not both. Eliminate (D) because, though the first paragraph says that a species threatened by competition may *adapt to find a new niche*, this was not proven by Gause's experiment. The correct answer is (A).

CHAPTER 10

Math Basics Drill 1 (page 203)

1. **c**   Examples: –7, 0, 1, 8

2. **d**   Examples: .5, 2, 118

3. **g**   Examples: –.5, –2, –118

4. **f**   Examples: –4, 0, 10

5. **b**   Examples: –5, 1, 17

6. **a**   Examples: Factors of 12 are 1, 2, 3, 4, 6, and 12. Factors of 10 are 1, 2, 5, and 10.

7. **i**   Examples: Multiples of 12 include –24, –12, 0, 12, 24, and so on. Multiples of 10 include –20, –10, 0, 10, 20, 30, and so on.

8. **h**   Examples: 2, 3, 5, 7, 11, and so on. There are no negative prime numbers, and 1 is not prime.

9. **e**   Examples: 3 and 4 are distinct numbers. –2 and 2 are also distinct.

10. **j**   Examples: In the number 274, 2 is the digit in the hundreds place, 7 is the digit in the tens place, and 4 is the digit in the ones place.

11. **p**   Examples: –1, 0, 1, and 2 are consecutive numbers. Be careful—sometimes you will be asked for consecutive even or consecutive odd numbers, in which case you would use just the odds or evens in a consecutive list of numbers.

12. **n**   Examples: 6 is divisible by 2 and 3, but not by 4 or 5.

13. **l**   Examples: When you divide 26 by 8, you get 3 with a remainder of 2 (2 is left over). When you divide 14 by 5, you get 2 with a remainder of 4 (4 is left over).

14. **k**   Examples: When you add 2 and 3, you get a sum of 5. When you add –4 and 1, you get a sum of –3.

15. **r**   Examples: When you multiply 2 and 3, you get a product of 6. When you multiply –4 and 1, you get a product of –4.

16. **m**   Examples: When you subtract 2 from 3, you get a difference of 1. When you subtract –4 from 1, you get a difference of 5.

17. **q**   Examples: When you divide 2 by 3, you get a quotient of $\frac{2}{3}$. When you divide –4 by 1, you get a quotient of –4.

18. **o**   Examples: The absolute value of –3 is 3. The absolute value of 41 is 41.

Math Basics Drill 2 (page 212)

3. **B** The question asks for the value of a number with certain properties. Start by translating the English into math. Use x for *value*. The question states that one of the *following values is 6 less than 5 times itself*. The phrase *5 times itself* can be translated as $5x$. The correct answer will be *6 less than* $5x$, which can be written as $5x - 6$. All together the equation can be written as $x = 5x - 6$. Solve for x by first subtracting $5x$ from both sides to get $-4x = -6$. Then divide both sides by -4 to get $x = \frac{-6}{-4}$ and reduce to $x = \frac{-3}{-2}$. The negative signs cancel to get $x = \frac{3}{2}$. The correct answer is (B).

5. **A** The question asks for an inequality that models a specific situation. Translate the English to math in bite-sized pieces. David is trying to take up to a certain number of photographs, p, so that he has *up to 31 unique photographs*. Since David can take up to 31 photographs and has already taken 11 photographs (*4 nature photos and 7 architectural photos*), these will need to be subtracted from the possible total of 31 as will the remaining photographs, p, he could take. This situation can be expressed as $31 - (4 + 7) - p$. Eliminate (B) and (D). The difference between the remaining answers is the direction of the inequality symbol. To determine which is right, try picking a number for p and using it in the remaining answer choices. Set $p = 2$ and solve to get $31 - (4 + 7) - 2 = 18$. Only (A) represents this situation since $0 \le 18$. The correct answer is (A).

9. **C** The question asks for the value of a variable in an equation. Begin by distributing the terms in front of the parentheses on both sides to get $16 - 8x = 10 - 5x - 15$. This simplifies to $16 - 8x = -5x - 5$. Gather like terms by adding $5x$ to both sides to get $16 - 3x = -5$, then subtracting 16 from both sides to get $-3x = -21$. Divide both sides by -3 to get $x = 7$. The correct answer is (C).

7. **D** The question asks for the value of a variable in an equation. Combine like terms on both sides of the equation to yield $-3c + 7 = -2c - 2$. Add $3c$ to both sides to get $7 = c - 2$. Then, add 2 to both sides to get $9 = c$. The correct answer is (D).

10. **C** The question asks for the value of a variable in a system of equations. Since the question asks for a, look for a way to eliminate b. Multiply the first equation by -1 so that the b terms will have the same coefficient with opposite signs. The new version of the first equation becomes $-2a + b = -11$. Keep the second equation as $4a - b = 7$. Stack and add the two equations together.

$$
\begin{array}{r}
4a - b = 7 \\
\underline{-2a + b = -11} \\
2a = -4
\end{array}
$$

Divide both sides by 2 to get $a = 2$. The correct answer is (C).

19. **A** The question asks for an equivalent form of the provided expression. Use Bite-Sized Pieces and Process of Elimination to tackle this question. Begin with the integer term in the first set of parentheses, -2, and combine it with the like term in the second set of parentheses, paying attention to sign changes: $-(-2) + (-8) = 2 - 8 = -6$. Choices (B) and (C) can be eliminated since they do not contain this

term. One difference between (A) and (D) is the x^4 term. In the original expression, there is only one term with a power of 4, and it is not multiplied or raised to a power, so this term will remain as is. Eliminate (D), which doesn't contain an x^4 term. The correct answer is (A).

20. **C**   The question asks for the cost of a certain number of items. The price of the item is unknown, so begin by translating the English to math in bite-sized pieces. The cost of one hockey puck can be represented as p and the cost of one water bottle as w. The question states that *Bill can purchase eight hockey pucks and two water bottles for $22*, so this can be represented as $8p + 2w = 22$. It also says that he can buy *twelve hockey pucks and ten water bottles for $54*, which can be represented as $12p + 10w = 54$. The question asks about the cost of water bottles, so solve the system for w. To do so, get the first equation, $8p + 2w = 22$, in terms of p and then substitute that into the second equation. Start by subtracting $2w$ from both sides to get $8p = 22 - 2w$, then divide both sides by 8 to get $p = \frac{22}{8} - \frac{2}{8}w$ or $p = \frac{11}{4} - \frac{1}{4}w$. Substitute $p = \frac{11}{4} - \frac{1}{4}w$ into $12p + 10w = 54$ to get $12\left(\frac{11}{4} - \frac{1}{4}w\right) + 10w = 54$. Distribute to get $(33 - 3w) + 10w = 54$, then combine like terms to get $33 + 7w = 54$. Subtract 33 from both sides to get $7w = 21$. Divide both sides by 7 to get $w = 3$. This is the cost of one water bottle, and the question asks for the cost of 16 water bottles, so multiply 16 by $3 to get $48. The correct answer is (C).

Math Basics Drill 3 (page 220)

a. **6**

b. **6**

c. **–1**

d. **–1**

e. **1**

f. **$6\sqrt{2}$**

g. **(0, 1)**

4. **D**   The question asks for the value of the y-intercept. For any graph in the xy-plane, the y-intercept will occur when $x = 0$. Plug in $x = 0$ to get $y = (0)^2 + 8(0) + 23$ and simplify to $y = 23$. The correct answer is (D).

9. **C**   The question asks for the number of solutions to a system of two equations represented on a graph in the xy-plane. Given the two equations of the graph, a solution to the system would be a point that satisfies both equations when it is plugged in. Given a picture of the graphs, the solutions are the intersections of the graphs of the equations. Circle the intersections of the line and the curve on the graph. There are two, near $(0.75, 1.5)$ and $(5.25, 10.5)$. The correct answer is (C).

6. **C**   The question asks for an equation that represents a line parallel to the one in the graph. A parallel line will have the same slope as the given line but a different y-intercept. The graph for this question has a y-intercept of 4 and a positive slope. Eliminate (A) and (B) which both have negative slopes. Calculate the slope of line a using the formula $slope = \dfrac{y_2 - y_1}{x_2 - x_1}$. The graph goes through the points $(-7, 0)$ and $(0, 4)$, so $slope = \dfrac{4 - 0}{0 - (-7)}$, which is $\dfrac{4}{7}$. The answers are in $y = mx + b$ form, in which m is the slope. Only (C) has a slope of $\dfrac{4}{7}$. The correct answer is (C).

9. **D**   The question asks for an equation that represents a graph. To find the best equation, compare features of the graph to the answer choices. The graph for this question has a y-intercept of 1 and a negative slope. Eliminate answer choices that do not match this information. All the answers are in $y = mx + b$ form, in which m is the slope and b is the y-intercept. The equations in the answers all have a negative slope, so nothing can be eliminated based on that. Eliminate (A), which has a y-intercept of 2. Choice (B) has a y-intercept of -2, so eliminate (B). Choice (C) has a y-intercept of 3. Eliminate (C). Choice (D) has a y-intercept of 1, which matches the graph. The correct answer is (D).

17. **C**   The question asks for an equation that represents a graph. Pick a point that is on the graph and plug it into the answer choices to see which ones are true. The graph contains the point $(7, 1)$, with 7 on the x-axis, so plug $a = 7$ and $t = 1$ into the answers. Eliminate answer choices that contain false equations. Choice (A) becomes $1 = -(0.5)(7) - 2.5$, then $1 = -3.5 - 2.5$, so $1 = -6$. This is not true, so eliminate (A). Choice (B) becomes $1 = -(2.5)(7) - 0.5$, then $1 = -17.5 - 0.5$, or $1 = -18$. Eliminate (B). Choice (C) becomes $1 = (0.5)(7) - 2.5$, then $1 = 3.5 - 2.5$, or $1 = 1$. This is true, so keep (C), but check (D) just in case. Choice (D) becomes $1 = (2.5)(7) - 0.5$, then $1 = 17.5 - 2.5$, or $1 = 15$. Eliminate (D). The correct answer is (C).

19. **C**   The question asks for the value of r in the provided equation $y = tx - r$. The graph shows that the line crosses the y-axis at the point $(0, -4)$, meaning that the line contains this point. Plug the coordinates of the point, $x = 0$ and $y = -4$, into the equation to get $(-4) = t(0) - r$. This simplifies to $-4 = -r$, so $4 = r$. The correct answer is (C).

20. **D**   The question asks for a system of inequalities that represents the graph. The graph is represented by the equation $y = mx + c$ where m is the slope and c is the y-intercept. The graph has a negative slope and a y-intercept of 2. Eliminate answer choices that do not match this information. Start with

either the slope or the *y*-intercept and use Process of Elimination on the answers. For example, if the slope must be negative, (B) and (C) can be eliminated, as those have positive values for *m*. Next, focus on the values of *c* in the remaining choices, values that represent the *y*-intercept. Choice (A) has a *y*-intercept of less than −4, so eliminate (A). It is also fine to start by eliminating choices with the wrong *y*-intercept before moving on to the slope. Either way, the correct answer is (D).

Math Basics Drill 4 (page 231)

11. $\frac{1}{3}$ The question asks for the slope of a line perpendicular to the graph of a linear equation. Perpendicular lines have negative reciprocal slopes. The equation, $f(x) = -3x - 2$, is given in $y = mx + b$ form, in which *m* is the slope. The slope of $f(x)$ is −3. Since line *b* is perpendicular to $f(x)$), its slope is $-\left(\frac{1}{-3}\right) = \frac{1}{3}$. The correct answer is $\frac{1}{3}$.

12. **3** The question asks for the value of a variable in an equation. Distribute the −8 through the parentheses on the left side of the equation to yield $-8g + 24 = -2g + 6$. Add $8g$ to both sides to get $24 = 6g + 6$. Then, subtract 6 from both sides to get $18 = 6g$. Divide both sides of the equation by 6 to get $3 = g$. The correct answer is 3.

3. **B** The question asks for the difference between two values on a graph. *Years* are listed along the horizontal axis, so find 2003 on that axis. Trace up to find the intersection with the graphed line. From this point, trace left to find the intersection with the vertical axis, using the answer sheet as a straight edge if necessary. It is between the horizontal gridlines for $1.50 and $2.00 on the *Cost per Gallon* axis, so ballpark this value as $1.75. Then, find 2007 on the horizontal axis. Trace up to the graphed line, then trace left to get a value of $3.00. The question asks for the *difference*, so subtract $3.00 − $1.75 to get $1.25. The correct answer is (B).

12. **25** The question asks for a possible value of 5*x*. Take the equation $5x^2 = 125$ and divide both sides by 5 to get $x^2 = 25$. Take the square root of both sides to get $x = \pm 5$. The possible values of 5*x* are 5(5) = 25 and 5(−5) = −25. Only positive values can be gridded in, so the correct answer is 25.

14. **B** The question asks about which intervals on the graph demonstrate a positive relationship. A positive relationship is one in which both variables increase together, resulting in a positive slope. From the graph, the only intervals that demonstrate a positive relationship between caffeine intake and reading speed are between 40–60 mg/hour and 80–100 mg/hour. The correct answer will contain only these intervals. Eliminate (A), (C), and (D). The correct answer is (B).

15. **C** The question asks for a certain value on a graph given an observed trend. There is no line of best fit for the interval between 40 and 60 mg/hour, so draw one in using the answer sheet as a straight edge if necessary. The variable *mg/hour* is listed along the horizontal axis, so find 45 on that axis. From this point, trace up to find the intersection with the line of best fit, again using the answer sheet as

a straight edge. Now trace over to the vertical axis to find the corresponding value on the *Reading Speed* axis. The intersection will be somewhere between 15 and 20 pages/hour. Only the value in (C) falls between 15 and 20 pages/hour. The correct answer is (C).

16. **D** The question asks for the difference between two values on a graph. The *x*-values are listed along the horizontal axis, so find 4 on that axis. From this point, trace up to find the intersection with the line of best fit, using the answer sheet as a straight edge if necessary. Trace left to find that this corresponds with 6 on the *y*-axis. Now, find the dot for the data point at $x = 4$ just above the line and trace left to find the *y*-value on the vertical axis. This is halfway between 6 and 7 on the *y*-axis, or 6.5. The difference is $6.5 - 6 = 0.5$. The correct answer is (D).

23. **2** The question asks for the value of a variable in an equation. Since the amount of apple juice is given as 5 liters, plug 5 in for *a*. The new equation becomes $1.9(5) + 2.2c = 13.9$, or $9.5 + 2.2c = 13.9$. Subtract 9.5 from both sides of the equation to get $2.2c = 4.4$, then divide both sides by 2.2 to get $c = 2$. The correct answer is 2.

CHAPTER 11

Math Techniques Drill 1 (page 243)

8. **D** The question asks for the height of a cylinder in terms of its volume and radius. There are variables in the answer choices, so plug in. Make $r = 2$ and $h = 4$. The volume becomes $V = \pi(2)^2(4) = V = 16\pi$.

The question asks for the equation to be solved for *h*, so the target value is 4. Now plug $r = 2$ and $V = 16\pi$ into the answer choices to see which equation makes $h = 4$. Choice (A) becomes $h = \pi(16\pi)(2^2)$.

Even without multiplying out the right side, this clearly will not make $h = 4$. Eliminate (A). Choice

(B) becomes $h = \dfrac{\pi(2^2)}{16\pi} = \dfrac{4\pi}{16\pi} = \dfrac{1}{4}$. Eliminate (B). Choice (C) becomes $h = \dfrac{\pi(16\pi)}{2^2} = \dfrac{16\pi^2}{4} = 4\pi^2$.

Eliminate (C). Choice (D) becomes $h = \dfrac{16\pi}{\pi(2^2)} = \dfrac{16\pi}{4\pi} = 4$. This matches the target value of 4. The

correct answer is (D).

9. **A** The question asks about the graph of the data representing a certain situation. Label the parts of the equation to determine what they represent. In this question, *P* represents the cost of caring for Patches for a given number of weeks, and *w* represents the number of weeks. The equation is not quite in $y = mx + b$ form, where *m* is the slope of a graph, but it can be rewritten as $P = (20 + 30)w + 55$. In this form, the slope is $(20 + 30)$. According to the table, 20 and 30 represent the cost of dog food per week and the cost of dog walking per week, respectively. Only (A) reflects this. The correct answer is (A).

4. **D** The question asks for an equation that models a specific situation. There are variables in the answer choices, so plug in. Make $h = 2$. According to the question, *each hour of play costs $1.50*, which means that for 2 hours of play, James will pay $1.50(2) = $3. There is a *monthly membership fee of $15*, which will need to be added to his charge for 2 hours of play to get $3 + $15 = $18. This is the target value; circle it. Now plug $h = 2$ into the answer choices to see which one matches the target value. Choice (A) becomes $(15 + 2)(1.50) = (17)(1.50) = 25.50$. This does not match the target value, so eliminate (A). Choice (B) becomes $(15 + 2)(0.50) = (17)(0.50) = 8.50$. Eliminate (B). Choice (C) becomes $(0.50)(2) + 15 = 1 + 15 = 16$. Eliminate (C). Choice (D) becomes $(1.50)(2) + 15 = 3 + 15 = 18$. This matches the target value. The correct answer is (D).

10. **D** The question asks for a true statement about two equations. The equations compare the number of trees chopped, t, to the number of hours, h, for two lumberjacks. Plug and play to determine the relationship between the two equations. Make $h = 1$. In that case, Albert chops $9(1) = 9$ trees and Buster chops $3(1) = 3$ trees. In the same amount of time, Albert chops three times as many trees as Buster. Eliminate answer choices that do not match this information. Choice (A) states that the rate at which Buster chops trees per hour decreases at a slow rate than Albert's, and (B) states that the rate at which Albert chops tress per hour decreases at a slow rate than Buster's. Not enough is known at this point to see how the rate will change over time, so keep (A) and (B) for now. Choice (C) states that for every hour of chopping, Albert chopped one-third as many trees as Buster. Albert chopped more trees than Buster in one hour, so eliminate (C). Choice (D) states that for every hour of chopping, Buster chopped one-third as many trees as Albert. This is true and likely the correct answer, but to double-check (A) and (B), plug in $h = 2$ to determine what happens to the rate for each lumberjack. If $h = 2$, Albert chops $9(2) = 18$ trees, which is the same as 9 trees/hour. In 2 hours, Buster would chop $3(2) = 6$ trees, which is the same as 3 trees/hour. Each lumberjack's rate is the same as when $h = 1$, which means there is no decrease in either Albert's or Buster's rate. Eliminate (A) and (B). The correct answer is (D).

17. **A** The question asks for the effect on the power when there is a change to the resistance. No values are given for the variables, but the question is about the relationship between variables, so plug in. Make the initial $V = 2$ and the initial $R = 3$. The power becomes $P = \dfrac{2^2}{3} = \dfrac{4}{3}$. Now multiply the value of R by 2 to get a new R of $2(3) = 6$. Keep the value of $V = 2$, as the voltage remains the same. The new power becomes $P = \dfrac{2^2}{6} = \dfrac{4}{6} = \dfrac{2}{3}$. This value is less than the initial value for power, so eliminate (C) and (D), which indicate an increase in power. The new power is one-half the initial power, so the power was divided by 2. The correct answer is (A).

19. **A** The question asks about the interpretation of the line of best fit for a graph. The horizontal axis represents minutes, m, and the vertical axis represents the number of bacteria, b. The resulting graph would have a negative slope since b decreases as m increases. The question asks about the y-intercept, which would occur when $m = 0$. Therefore, the y-intercept must represent the number of bacteria at the start of the experiment. Only (A) reflects this. The correct answer is (A).

20. **D**   The question asks for the value of g in terms of F. There is a variable in the answer choices, so plug in. Make $g = 2$. The equation becomes $F = 5(2 + 2) - 3 = 5(4) - 3 = 20 - 3 = 17$. The question asks for the equation to be solved for g, so the target value is 2. Now plug $F = 17$ into the answer choices to see which equation makes $g = 2$. Choice (A) becomes $\frac{17 - 2}{5} = \frac{15}{5} = 3$. This does not match the target, so eliminate (A). Choice (B) becomes $\frac{17 + 3}{5} = \frac{20}{5} = 4$. Eliminate (B). Choice (C) becomes $\frac{17 - 2}{5} + 3 = \frac{15}{5} + 3 = 3 + 3 = 6$. Eliminate (C). Choice (D) becomes $\frac{17 + 3}{5} - 2 = \frac{20}{5} - 2 = 4 - 2 = 2$. This matches the target value of 2. The correct answer is (D).

Math Techniques Drill 2 (page 248)

3. **A**   The question asks for the solution to the equation. Since the question asks for a specific value and the answers contain numbers in decreasing order, plug in the answers and look for the answer choice that makes the equation true. Begin by labeling the answers as "z" and start with (B), 7. Plug (B) into the equation to get $4(7 + 3) - 6 = 5(7 - 1)$. Simplify both sides to get $4(10) - 6 = 5(6)$ and then $34 = 30$. Since this is not true, eliminate (B). Even though both sides are not equal, they are close, so choose an answer choice close in value to (B), 7. Since (A), 11 is closer in value to (B), 7, than (C) –2, plug (A) into the equation next. The equation becomes get $4(11 + 3) - 6 = 5(11 - 1)$. This simplifies to $4(14) - 6 = 5(10)$ and then $50 = 50$, which is true. The correct answer is (A).

6. **A**   The question asks for the value of x. Since the question asks for a specific value and the answers contain numbers in increasing order, plug in the answers. Begin by labeling the answers as "x" and start with (B), 3. The equation becomes $\frac{7 - 3}{3 + 2} = \frac{5}{4}$, which simplifies to $\frac{4}{5} = \frac{5}{4}$. This is not true, so eliminate (B). To make the numerator larger and the denominator smaller, a smaller number is needed, so check 2, the value in (A). The equation becomes $\frac{7 - 2}{2 + 2} = \frac{5}{4}$, which simplifies to $\frac{5}{4} = \frac{5}{4}$. This is true, so stop here. The correct answer is (A).

9. **B**   The question asks for a solution to the equation. Since the question asks for a specific value and the answers contain numbers in increasing order, plug in the answers and look for the answer choice that makes the equation true. Begin by labeling the answers as "p" and start with (B), –15. Plug –15 into the equation for x to get $(-15)^2 + 20(-15) + 75 = 0$. The equation simplifies to $225 - 300 + 75 = 0$ or $-75 + 75 = 0$. Since this is true, stop here. The correct answer is (B).

12. **D**   The question asks for the amount of green tea needed to make a pitcher of iced tea. Since the question asks for a specific value and the answers contain numbers in increasing order, plug in the answers. Begin by labeling the answers as "amount of green tea" and start with (B), 207. If there are 207 mL of green tea in a pitcher of 900 mL, the remaining amount is the volume of raspberry purée. This means there are $900 - 207 = 693$ mL of raspberry purée. The ratio of green tea to raspberry purée

becomes 207 : 693, which reduces to 23 : 77. The ratio is supposed to be 23 : 7 , so this does not work. Eliminate (B). A much larger volume of green tea is needed, so try (D) next. If there are 690 mL of green tea in a pitcher of 900 mL, there are 900 – 690 = 210 mL of raspberry purée. The ratio of green tea to raspberry purée becomes 690 : 210, which reduces to 23 : 7. Since this is the given ratio, stop here. The correct answer is (D).

15. **B** The question asks for a solution to an equation, which is a value for the variable that will make the equation true. Since the question asks for a specific value and the answers contain numbers in increasing order, plug in the answers. Begin by labeling the answers as "x" and start with (C), 32, which is the middle of the numerical answers. The equation becomes $\frac{7}{4}(32+8)=56$, which simplifies to $\frac{7}{4}(40)=56$. Use a calculator to multiply the left side of the equation to get $70 = 56$. This is not true, so eliminate (C). A smaller number is needed, so check 24, the value in (B). The equation becomes $\frac{7}{4}(24+8)=56$, which simplifies to $\frac{7}{4}(32)=56$. Use a calculator to multiply the left side of the equation to get $56 = 56$. This is true, so stop here. The correct answer is (B).

17. **A** The question asks for a value that decreases the mean but increases the range. Since the question asks for a specific value and the answers contain numbers in increasing order, plug in the answers. Begin by labeling the answers as "chocolate coating in grams." Before plugging in the answers, calculate the original mean and range. Since the range is easier to calculate than the mean, start with range. The range of a list of values is the greatest value minus the least value. According to the table, the greatest value is 22.5 and the least value is 16.3. The greatest minus the least is 22.5 – 16.3, or 6.2. To find the value that increases the range, the value must not be between the greatest and least values in the table. Eliminate (B) and (C) for this reason. For averages, use the formula $T = AN$, in which T is the total, A is the average, and N is the number of things. The *Total* is 17.8 + 22.5 + 19.1 + 20.6 + 16.3 + 18.9 = 115.2 and the *Number of things* is 6, so the formula becomes 115.2 = A(6). Divide both sides by 6 to find that A = 19.2. Since (A) and (D) satisfied the requirement for an increased range, use them to find the new mean. To find the new mean using 15.8, use the formula $T = AN$. The new *Total* is 115.2 + 15.8 = 131, and the new *Number of things* is 7. The formula becomes 131 = A(7), then divide both sides by 7 to find the new A = 18.7, which is lower than the original average. Since the value in (A) also satisfies both requirements, stop here. The correct answer is (A).

18. **B** The question asks for the value of c in two equivalent expressions. Since the question asks for a specific value and the answers contain numbers in decreasing order, plug in the answers. Begin by labeling the answers as "c" and start with (B), 2. The first expression becomes $x^2 + 2x - 8$ and the second expression becomes $(x - 2)(x + 4)$. There are a few ways to determine if these expressions are equivalent. One is to use FOIL to multiply the binomials in the second expression, which results in $x^2 + 4x - 2x - 8$. This simplifies to $x^2 + 2x - 8$, which matches the original expression. Another method to check if the expressions are equivalent is to plug in a value for x, as the expressions should be true for any value of x. If $x = 2$, the first expression becomes $2^2 + 2(2) - 8 = 4 + 4 - 8 = 0$. The second expression becomes $(2 - 2)(2 + 4) = (0)(6) = 0$. The expressions are equivalent. Either way, the correct answer is (B).

Math Techniques Drill 3 (page 261)

a. **90**

b. **320**

c. **6**

d. **$x = 8$**

e. **5**

f. **3**

g. **10**

h. **120%**

i. **108**

j. **10%**

k. **$\dfrac{2,600}{18,600}$ = approximately 14%**

l. **40**

m. **1.5**

n. **5 kPa**

4. **C** The question asks for the approximate amount of cream, in liters, needed for a recipe, given amount in quarts. The question states that Kendall needs 0.8 quarts of cream, and that *there are 1.06 quarts in one liter.* To deal with unit conversions, make a proportion. The proportion is $\dfrac{1.06 \text{ quarts}}{1 \text{ liter}} = \dfrac{0.8 \text{ quarts}}{x \text{ liters}}$. Cross-multiply to get $1.06x = 0.8$, then divide both sides of the equation by 1.06, which gives $x \approx 0.754$. Since the question asks for an approximate number, look for the closest answer choice. The correct answer is (C).

5. **B** The question asks for an approximate number of flashcards that is determined by a specific percentage. "Percent" means to divide by 100, so change the given percent, 18%, to a decimal, 0.18. Multiply the total number of flashcards, 398, by 0.18 to find the approximate number of flashcards Jeshua can make in an hour. The result is $398 \times 0.18 = 71.64$, and the questions asks for an approximation, so round to the nearest whole number, 72. The correct answer is (B).

8. **C** The question asks for the average of a set of numbers. Since the question only refers to the stuffed animal, refer to the top row of data values in the two-way table. For averages, use the formula $T = AN$, in which T is the total, A is the average, and N is the number of things. Calculate the total of the original set of numbers. The *Total* is $10 + 8 + 13 + 14 = 45$ and the *Number of things* is 4, so $45 = A(4)$. Divide both sides by 4 to find that $A = 11.25$. The correct answer is (C).

11. **B** The question asks for a set of measurements and gives conflicting units. When dealing with unit conversions, make a proportion, being sure to match up units. There are 3 measurements, so deal with one at a time. The proportion for the length is $\dfrac{1 \text{ centimeter}}{10 \text{ millimeters}} = \dfrac{x \text{ centimeter}}{1{,}219 \text{ millimeters}}$. Cross-multiply to get $10x = 1{,}219$, then divide both sides by 10 to get $x = 121.9$ centimeters. The question says that the length is given first, so (C) and (D) can be eliminated, since these have a length of 12,190 cm. The remaining answers have the same value for the width, 30.5 cm, so skip that proportion and go right to the one for depth. The proportion for depth is $\dfrac{1 \text{ centimeter}}{10 \text{ millimeters}} = \dfrac{x \text{ centimeter}}{406 \text{ millimeters}}$. Cross-multiply to get $10x = 406$, then divide both sides by 10 to get $x = 40.6$ centimeters. The correct answer is (B).

15. **A** The question asks for an amount that is based on a specific percentage every year. To find the percentage, divide the amount donated by the firm last year by the amount of profit in that same year. The specific percentage is $\dfrac{\$52{,}320}{\$654{,}000} = 0.08$. This same percent will be applied to the current year's profit, so there is no need to convert it to the value 8%. To find the amount donated for this year, multiply this year's profit of $575,000 by 0.08 to get $\$575{,}000 \times 0.08 = \$46{,}000$. The correct answer is (A).

24. **50** The question asks for a percent based on data. Find the numbers on the table to set up the percent. The question asks what percent of the batch of hand sanitizer Jack used, so the percent is $\dfrac{\text{amount used}}{\text{amount in batch}} \times 100$. The table indicates that one batch contains 0.5 mL of essential oil, and Jack used an amount of hand sanitizer that contained 0.25 mL of essential oil. Plug the two values into the percent to get $\dfrac{0.25 \text{ ml}}{0.50 \text{ ml}} \times 100 = 50\%$. The correct answer is 50.

25. **0.04** The question asks for the amount of rubbing alcohol, in liters, in one dose of hand sanitizer, given the values given in the table. The table states that 0.16 liters are needed for *one batch of hand sanitizer*, and that *one batch of this recipe makes 4 doses*. To deal with unit conversions, make a proportion. The proportion is $\dfrac{4 \text{ doses}}{0.16 \text{ liters}} = \dfrac{1 \text{ dose}}{x \text{ liters}}$. Cross-multiply to get $4x = 0.16$, and divide both sides of the equation by 4, which gives $x = 0.04$. The correct answer is 0.04.

CHAPTER 12

Advanced Math Drill (page 280)

3. **B**   The question asks for the relationship between two variables. When given a table of values and asked for the correct equation, plug values from the table into the answer choices to see which one works. According to the table, $f(x) = 10$ when $x = -2$. Choice (A) becomes $10 = -5(-2)$, which simplifies to $10 = 10$. This is true, so keep (A) but check the remaining answer choices just in case. Choice (B) becomes $10 = -4(-2) + 2$ or $10 = 8 + 2$. This is also true, so keep (B). Choice (C) becomes $10 = -2(-2) - 4$ or $10 = 4 - 4$. This is not true, so eliminate (C). Choice (D) becomes $10 = 2(-2) + 2$ or $10 = -4 + 2$. This is not true, so eliminate (D). Since there are two answer choices remaining, plug in another point. According to the table, $f(x) = 6$ when $x = -1$. Choice (A) becomes $6 = -5(-1)$ or $6 = 5$. This is not true, so eliminate (A). Choice (B) becomes $6 = -4(-1) + 2$ or $6 = 4 + 2$. This is true, so keep (B). The correct answer is (B).

7. **B**   The question asks for an equation that represents a graph. Pick a point that is on the graph and plug it into the answer choices to see which ones are true. The graph contains the point $(0, -4)$, so plug $x = 0$ and $y = -4$ into the answers. Choice (A) becomes $-4 = -(0 - 4)^2$ or $4 = (-4)^2$. This becomes $4 = 16$, which is false, so eliminate (A). Choice (B) becomes $-4 = -0^2 - 4$ or $-4 = 0 - 4$. This becomes $-4 = -4$, which is true, so keep (B), but check the other answers just in case. Choice (C) becomes $-4 = (0 - 4)^2$ or $4 = (-4)^2$. This becomes $4 = 16$, which is false, so eliminate (C). Choice (D) becomes $-4 = 0^2 - 4$ or $-4 = 0 - 4$. This becomes $-4 = -4$, which is true. To differentiate between (B) and (D), either plug in another point or remember that parabolas that open downward correspond to a quadratic equation with a negative sign in front of the x^2 term. In (D), the sign of the x^2 term is positive. Eliminate (D). The correct answer is (B).

12. **18**   The question asks for a specific value when the function is equal to 6. In function notation, the number inside the parentheses is the x-value that goes into the function, and the value that comes out of the function is the y-value. Plug $x = c$ into the q function to get $q(c) = -\frac{1}{3}c + 12$. The value of $q(c)$ is 6, so this becomes $6 = -\frac{1}{3}c + 12$. Subtract 12 from both sides of the explanation to get $-6 = -\frac{1}{3}c$, then multiply both sides by -3 to get $c = 18$. The correct answer is 18.

5. **B**   The question asks about a population based on information about a study of a sample from that population. Since the members were randomly selected, the rate of exercise equipment ownership found in the study should match that of the larger population. To extrapolate the study results, set up a proportion. In this case, the proportion is based on the number of exercise equipment owners out of the total of each group: $\frac{7}{30} = \frac{x}{210}$. Cross-multiply to get $30x = 1,470$. Divide both sides by 30 to get $x = 49$. The correct answer is (B).

10. **B** The question asks for a probability, which is defined as $\frac{\text{\# of outcomes you want}}{\text{\# of possible outcomes}}$. Read the table carefully to find the numbers to make each probability. The astronomer will select *one of these planets*, and there are 5 + 1 + 1 + 2, or 9, planets, so that is the *# of possible outcomes*. The question asks about planets *greater than 999 million miles* from the Sun. Of these planets, 1 is between 1,000 and 1,999 million miles away and 2 are more than 2,000 million miles away, so the *# of outcomes you want* is 3. The probability is $\frac{3}{9}$, or $\frac{1}{3}$. The correct answer is (B).

13. **C** The question asks for the average hourly increase in the number of cells. When a question asks for a rate of change, it is asking about the slope of the graph. For slope questions, use the equation $slope = \frac{y_2 - y_1}{x_2 - x_1}$. Find two points on the best-fit line and plug them into the slope equation. Use the points (0, 50) and (5, 80), where $y_2 = 80$, $y_1 = 50$, $x_2 = 5$, and $x_1 = 0$. The slope is $\frac{80 - 50}{5 - 0} = \frac{30}{5} = 6$. The correct answer is (C).